IN SEARCH
OF A PRINCE

IN SEARCH OF A PRINCE
– My Life with –
Barbara Hutton

MONA ELDRIDGE

SIDGWICK & JACKSON
LONDON

First published in Great Britain in May 1988
by Sidgwick & Jackson Limited

First reprint, July 1988

ISBN 0-283-99500-9

Typeset by Hewer Text Composition Services, Edinburgh.
Printed in Great Britain by Butler & Tanner Limited
Frome and London
for Sidgwick & Jackson Limited
1 Tavistock Chambers, Bloomsbury Way
London WC1A 2SG

To the memory of Barbara

Contents

Acknowledgements

In writing this book, I would like to express my gratitude to:

Phoebe Phillips and Carey Smith for their professional advice; Bernadette Lichodziejewski and Françoise Loutreuil-Serre, both friends from my Paris days, for their help with the research; my niece, Roseanne Hoo, for doing the research in the USA and for providing me with the vital moral support throughout the project; Glynis Robinson for her help at the typing stage; Jeremy Eldridge, my ex-husband, for contributing his recollections and reminding me of many interesting incidents.

Chronology

BH = Barbara Hutton

14 Nov 1912	Birth of BH, in New York
2 Feb 1917	Mother's suicide
8 Apr 1919	Death of F. W. Woolworth (grandfather)
May 1924	Death of Jennie Woolworth (grandmother)
19 May 1931	BH presented at British Court
20 June 1933	Civil ceremony marriage to husband no. 1, Prince Alexis Mdivani
22 June 1933	Religious ceremony marriage to Prince Alexis Mdivani
14 Nov 1933	BH reaches majority and inherits $42,077,328.53
13 May 1935	Divorce hearing in Reno
14 May 1935	Marries husband no. 2, Count Kurt Haugwitz-Reventlow
25 Feb 1936	Birth of son Lance in London
Dec 1937	BH renounces American citizenship
1937	Meets Baron Gottfried von Cramm
1938	Refurbishment of Winfield House in Regent's Park, London
1938	Trial of Reventlow
1940	Liaison with Bobby Sweeney
6 June 1941	Divorce from Reventlow finalized
10 July 1942	Marries husband no. 3, Cary Grant
30 Aug 1945	Divorce from Cary Grant
1946	Buys Sidi Hosni in Tangier
1 Mar 1947	Marries husband no. 4, Prince Igor Troubetzkoy
Mar 1950	Meets Prince Henri de la Tour d'Auvergne
Oct 1951	Divorce from Troubetzkoy
30 Dec 1953	Marries husband no. 5, Porfirio Rubirosa

Aug 1954	Brief liaison with Michael Rennie
30 July 1955	Divorce from Rubirosa
Aug 1955	Invites von Cramm to Tangier
8 Nov 1955	Marries husband no. 6, von Cramm, in Versailles
Nov 1957	Liaison with Philip van Rensselear
Dec 1957	Meets Jimmy Douglas
Mar 1959	BH employs Mona Eldridge
12 Jan 1960	Divorce from von Cramm
24 Mar 1960	Lance marries Jill St John in San Francisco
July 1960	Meets Lloyd Franklin
Aug 1963	Raymond Doan's exhibition in Marrakesh
1963	Lance divorces Jill St John
3 Feb 1963	Mona Eldridge leaves BH's employment
7 Apr 1964	Marries husband no. 7, Raymond Doan, in Cuernavaca
Nov 1964	Lance marries Cheryl Holdridge
July 1965	Rubirosa is killed in car accident in Paris
6 Dec 1966	Jimmy Donahue dies
1968	Lloyd Franklin killed in car crash
Aug 1969	Reventlow dies during heart operation
1969	Marriage to Doan legally over
4 Nov 1971	Aunt Jessie Donahue dies
Feb 1972	BH visits Palm Beach after twenty years absence
24 July 1972	Lance killed in air crash
Apr 1973	Cousin Wooly Donahue dies of cancer
1975	BH's last visit to Tangier
8 Nov 1976	Von Cramm killed in car crash in Cairo
11 May 1979	BH dies in San Francisco
25 May 1979	Funeral

Introduction

It is now over twenty-four years since I lived in Barbara Hutton's world, in daily and continuous contact with this much-publicized woman. As her social secretary I was in a unique position to observe her activities and her reaction to her environment. I had, for four years, her complete trust. I was responsible for all the financial expenditure involved in running her three beautiful homes; I witnessed the legendary manner in which she threw away her fortune, and the vast amount spent on hangers-on who lived off her pathological generosity.

I left that hot-house atmosphere because I was stifling among people whose values I did not share, whose behaviour made me uncomfortable, and because I needed the freedom to lead my own life. Still, I felt affection and loyalty to Barbara who was more a friend than an employer. She had such a beautiful nature, but it was trapped in her own weaknesses. This only increased a certain sense of protection and caring which I felt for her.

The opportunity to leave came when I married and went to London to become a housewife. Strangely, at the time, being a home-maker was the most exciting and glamorous role I could imagine.

Since then, I have at various times been asked by popular tabloids and magazines of many countries to write articles about Barbara Hutton. Even if I had needed the money, I would never have considered it. Barbara had convinced me totally and absolutely that the press was not to be trusted. I could not possibly betray her, especially while she was living. After her death, I continued to feel the same until recently when I read a series of published 'facts' about Barbara Hutton. I had been aware all along, of course, of the sensational myths that appeared in the press, but whichever journalist wrote on the subject, however juicy and well-told a story it was, none of them could tell the truth from the inside.

My purpose in writing this book is to try to portray the real Barbara Hutton as I knew her – neither a good person nor a bad person, just a real person. I do not mean it to be an act of hero-worship nor a justification of what was undoubtedly a wasted life. I mean it to be a truthful reflection of my years with Barbara Hutton. As such, I hope it will also be an affectionate tribute to a much misunderstood woman whom the world despised, reviled, condemned, envied, pitied, vilified. She gave me a warm and trusting relationship; she was a mother-figure to me when, at the age of twenty-one, I needed a worldly and sophisticated role-model, for my own mother was a rather cold, remote figure who, because of poor health, had had little to do with bringing me up. She opened my life to the beauty and ugliness of the human spirit. In practice, she inadvertently set the course for the rest of my life, for through her I met my future husband who gave me the roots I have formed in the UK.

There are many personal benefits which I gained from my job with Barbara Hutton. The job gave me responsibility early in life and transformed an extremely under-confident and sheltered girl into a person of many more dimensions. It gave me the opportunity of experiencing life's rich resources at many levels and greater scope than I would ever have found in the usual course of events.

Money represents many things to many people. For most people, in my experience, it assumes an inordinate place in their imagination and they cannot cope with it in a reasonable manner. Every one of us has our price, which may not be in monetary terms. I was given a chance early in life to discover the importance of money to me. I found that freedom and being true to myself was more important than having more money than I needed at the expense of my self-respect. Thanks to my unusual apprenticeship I came to realize that having nothing more than money and privilege is empty.

I became more and more disillusioned at the lengths to which people – even the wealthy and titled – will go to acquire more goods and more favour among the rich. I began to despise money and all the people who sought it. Realizing that wealth, like power, has a corrupting influence on people, I became extremely arrogant in my rejection of it. Yet, within the same milieu, I saw wealth being used for intrinsically good purposes. The unpublicized and anonymous donations that Barbara made brought hope and assistance to the needy. In her kindness, she gave pleasure, and an expression of love and friendship to those around her. I have also found that money carries more than material considerations. Especially for women, wealth can represent freedom of choice and action, self-respect, status, security and an interesting social life.

I'd like to think that some of Barbara's characteristics have rubbed off on me. They say that we learn by copying others. I think that without her I would have been narrow-minded and priggish. Barbara's nature was unbigoted; she had a remarkably open mind. I have it in myself since I have known her. It has helped me a great deal in my work with the younger generation, and I believe it has contributed to the quality of my life.

This book is not meant to be a documentary account of Barbara Hutton's life – I was part of her life for only a brief period. The account comes from my own personal experience of Barbara, for we had a very close relationship. I remember my conversations with the people who were closest to Barbara, such as Tiki, her governess, Hélène, her personal maid, Bill Robertson, her life-long friend, Colin Fraser, her faithful minder. I knew some of her ex-husbands: Cary Grant, Prince Igor Troubetzkoy, Porfirio Rubirosa, Baron Gottfried von Cramm and Raymond Doan. I shared a daily life with two of Barbara's long-term companions, Jimmy Douglas and Lloyd Franklin. I worked for Barbara's attorney, Graham Mattison. I was on friendly terms with most of Barbara's friends of that time, and, last but not least, her son Lance.

These are my recollections . . .

1

How Not to Start a Job

I really didn't have time to fret about my interview with Barbara Hutton in the spring of 1959 because there was such a rush about getting ready to fly to Paris at short notice. It was general excitement, not specific panic. What worried me most, I remember, was what I should wear. I was going through a phase of wearing black, but my mother talked me out of it. She always said that I would have plenty of time to wear black when I was old. Being twenty-one I compromised, and decided on a navy suit and white gloves. In those days you were expected to wear a hat to an interview but I looked so ridiculous in one that I waived the rule. Gloves, however, could not be so lightly discarded.

On arriving at the Hôtel Meurice in Paris that evening, I rang up Philippe, my French fiancé, who did not expect me. When I told him my news, he sounded somewhat put out. I then rang some girl friends; they all thought the whole proposition most fascinating and romantic. But for me a heavy and momentous decision had to be made. As such, I kept putting it off – 'I'll see how it goes; I'll weigh up the pros and cons and then decide . . .'

The following morning, I crossed Paris by bus. It was all very familiar to me since I had been a student there less than a year earlier. It was March, and the first rays of sunshine were coming through a light fog. My appointment was 11 am. I had allowed myself ample time and, as I walked down the Avenue Victor Hugo, I wondered if it would be appropriate for me to take Miss Hutton a bunch of flowers for paying my expenses on this trip. I decided against it as it might appear sycophantic. By the time I arrived at the door of 31 rue Octave Feuillet in the 16th Arrondissement, the smart area near the Bois de Boulogne, I had fifteen minutes in hand so I walked up

1

and down for ten minutes before entering and taking the lift to the third floor. It was one of the ornate, open lifts with a heavy wrought iron door and double swing internal doors, typical of turn-of-the-century Parisian apartment blocks. The building was extremely quiet; there was heavy dark red carpet on the wide staircase. I rang the bell of the third floor apartment; there was no indication of who might be living behind the moulded oak doors.

The butler, dressed in black suit and white gloves, opened the door and I found myself in a bright entrance lobby. I gave my name and said I had an appointment. Asking me if 'Mademoiselle' cared to sit down, he pointed to the sofa under a large portrait of Barbara Hutton by the artist Sorine, and told me 'kindly' to wait there. Despite his formality, his manner was nevertheless friendly and deferential at the same time, which reassured me. There was an unusual stillness about the place, as if uninhabited. I found out later that all the rooms had double doors so muffling the noise. While I waited in the entrance hall, I noticed that opposite the sofa there was a door which was ajar. I took a look and saw the most adorable little guest cloakroom I had ever seen. It was done up in pink with a small marble wash basin with gold taps shaped like fish. And it smelled so good. So far, I had liked everything I had seen.

The butler returned and asked me to follow him into the salon. At the door, he bowed and withdrew. Barbara Hutton was sitting on a very ornate Louis XV sofa. She stood up and greeted me almost shyly, and asked me to sit down. I thought how small she looked in this elaborate framework. Well into her forties, she was wearing a simple aubergine-coloured Lanvin suit with matching blouse. Her blond hair was wound rather severely around the crown of her head, and the pearls in her earrings were enormous – quite the largest I had ever seen. She apologized as she took a couple of aspirins and drank some water from a heavy Venetian cut-glass tumbler. She said, with a laugh, that she had never had to interview anyone before. She said that she had received an excellent recommendation from her lawyer, Graham Mattison, and that she hoped very much that I would take the job. Graham would be arranging all the details. I realized that my visit was merely a formality, so that she could have a look at me. She did not ask me any questions about myself, nor did she mention salary or conditions.

My first impression of Barbara Hutton was that she had a simple manner with no airs and graces. She was extremely polite and seemed strangely unsure of herself. I also noticed that she had lovely, small and elongated hands, and long nails perfectly shaped and manicured. The interview lasted only about ten minutes. Barbara said she had to go to the dentist and I took that as my cue to get up and thank her and leave. As we shook hands, for the second time, she held my hand in both hers and thanked *me* for coming all the way from New York so we could meet. There was a warmth in her smile which was very flattering.

The butler showed me to the door, and as I returned to the normal world outside, I knew that I would accept the job. I could not envisage saying no to the charming person I had just met.

I was born in Shanghai in 1938, to a couple from the privileged class of old China. Mother's father had been Mayor and Foreign Commissioner of Shanghai in the days when that city was divided into international zones. Although not exceptionally wealthy, he commanded respect both professionally and socially. In that milieu my mother, Marguerite, enjoyed her position as the most eligible débutante of the 1920s. The fact that she was very beautiful, educated in the English system, and spoke English and French, enabled her to pick and choose from a host of suitors. My mother was still single when, at the age of twenty-four, she went to a ball at the French Embassy and met young Dr Victor Hoo, a brilliant young diplomat and the darling of the international set.

Victor Hoo's ancestors were from the noble Mandarin class. The men in his family had all held high governmental positions and had moved in the inner circle of the Emperors. Victor was inculcated with a high sense of duty; throughout his life he was dedicated to the idea of service. It was part of the *noblesse oblige* ethic of his forebears.

Marguerite immediately felt an attraction for this young man who obviously had a brillant future. He was neither tall nor handsome, but he had an unmistakable cachet; today it would be called charisma. All his life, there were hoards of people, men and women, who fell under his charm.

Victor's father, Dr Hoo Wei Teh, was one of the few Mandarins at the Court of the Empress Dowager Tzu-hsi who was asked to serve office in the government of the new Republic after the revolution of 1911 which swept away all titles with the Manchu Dynasty. A few members of the Hoo family emigrated to Thailand in order to hang on to their titles and privileges. As far as my family were concerned, they were stupid and vain; and we had nominally

3

written them off. By coincidence, I discovered two years after entering Barbara's household that she had become friends with them on her visits to the Far East. At that point I admitted to her that we were related. Until then I had grown up feeling ashamed of them.

When Victor and Marguerite met in 1927, Dr Hoo Wei Teh was Foreign Minister (later to become Prime Minister) and living in the first Western Villa in Peking. Today that house is occupied by Deng Hsiao Ping.

Victor had been born in Washington DC, and educated up to the age of seventeen in St Petersburg, thereafter continuing his studies in Paris. Following his parents around from embassy to embassy, Victor developed a gift for languages. He joined the Chinese delegation at the Versailles Peace Treaty in 1919 and subsequently joined the Chinese Embassy in Berlin as Third Secretary. During this posting, he fell in love with the daughter of a German nobleman. They wanted to get married and the girl's family gave their consent. Back in Peking, however, Dr Hoo Wei Teh was not so amused. As Foreign Minister, he recalled his son to the Ministry in Peking, giving him twenty-four hours to pack his bags and board the next ship from Hamburg. Despite his Westernized nature, Victor obeyed and, once in Peking, was ordered to buckle down to routine work, take private lessons in Chinese calligraphy (at which he was not very competent due to his Western education) and look for a suitable Chinese wife to take him in hand.

It seems that the minute he set eyes on Marguerite, he knew he wanted her, and no one else, for his wife. How lucky for him that this time his father approved of his choice! The wedding was the occasion of the year.

However, if the old Chinese family expected a compliant daughter-in-law they had a shock in store. They were scandalized that the wedding should take place in my mother's home town of Shanghai, and that the bride wore a modern (i.e. short) white wedding dress, flapper-style (white in China is traditionally worn for funerals). Furthermore, Marguerite demanded her own house. No Chinese daughter-in-law had *ever* been allowed the freedom of her own house; she was by strict tradition part of her in-laws' domain. But this bride got what she wanted. The couple settled in Peking in a modern house and did everything by the book, in the hope of getting an early foreign posting. Within a year they were

4

rewarded. Victor was named as the delegate at the League of Nations in Geneva, with special responsibility for narcotics.

Geneva was to be their home for close to twenty years. Still, when my brother and I came on the scene, Marguerite took herself off to her family in Shanghai. At those times, she felt the need for her old servants and her family. She also felt that she wanted her children to be born on Chinese soil. Both of us were, therefore, conceived in Geneva and born in Shanghai.

We returned to Geneva after a few months and my earliest recollections are completely Swiss. We had a governess, Martha, who raised us in the strict Calvinist ethic. I went to Swiss State schools until the age of fourteen and French became my first language.

The first big trauma I experienced was when we had to move to New York: my father had been asked to join the United Nations. I knew no English and it took me a year to learn the language and the customs. And yet the American way of life was an attractive one for a teenager – especially one like me who had had a severe and restricted home life – and I took to it like a duck to water.

After high school, I went on to take two degrees at Columbia University in Politics and Economics. My ambition was to be an international spy although I had neither the looks nor the discreet personality for such a profession. I so much enjoyed my student life that I went on to study at the Institut d'Etudes Politiques in Paris; my early European influence could not be denied and I wished to study where my father had studied. In Paris I found freedom from my parents; I became my own person. By the time I finished my course in 'Sciences Po' (Political Science) I was engaged to a Frenchman and firmly rooted in European life.

After all those years of academic life, how does one become social secretary to one of the world's richest women? In my case, having finished my studies at the Institut d'Etudes Politiques, I found a job as a bilingual secretary at the Paris branch of Dominick & Dominick, one of the leading investment firms on Wall Street. The Paris Director was a Mr Giovanni Pagnamenta. He had been Vice President of Bankers Trust in New York and had retired, but had come out of retirement to head the small representative office in Paris. Mr Pagnamenta was an elderly Swiss who took a fatherly interest in his staff's welfare. After I had been working there only a month, he called me in to tell me that he was increasing my salary as

5

he did not like the area where I was living and that I should find my-self better accommodation in a classier area of town. When I became engaged to my French boyfriend, Mr Pagnamenta asked to meet his parents. I could not have had a kinder boss in this my first job.

Graham Mattison was the partner in Wall Street responsible for the foreign branches of Dominick & Dominick and as such was Mr Pagnamenta's superior. Mattison handled the accounts of several very rich clients and was in a position to manipulate the stock market with his dealings. Besides being a very successful investment broker he was also a brilliant lawyer. Whenever he came to Paris from New York on one of his flying visits, we knew he would be seeing Barbara Hutton at the Ritz; he acted as her lawyer and business manager and we had heard that he had been one of her lovers. We also heard that Mattison had invested Barbara's money so well that he had increased her capital tenfold in fifteen years in spite of her extravagant spending.

After I had been working at Dominick & Dominick for some months, Graham Mattison started taking me with him to some of his European business meetings. I was fascinated, finding it all so vital and exciting.

One day, Graham asked me to work in his New York office for three months on a particular, confidential project in the Foreign Department of the Wall Street office. I was very flattered that he felt it worth the company's while to transport me across the Atlantic and back for a project; there was, too, a bonus of $5,000. It also allowed me to visit my parents in New York at the firm's expense. I greatly enjoyed my initiation into big institutional business, and I threw myself into the challenge.

I had only been in New York three weeks when Mattison called me into his office one Thursday afternoon and closed the door. 'There's a job offered to you in Paris as social secretary to Barbara Hutton,' he said. 'She knows all about you and I know she will be happy with you. It will be up to you to decide if you want the job.' Of course I had heard all about Barbara Hutton – everyone had in the 1950s – and I was flattered by the offer. But this kind of job was the last thing I wanted: I was engaged to a young French banker and we had already bought an apartment in Paris. I was intending to give up work shortly to take a permanent role as a bourgeois housewife and mother. I told Mattison this and he replied, 'You don't need to stay with her for ever and you could arrange with her not to do any travelling. Why don't you go to Paris this week-end for an interview? It won't cost you anything and then you can make up your mind. Miss Caton [his personal assistant] has arranged a first-class flight leaving tomorrow morning at 9 am and there is a room booked for you at the Meurice.' If I was going to refuse, I had to do it then and there, but the idea of going to Paris for the week-end, seeing my fiancé and meeting Barbara Hutton was too much – I couldn't refuse! I could always say no afterwards. Mattison had used the right mixture of timing, delivery and bait. He knew very well that I would take the job, if only out of curiosity.

One month after my interview with Barbara, I arrived back in Paris from New York to start work as social secretary to the Baroness von Cramm. Barbara preferred to be addressed as 'the Baroness' rather than 'Miss Hutton' although she had just divorced Gottfried von Cramm and at the time hated any reference to him. She did like titles and some people still called her 'Princess', harking back to the days when she was Princess Mdivani or Princess Troubetzkoy.

I was to take charge of the Paris household, deal with Barbara's suppliers, pay her bills, arrange all her travel and manage the staff (over fifty in all) at her homes in Paris, Tangier, and Cuernavaca in Mexico. Although I aimed to make myself as useful as possible, the most unpleasant part of the job was having to pander to Barbara's so-called friends; the most difficult part was dealing with Graham Mattison who had got me the job so that I could keep the accounts tidy and curb Barbara's mania for spending money. I was doomed from the start because no one had been able to stop her habit of throwing her money away. For someone who had led a relatively sheltered life up to that point, it all came as quite a shock. Indeed, people who knew me both before and after I worked for Barbara tell me that my personality changed quite markedly, and that I became hard. Certainly I know that the next four years of my life were to change my view of people and life in general.

I found that Barbara had no notion of employer/employee relationships. At times she treated me as a friend and her friends as employees. I remember once she saw me at my desk and asked what I was doing. I said I was writing out the salary cheques. She asked if I got one too. I said yes. She said, 'Oh, I'm pleased you get paid; I hope it's a good salary!'

Despite my job title, I found myself cast more in the role of useful companion. Barbara expected me to keep her company through the night when she wanted someone to talk to and to share all the ups and downs of her life. She also used me as a shield against the media and as a link with the outside world. I had to become totally involved in the job – there was no other way. I had to do everything from co-ordinating the Annual Ball (booking the bands, ordering the flowers, supervising the seating, finding accommodation for more than a hundred guests) to reminding Barbara of who was coming to lunch. The only thing I did not get involved with was the actual domestic work: the cleaning, the care of clothes, organizing transport and the buying of food and drink were all dealt with by others in her household.

My first experience of my new job and the Paris apartment was in the absence of Barbara who had gone on a trip to the Far East with her current partner, Jimmy Douglas. Jimmy was a handsome and cultured young American who had a taste for beautiful and rare things. This was perhaps his attraction for Barbara, but two of his rare possessions were to cause me dreadful anxieties.

He had in his room a sophisticated aquarium and had left instructions for me to look after his fish, in particular two of a species known as *Symphysodon acquifasciata*: despite their fancy name they looked to me like a pair of ordinary angel fish. However, they were not in the least ordinary; he had paid $4,000 each for them in Japan and had brought them to Paris in a plastic bag, holding the bag in his hand all through the twenty-two-hour flight from Tokyo. I could hardly sleep at night worrying about those expensive, and as it was stressed, delicate creatures. Every morning the butler had to go to a special pet shop to get a particular type of worm for them; sometimes the shop did not have any. I dared not have my own lunch until I saw with my own eyes that each had eaten its meal.

Barbara and Jimmy had been away for a few weeks when the fish began to give me trouble. One of them was not eating. It was obviously ailing. I rang the vet who told me to hold the fish in my hand and shove the food into its mouth. This is easier said than done, so I got the vet to come round and show me how to do it. I was very upset, but the vet did not seem to understand my sense of panic and urgency. He looked around the place and, seeing all the luxury, sarcastically remarked that the death of a fish would not be a great loss to such people. I could not make him understand that my credibility and reputation were at stake. It took three days for the other fish to catch whatever disease it was and they both died in spite of my efforts. I felt crushed, defeated. It seems strange, when I look back now, how important it was to me to prove that I could look after two little fish.

Another important charge left behind in my care was Tiki, Barbara's old governess. She was by then a woman in her late seventies who had had two heart attacks and it was my responsibility to watch that she did not indulge in her favourite rich foods and drink because the doctor said her blood pressure and arteries were in bad shape. I was quite unsuccessful for on the matter of her stomach this sweet little old lady would not be dictated to.

She was a very pleasant woman, small and dumpy, who had lived all her life surrounded by gossip, intrigue and tittle tattle. She had been in the household since Barbara was about ten years old. Tiki had seen at first hand all the comings and goings of successive husbands, lovers, friends, employees. She loved talking about them like a proud parent boasting of their children's achievements. She was at that time in life when only the past counted. I was a new person and she relished telling me the stories that the others had heard dozens of times. Tiki's real name was Germaine Toquet and she was the reason why Barbara spoke perfect French. Tiki's origins were obscure and no one really knew the truth about her. It was obvious that she had had no formal education; she could hardly write and made obvious grammatical mistakes in her own language. In spite of all her travelling with Barbara (who had learned French as a child and spoke the language perfectly, with no trace of an accent), she never learned any other languages. She admitted that she started life as a servant in a rich household. Rumour had it that she became pregnant by the master of the house and had had a daughter but that could have been fabrication. She never denied nor affirmed this story, although she did admit with a twinkle in her eye that men used to be attracted to her. She mischievously kept her cards close to her ample chest. Now that she was old, Barbara treated her like a mother.

In Paris Tiki had her own chambermaid, Louisette, her own small circle of friends, generally people who wished to approach Barbara through the back door or former friends of Barbara who hoped to regain her favours. They only dared to come around when Barbara was absent. Barbara had stopped including Tiki in her travels or her social activities due to Tiki's failing health. Instead she lavished Tiki with jewellery, clothes and money. Many people

9

were jealous of Tiki, of the luxury that she enjoyed and all the gifts that she received.

I was told by Basile, the butler, on my first day in my new job, that I could have my meals in the dining-room, in my office, or accept Tiki's invitation to eat in her room. She was a lonely person who loved company and gossip. I decided to take my meals with her. I was glad I made that decision, because my meals with Tiki were very interesting and informative. She loved talking about Barbara and the past. She made me feel that I was now part of the clan.

Occasionally, we would be joined by one of her friends. One of these was Monsieur André Denet, Barbara's salesman at Cartier. Barbara had recently visited Cartier and as she was used to being showered with attention and flattery, she was very upset when Monsieur Denet had to abandon her to serve the Duchess of Windsor who had an appointment with him. The Duchess, too, was a good customer. Barbara was so upset that she immediately went to Van Cleef and Arpels across the Place Vendôme and did her Christmas shopping there. Now, Monsieur Denet was making a point of fussing over Tiki. He invited her to dinner, sent her flowers, rang her up for chats. He wanted to be able to tell Barbara on her return that he had kept an eye on Tiki, that he had spent a great deal of time seeing that Tiki was happy. He also made a point of courting my goodwill; he invited me to dinner with my fiancé, Philippe. Coincidentally we found out that Madame Denet's two brothers had gone to the same Jesuit boarding school in Toulouse as Philippe.

One evening, I was enjoying a quiet meal with Tiki when, in the middle of the main course, she clutched at her chest, apparently in great pain. I guessed immediately that she was having her third heart attack. Everyone had warned me to expect it. I rang her heart specialist, Dr Henri Deschamps, but he was out for the evening and I had to wait three hours before he could be reached. When he arrived, he gave Tiki an electrocardiogram and ascertained that she had indeed had a heart attack. In spite of being in extreme pain she managed to stay calm. She refused to go to hospital and it was up to me to make the decision, against the doctor's wishes, to turn Tiki's room into one. With enough money, anything is possible. For the next few days we had regular deliveries of oxygen cylinders. There was not only a regular rota of nurses around the clock, but also a rota of young doctors, chosen by the heart specialist from those who needed the money. No expense was spared. Tiki appeared comfortable, and I truly believed that as everything possible was being done we would save her. Tiki was even well enough to play cupid. She paved the way for a happy though short-lived, love affair between me and Dr Deschamps.

Tiki was kept comfortable with regular doses of pain-killers. Most of the time she was resting in an oxygen tent. Still I thought that she was on the mend. I felt she was improving every day. On the ninth day, she died peacefully with a smile on her face. The young doctor on duty and I were chatting in front of the open window in Tiki's room. It was a glorious spring day. Every fifteen minutes he would check Tiki's pulse, but on this occasion said calmly, 'She is no more.' It was a great shock to me and also, for some reason, I felt a great sense of failure; in spite of all the efforts made by so many people, we had failed. It seemed so unfair.

I had no real or deep feelings for Tiki, after all I had only known her for a few weeks, but it took me a long time to get over her death. It was a turning point in my life. It was the first time that I had felt deep disappointment and failure. It left me with some bitterness which was to influence my whole outlook.

I had, of course, kept Barbara informed in Japan (where she now was) of all that was happening. Her messages seemed rather unfeeling. When I had to tell her on the telephone of Tiki's death, I was certain that she would want to attend the funeral. Instead – and to my surprise – she did not seem distressed and did not wish to discuss the funeral arrangements; she left me to decide on everything. Hélène, Barbara's personal maid, insisted on a Catholic mass and funeral. I knew that Tiki was not only an atheist but that she had been very anti-Catholic. However, Hélène said, just in case, you never know . . . she might have repented at the last minute. The funeral directors were very helpful, and a man came every hour to put ice on Tiki's body. Before the funeral came the 'mise en bière', the placing of the body in the coffin. Apparently, someone had to witness this. It had to be me, as the person in charge. Before they closed the lid, I felt choked. How will she breathe? I thought. Tiki had a Catholic funeral, a mass with an orchestra and singers and a proper funeral cortège – it was the best package offered. I received condolences from the crowd that had come out of curiosity. During the mass, I thought how incongruous that I should be leading this funeral, I who had known her a short time, and I felt an overwhelming sorrow for her. She had no family, no real friends.

The choir of boys sang beautifully, the past two weeks had stretched all my emotions and I wept warm and bitter tears.

The Paris cemeteries were all full to capacity and I was unable to arrange for one to accept poor Tiki's mortal remains. We had to leave the body somewhere until we could find a plot. The funeral parlour had no room. I finally arranged for a local church that had a small unused annexe to accept the body for an indefinite time. We paid them a high rent and Tiki remained there for four months. Then an acquaintance of hers who had fallen on hard times accepted a substantial payment in return for allowing Tiki to be buried in her family plot in northern France. By that time, all Tiki's 'friends' had vanished. I asked Hélène and Herminie, the chef, to come with me. The three of us accompanied the coffin to its final resting place. It was a beautiful day and we made it into a picnic. Tiki had once said, on seeing the beautiful cemetery on the island of Torcello near Venice, 'I would love to be buried here but I don't speak the language.' Now, at least she was among her own people.

After Tiki's death, I had to go through her belongings and found myself in the position of having to dismiss her chambermaid who had only been with her a few months. She seemed to me to be an uncaring, coarse woman who only did the minimum. I tried to break it to her gently and offered her three months' wages. She flew at me in a rage. What had she done to be treated like a criminal? She had her rights; she wasn't about to be thrown into the street. It was a traumatic experience for me; I was easily intimidated and tongue tied. The woman was threatening violence, shouting obscenities about foreigners. She said that she would see that I would be barred from France forever. I looked up the employment laws and found that she was entitled to a month's wages. I had to find some inner strength to impose my view but it was her or me and I could not afford to go under at this first crossroad. I found the strength and with the help of Basile she was out the same day. After that I found it easier to deal with the staff, most of whom gave me their support.

It has been reported that when Tiki died, she left a fortune. She certainly *should* have left a fortune for Barbara had given her no end of money and jewellery over the years. Tiki had no need to spend anything; everything was paid for her. Yet she was receiving several thousands of dollars per month which went regularly into the bank. Occasionally Barbara had given her five-figure sums for Christmas or her birthday. And Barbara also gave Tiki fabulous pieces of jewellery when she herself had grown tired of them. On

12

Tiki's death, however, the big mystery was what had happened to it all? There was no trace of any bank account and the few pieces of jewellery which Tiki wore every day were all there was. Where was the rest? In retrospect, the people around Tiki realized that they had not seen the pieces of jewellery for some time. What was incredible was that especially in her latter years, Tiki was almost bedridden and she was never left alone for a minute. She could not even write a letter without someone knowing as she could not post it herself. She never went anywhere without being accompanied. This was indeed a real mystery and I wanted to know the truth. Barbara asked me to leave the subject alone; she appeared to want the matter closed. Did she suspect something? Was she afraid of finding out something unsavoury? If she had an inkling of what had happened to this small fortune, she never told anyone. Perhaps we would never have found out anyway. Still, I was very curious. To my knowledge, no one has ever fathomed the mystery.

After Tiki's death, Barbara's maid Hélène became concerned with the health of Cocotte, a long-haired dachshund, originally given to Barbara by her fourth husband, Prince Igor Troubetzkoy. Typically, Barbara had, at first, lavished money and attention (including a mink coat and diamond necklace) on the little dog. However, as it was Hélène who always had to feed Cocotte and take her for walks, she eventually preferred Hélène to Barbara, whereupon Barbara lost all interest in her. Now it was found that Cocotte was suffering from cancer and that she had not long to live. Hélène tried every kind of remedy – faith healing, homoeopathy, acupuncture. There was no cure and the vet advised that Cocotte be put to sleep. Hélène refused to lose hope and spent her days clutching Cocotte wrapped in a blanket, praying in church for a miracle. When Cocotte finally died, probably in pain, Hélène was inconsolable. She was blaming herself for allowing Cocotte to suffer. My room had a connecting door to Hélène's and she used my shoulder for laying bare all her problems. We became very close during that time.

Two months after the start of my employment in Barbara Hutton's household, she and Jimmy returned from their trip, full of joy and cheer. I had just gone through the worst two months of my life; I felt responsible for the deaths of the fish, Tiki and Cocotte. What a record! What a way to start a job when I wanted to make a good impression! In such a short time I felt I had aged twenty years.

13

2

Life at 31 rue Octave Feuillet

When I first began working for Barbara, she and her staff had only been living at 31 rue Octave Feuillet for only two months. Before that, indeed from her very first childhood visits to Paris, she had always had a suite at the Ritz. However, two things occurred to alter that pattern.

Through an acquaintance she met a handsome, impeccably-mannered young man, who could be invited to her dinner parties. This young man's boyfriend worked for Jensen, the most prestigious interior decorators in Paris. He was determined that he would persuade Barbara to get an apartment of her own, and naturally the décor would be by Jensen. He was lucky in his timing, for it was about this time that Barbara's unique collection of Chinese porcelain was returned to her after being on loan to a museum in Hawaii and the idea of finding a place worthy of the collectiion was attractive.

Graham Mattison, too, was in favour of Barbara buying an apartment. The bills incurred at the Ritz had been astronomical, especially as Barbara was in the habit of putting all her friends up there too. The 'friends' would do all their shopping in Paris and charge it to Barbara's account. There was no limit to the way people took advantage of her. At least, Mattison thought, if she had an apartment, her friends could stay with her at no further expense, and bills could be dealt with by a member of the household, rather than by the concierge of the Ritz.

As a result of this move Barbara told Mattison that Margaret Latimer (but always known as Sister), who had originally joined the staff when Lance was born in 1936, was no longer suitable as a secretary, and that what she really needed now was someone who

14

could keep accounts and speak French. And that is where I came in. Mattison knew that he could sell me to Barbara for she had always been a lover of the Orient and a believer of fairy tales, and there he was offering her a Chinese girl who was a tri-lingual university graduate and whose father had been a prince.

Everything turned out as Mattison had intended: Barbara responded, as always, to the Orient. I rose to the challenge of the unexpected and the intriguing and Sister was pensioned off for the hard work she had given over twenty-five years of service. She was quite pleased to leave under the circumstances. She was to continue to receive her salary, unchanged, and in addition she asked for a large house in Hampstead, London, with a lump sum to convert the house into a boarding house. She was thus able to have a new source of income, her old salary and a house, for which she had not had to pay, as an investment. We discovered later, when the conversion was done, that Sister had kept only a tiny room for herself. That did seem to be taking the legendary Scottish frugality to extremes.

Starting my new job while Barbara was away in the Far East with Jimmy Douglas was really rather convenient as it was a good way to become familiar with my new duties, for I had been left in sole charge. It also gave me the chance to get to know the rest of the staff. The biggest problem I had with the staff in Paris was how to deal with people who had nothing to do for at least nine months in the year. Discontent would become endemic, arguments and bad feelings would proliferate.

In the hierarchy of staff, the top-ranking person was Basile, the butler. Basile was a White Russian, and the embodiment of correct protocol. We could count on him for everything. There is an implicit understanding in certain circles that the butler's word is law, but in the event, Basile happened to be a very gentle and discreet person; not at all the kind of person to lay down the law. Yet, he commanded everyone's respect by being kind, fair, efficient and impartial. He minded no one's business but his own.

During Barbara's absences when the staff were on full pay, Basile would spend hours studying the odds at the races and investing in lottery tickets. He was very circumspect about his dealings and although we did not know how much he gambled, the word was that he amassed quite a sum from his winnings. Basile belonged to some sort of *émigré* White Russian society. Every week he would go to secret meetings which, as far as we could fathom, involved the Russian Orthodox church, anti-Soviet activities and plans to restore the Tsar to his rightful place. It was all a hush-hush type of activity but I managed to worm out of him that the Tsar was alive and would soon be vindicated. This fervent belief was Basile's mainstay in life.

When there was a need for extra staff, for instance when there was to be a large reception, Basile would call in a Frenchwoman to help with the silverware. She was a wretched looking person who had obviously suffered ill health and misfortunes in her life. She had a small daughter and it was said that she was Basile's child. He denied it, but when the woman died Basile took full charge of the girl's education and upbringing.

Basile had under him an Italian footman, Giovanni, who was jolly and a good worker but had little initiative or refinement. He had aspirations of marrying Barbara and achieving fame and fortune. Basile had to watch that Giovanni did not forget his place. In fact, there was little chance for the footman to come into contact with Barbara. His station was in the pantry.

Herminie, the chef, was the real boss whom no one dared cross. She was in her mid-seventies, short and plump, with unruly grey hair that refused to remain in a chignon. She had the volatile nature of her Mediterranean background and a tremendously powerful personality which had driven her from being an illiterate shepherd girl to achieve recognition as the top woman chef in Paris. Her flashes of anger would see crockery crashing across the room and woe betide anyone standing in its path. These moods would go as quickly as they came. In truth, Herminie had a creative temperament for she was truly a master craftsman. I thought this was my golden opportunity, when Barbara was away, to pick up some good tips, if not some fantastic recipes. But I soon found out that Herminie's type of cooking was far beyond anything I would be capable of in my lifetime. Her cooking required the best specialized equipment, mostly heavy copper saucepans. Then, she had an intuitive genius that had nothing to do with following a recipe. I tried, with Herminie's consent, to write down one of my favourite dishes, *veau sauté aux champignons*. She cooked the dish in front of me and gave a running commentary for me to take notes. But if I put such questions as 'How much of that?' or 'How long for?' she could not answer. It had to *look* or *feel* right. There were no definite ingredients or measurements. Herminie cooked as a painter paints. I was defeated.

Herminie never used stock or sausages that she had not made

personally with her own most secret ingredients. My friends all urged me to learn what I could, but I came to the conclusion that only certain people had the talent and I was not one of them. However, I did learn that what I used to think difficult to cook – pastry, cakes, sauces – were really easy. With the right ingredients and the proper temperature these will always come out perfectly – like a result from a laboratory. The most difficult thing to cook is meat because there are never two pieces the same so the result can always be a surprise. I tried to argue that it was easier to cook a steak than make one of her fancy *baba au Savarin*. No, she said, it depends on the result you expect.

One of Herminie's former employers was the Minister of the Navy, Louis Jacquinot. He and my father had been at university together and Herminie remembered having cooked dinners in the Jacquinot house attended by my father. It seems that my father had once written on the menu *'Qui est cette fée qui existe dans la cuisine?'* She had kept it and I recognized my father's handwriting. Herminie enjoyed talking to me about the political scene; we had a common interest in gossiping abut the people she knew who were my father's colleagues or old friends.

Once, when I was about to go to New York to visit my family, Herminie said she wanted to make a *pâté de foie d'oie* to take to my father. Although this was her great speciality, I was reluctant to accept as I knew there were restrictions on taking food into the US. She insisted and said she would put it in a sealed jar wrapped in some clothing so I could smuggle it in my hand luggage. She was totally determined to go through with it. At the customs my face must have betrayed my cold feet as I went through the 'Nothing To Declare' side for I was stopped. 'Do you have anything in your luggage which appears on this list?' said the customs official thrusting a list mounted on cardboard at me. The list included fruit, plants, meats, food, soil, birds, snails, other live animals, farm products. 'No,' I squeaked guiltily. 'Let's have a look in here.' He started to dig in my bag and discovered the jar. 'What's in here?' he asked. '*Foie d'oie*, goose liver,' I replied. 'What's that?' he looked baffled. 'Is it fresh meat?' I tried to talk my way out but to no avail. He was impervious to any pleas or explanations. He handed the jar to his assistant to dispose of, 'Unless,' he conceded, 'you want to eat it on this side of the barrier.' He had never heard of goose liver pâté, let alone tasted any. I said, 'Don't throw it away, *you* eat it. It's too good to waste.' 'It'll go straight down the toilet,' he said, 'you're

17

lucky I'm not pressing charges for smuggling illegal material.' I felt that on the contrary, *he* had committed the crime. How could I explain this to Herminie? I couldn't, so I asked my father to write a note complimenting her on it. I knew she would be pleased. Even someone as highly regarded as Herminie was sensitive to praise.

Herminie had worked for Coco Chanel for six years. Herminie, whose cynicism was great, had only admiration for this woman. Perhaps because she was a self-made woman, a woman with extraordinary talent and a single-minded will to succeed. That trait had made Chanel extremely attractive to men even though she was no beauty by any standards. Two stories about Chanel, as told by Herminie, struck me as significant. She enjoyed her food immensely. Yet, when she needed to lose weight she would stop eating altogether, taking only water. When she felt faint she would lie on her bed and conduct all her business from there until she had reached the required weight. Nothing would deter her from her goal. The only story which Herminie told with admiration was of the well-known love affair between Chanel and the Duke of Westminster. Herminie had been a witness to it. This was not just a social dalliance, it was true, passionate love on both sides. The Duke was reputed to be the richest man in England and he wanted Chanel to give up her business to be with him always. Even though she was deeply in love with him, she put her work first. What an example she was to future feminists!

Herminie bordered on the eccentric and was a great talker. She could tell fascinating stories of her humble origins, tending sheep in the Pyrenees. It was nothing like the romantic ideal of a curly-haired girl with a crook and fluffy white lambs grazing around her. She described it as the most degrading work because only the poorest people did it. However it gave her the determination to better herself at any cost. She landed a job as the kitchen maid in a household where the chef kicked and beat her. It reminded me of Cosette in *Les Misérables*. Her duties, at the age of twelve, were to do the heavy washing and there was no pay, just room and board. Her bed was a rug under the kitchen table. She said that she cried bitter tears every night and was determined to get her revenge. She found herself fascinated by the culinary art and obviously had an aptitude for it. So single-minded was she in her ambition that she enjoyed her hard apprenticeship, but when it was her turn to be boss in the kitchen, she was very hard on her subordinates. And though she was illiterate and could not keep even a simple account of her spending, she had all the shops jumping at her command. But her temper was her undoing – divine though her cooking was, it was usually an outburst of temper that led to employers dismissing her.

When I first joined the staff there was a kitchen maid from Alsace, Marise, who was bright and able. She, like Herminie at that age, had ambitions of becoming a chef. She accepted the job of kitchen maid because the salary was twice as high as for any other kitchen maid in Paris. Also, she wished to learn from Herminie, an apprenticeship worth a great deal to an ambitious girl. Marise stayed only one year; she could not stand Herminie's tyranny and she was never allowed to prepare the food. Herminie kept her only washing the heavy pots and pans and the dishes used for the staff. Everything used in the dining-room would be washed in the pantry by the butler or the footman. Was Herminie perhaps getting her revenge for her early torments?

Of all the staff close to Barbara, Hélène, her personal maid, was the most devoted. She would have laid down her life to make Barbara happy; she would have worked for no salary so entwined was her life with Barbara's. There are still a few Hélènes in the world, though not many: spinsters who have no family and who need to dedicate their caring to someone outside themselves. Had they got married, they would have been the ideal mothers and grandmothers. Their notion of service and duty produced something akin to a religious vocation. Towards Barbara, Hélène felt more than submission and respect, for she had no one else in her life.

Hélène was a mousy sort of person in constant turmoil. She spoke incessantly in her Germanic accent out of nervousness and suffered from a variety of nervous tics. Not only did she twitch but she constantly cleared her throat and sniffed. She appeared never to exhale completely, as if she was afraid to let go. Her constant worry about everything made it difficult to relax in her company. When Barbara was in Paris, Hélène would of course be very busy. Yet she would come to me every few minutes to tell me of her worries and to seek support. It would have been an intolerable irritant were it not for the fact that she had a heart of gold and one could not help being extremely fond of her because her intentions were always pure. Barbara herself would feel exasperated at Hélène's fussing and her very straight-laced views, but how could one deny such loyalty?

19

On occasions when Barbara was on sleeping pills, Hélène would empty the capsules and refill them half with sugar. She was the only person who dared face Barbara's anger at being duped. Of course, in her heart of hearts Barbara knew that Hélène was acting out of sincere concern. Hélène was also the only person who dared moralize with Barbara about her drinking, for health reasons.

Hélène never left France to accompany Barbara on her travels. In her other two homes the maids were in residence and Barbara would be in informal attire both in Mexico and in Morocco. On her trip to the Far East Barbara said Hélène would spoil her fun. So in Paris, Hélène would stay as self-appointed guardian of any calamity that might befall the household. Any little noise set Hélène into a panic. I believe that she enjoyed worrying. One evening as I prepared to go out, she stood there and said, 'I don't know how you can go out and enjoy yourself knowing that this place could burn down!'

One day I found Hélène writhing in pain on her bed. She had a dreadful pain in her abdomen. I called our doctor who called an ambulance and she was admitted to hospital. The diagnosis was an intestinal obstruction and they prepared to operate. She had to wait two hours during which time she was not allowed either pain-killers or water. It was agonizing for me, to have to witness her pain without being able to do anything about it. She remained in hospital for two weeks, in a private room, and every day I sat in that darkened room to keep her company because she was afraid they would steal her belongings. Two years later it happened again. The doctor had explained that there was no explanation why the obstruction should occur and that it might happen again or it might not. This second time, I found Hélène ashen with pain but quite composed. She was busily making little parcels of her belongings and putting names on the parcels to indicate the recipient after she died, for she was convinced that this time she was dying. She put her bits of jewellery in envelopes with rubber bands around them and she asked me to promise to carry out her wishes, apologizing that she was not leaving much to me. We then went through the same routine and fortunately she pulled through again.

The two chambermaids on the staff when I joined were Maria, a Frenchwoman of Spanish origin, and Araceli, a Spanish woman who spoke very little French. Both were expert ladies' maids. They knew how to care for the most delicate materials such as the finest crêpe de chine and hand-made lace. They were, however, only

20

allowed to assist Hélène, and do any tasks delegated by her. Their normal duties were to make beds, clean rooms and look after the linen. This last included looking after my clothes and guests' clothes. Both Maria and Araceli were in their early thirties and did not have the servile attitude of their elders. The older ladies' maids, like Hélène, born in the last century, lived only to serve their ladies. Maria and Araceli were not of the old school: they expected something for themselves first. They took their above-average salary for granted; they knew their skills were in demand.

When Barbara was not in residence the difficulties began. Araceli was not too much trouble. She was a pious and quiet person who joined the legions of Spanish maids in the 16th Arrondissement at the Eglise Espagnole in rue de la Pompe every Sunday morning. As she could not communicate well in French she wisely kept out of the discussions which sometimes degenerated into arguments. Araceli also used her free time making garments on a knitting machine in her room, which she sold for extra cash. She never talked about it, but at times Maria would throw it in her face in a fit of indignant rage and as the only criticism she could think of. Araceli sent most of her income to her widowed sister in Spain whose five children were sent to good schools through Araceli's savings and kindness.

Maria, on the other hand, was a born troublemaker. An excellent lady's maid and a beautiful woman with fiery, dark good looks, she would have fared well if she had been kept busy all the time, for she was an excellent worker. Unfortunately she suffered from an intensely jealous nature which led her to start arguments over any little thing. In her high-pitched strident voice, she would pick on a comment made by one of the other staff and twist it to make it imply an insult to herself, or to provoke a retort which she could use as ammunition. 'How much money have you made today, Araceli, with your knitting? You'll soon be as rich as *Barbara*!'

I had authorization not to restrict the staff expenses in any way, so Herminie would produce, as much for her own pleasure as ours, sumptuous four-course meals for the staff even in Barbara's absence. Most of the staff would beg her to cut down, for day in day out such a diet was too rich. As a result, Herminie would produce different dishes for different tastes. She would never serve any leftovers and I thought there was a criminal amount of waste. The leftovers were given to the concierge who no doubt had enough to feed her neighbours and her daughter's family as well. Having

21

done more than her best, Herminie did not take criticism kindly. At every meal time she could hear Maria's high-pitched voice: 'Is that all we get at *Barbara*'s? Don't we rate better at *Barbara*'s?' always emphasizing *Barbara*, the disrespectful way of addressing Madame. Another favourite complaint of Maria's came from the fact that after Tiki's death, I usually ate my meals in the kitchen with Herminie. 'The Duchess and the Princess are there again; *we're* not good enough for the likes of them.' The voice was deliberately loud enough so we could hear in the kitchen. In retrospect, it was an error on my part to eat in the kitchen. It showed favouritism. At the time, in Barbara's absence, I found it very cold and lonely to eat in the dining-room on my own. I felt uncomfortable with Basile standing behind waiting to serve the next course. It was impossible to ask for something simple, it was not within this household's frame of reference. There were always three wine glasses (just in case I changed my mind), although I never drank wine with meals – a habit left over from my days in America. The alternative was for Basile (always in his white gloves) to roll a table into my office. It would be a lot more trouble for him in a sense, for he would then lay the table with a tablecloth, flowers, silver, finger-bowl, all of which he had to carry some two hundred yards from the pantry. Similarly, he would have to bring each course from the kitchen area which was also a long way.

Since the staff ate in their dining-room and Herminie stayed in her kitchen, I found it ideal to join her where I could have just a snack, an omelette or a *salade niçoise*, as opposed to a meal which entailed several courses. Herminie never ate a meal. She was short and quite overweight – she said it came from having to taste all the time. I never saw her sit down with a knife and fork in front of a plate of food. At most she might cut off a piece of cheese and pop it into her mouth.

Herminie was full of interesting conversation. She listened to the news avidly and enjoyed discussing the politics of the day. She grew flowers on the window sills, including some magnificent double begonias which she tended with love and care. She used to ask me to bring back some horse manure to put in the pots when I went riding in the Bois de Boulogne and she would prepare a box lined with aluminium foil to make it easy to transport the manure. The box would usually be one from Lanvin, which had probably originally contained a ball gown. The stable boys almost died laughing the first time they were given the grand foil-lined box to put the manure in. Not only did they make jokes about it every time they saw me, but the story reached other stables, and has no doubt been exaggerated and become a legend.

It did not occur to me at the time that anyone should resent my having meals in the kitchen until I heard a sarcastic remark from Maria about Herminie and me being in a financial conspiracy. Herminie rendered her accounts to me and Barbara never limited the spending. Herminie took a rake-off from her suppliers as is the normal practice in France. What took me a while to learn was that the rake-off system had far-reaching ramifications. For example, I was told that Barbara's friend, Silvia de Castellane, who had originally selected Barbara's Paris staff, was receiving a regular percentage of their inflated salaries. Others would receive a percentage as soon as they found out that something had been bought at Lanvin. This remarkable system was explained to me by a fashionable antique dealer in the Faubourg St Honoré. He said that an awkward moment sometimes occurred when more than one of Barbara's friends came to claim their money. There might be an ugly scene to decide who was the legitimate 'friend' who had a right to the tipster's fee. Usually, however, they would agree to share the spoils. The shops, of course, would never voluntarily hand out the 'discount'. The House of Lanvin was particularly grateful to me for settling their bills promptly, and occasionally I would be offered an amount as 'my' part of the yearly bill. In my own priggish manner I always refused. It was only when I left Barbara's employ that I was told by Lanvin's accountant that the sums I had refused had gone directly to others.

By the late summer of 1959, Barbara had been away for eight weeks, and the staff had had a protracted period of leisure. Maria's behaviour showed more and more signs of hysteria and I thought some days she even looked ill, with dark circles under her eyes. One day I suggested that she looked tired. Her sharp retort was 'Yes, I have a mirror too.' I did not have the confidence to insist, but it gave me cause for worry. I was very angry particularly at Maria's constant harping about the meals not being good enough, knowing full well that nowhere else would she ever come across such luxury. This frustration threw me even more into confiding in Herminie to whom I could pour out my troubles, trusting her discretion. Through Maria's subsequent behaviour, I was to learn even more about the system of rake-offs for 'friends' of Barbara.

The apartment at 31 rue Octave Feuillet was, of course,

magnificent – decorated and furnished with exquisite taste and beauty. Friends would ask me if it wasn't a bit like living in Versailles, and no doubt the wonderful antiques did make the place seem rather like a museum. At first I was overwhelmed by all this opulence, but it did not take long for me to feel at home – especially in my own suite which was situated about halfway down the lengthy hallway.

My room was a large oval studio with French windows on to a balcony. It had an air of cheerfulness and brightness which was not to reflect the atmosphere of my job. The room was furnished with Louis XVI furniture, while the curtains and bedspread were made of Thai silk. I had a single bed which in the daytime was made to look like a sofa. The rest of the furniture was dominated by an enormous antique double desk made for two people to sit facing each other. That gave me ample room for all my files, and the four-line telephone exchange that was to take over my waking and sleeping hours.

The room also included the most modern hi-fi equipment. This was to give me a great deal of pleasure and Mozart soothed my temper many a time. Because my room was also my office, I was fortunate to have next to it a bathroom equally as large as my room. I once gave a dinner party for six people in it! Two walls had mirrors from floor to ceiling and behind one was a walk-in wardrobe. It was a cross between a bathroom, boudoir and dressing-room. An Irish college mate who came to visit commented, 'When you park yourself in someone's drawers, you sure choose the best.'

This suite was my sanctuary; no one broke my privacy except through the intermediary of the phone. Even Barbara never barged in unannounced; she used to say she would 'never walk into the pantry to look for the butler'.

I was often left in charge of the Paris household during Barbara's stay at her other homes: she would generally spend the winter in Cuernavaca, Mexico, the spring in Paris, and the summer in Tangier, usually devoting part of the autumn to Paris, and part to an annual trip to the Far East. The staff accepted me at first because I held the purse strings and I was their intermediary with their employer. Later, our friendship was based on mutual affection. Still, when things did not go their way, I took the blame – often. I had to learn to take criticism. I had a budget with no limit. Barbara encouraged me to give parties in her absence to keep the staff happy. Many of my friends had their most memorable meal at my place of work and still talk about it to this day. My father, while working for the United Nations, came to visit me on one occasion and I was able to give a superb cocktail party in honour of him and his diplomatic colleagues.

Except for Hélène, Barbara's personal chambermaid, whose bedroom was next to my office, the rest of the personnel were lodged on the sixth floor, in very comfortable 'chambres de bonnes'. These were the traditional living quarters for the servants in the better districts of all the large cities of France. Ironically, in most Paris buildings, these top floors have now been done up into very fashionable apartments. We also had storage space in the basement with a special room for a wine cellar.

It was wonderful to live in such truly elegant surroundings, but it was not just the work of that most prestigious firm of interior designers, Jensen of the Rue Royale, that made it so special. The feature which made Barbara's apartment unique and matchless was her collection of Chinese porcelain which she had started to acquire in her youth. Some time before she was married for the first time Barbara had found an affinity for Chinese literature and poetry. She also became interested in Chinese porcelain long before it had become fashionable in the West outside museums. By the time the Paris apartment was being fitted the collection comprised some 150 pieces. It was reputed to be the second largest private collection in the world.

Jensen was commissioned to use the large dining-room as the new setting to house the smaller pieces of this collection. At each corner of the dining-room they fitted pale yellow velvet-lined display shelves with subtle indirect lighting and there the collection, amassed with love, piece by piece over some thirty years, literally found its niche. The pieces, distinguished by their perfection of potting, glaze and decoration, included some notable pieces of the Ch'ing Dynasty (eighteenth century) with specimens of apple green, coral red and other monochrome glazes. There were thirty-two examples of paper-thin white porcelain of the Ming Dynasty, not to mention the splendid group of eighteenth-century 'ruby-backed' plates, with brilliant *famille rose* enamel decoration on a white background, made in the Imperial kiln in Kiangsi province. There were several pieces of jade-like 'milk glass', a type dating from the early eighteenth century. These pieces were not like objects in a museum; they came to life because Barbara loved them.

She had personally sought out and chosen each piece and she had the experience and knowledge to seek, and find, the telling combinations of form, potting methods, glaze and colour, distinguishing the real from the fake. She could read the six Chinese characters within a double circle or a double square painted in underglaze blue on the base of a piece which, on Imperial pieces, is the reign mark.

When the collection arrived in Paris most of the wooden bases had been broken and lost, so I had to find new ones to fit each different piece. It was very difficult, because Barbara wanted them to be ancient. I contacted porcelain houses and collectors all over the world and received many parcels. It was like a gigantic jigsaw puzzle, trying to fit the right sized bases to each piece of porcelain. In the process, I met and corresponded with most porcelain experts, all of whom marvelled at Barbara's specialized knowledge and interest in this field. I quote from the booklet on her collection written by the Director of the Honolulu Academy of Arts who wished:

. . . to call attention to the range of the collection and to emphasize the discriminating taste of its owner, who chose the pieces from the point of view of personal enjoyment . . . whose discerning taste for the exquisite has made it possible for so many people to enjoy [the collection at the museum].

The main feature of the Paris apartment, therefore, in spite of its predominantly French décor and contents, was this oriental treasure. So exquisitely subtle were the pieces and so beautifully were they fitted into the room, that many guests eating in the dining-room were unaware of the beauty and value of the objects in the corner recesses.

Barbara's collection of jade was another reflection of her love for and admiration of the Orient. Again, she knew a great deal about it and the staff at the jewellers, Cartier, admitted to me that Barbara knew a lot more than they did about it. She could assess and appreciate jade that was not green. I learned from Barbara that the purest jade is white jade; that colour comes from the presence of other minerals in the stone. Even in the most usual green jade there are dozens of distinct hues, bearing such colourful names as kingfisher, spinach, emerald, moss and young onion green. The quality of jade does not depend on its colour or lack of faults, as with emeralds. To judge jade one must be able to distinguish translucence from transparency and to see the right combination of each of these qualities. Barbara appreciated jade as part of the development of Chinese worship, court ceremonials, thought and art. Much of her knowledge had come directly from Chinese texts, because she had hired a translator to read Chinese books on the subject to her.

In Paris Barbara also housed her collection of Fabergé objects which at the time I worked for her she was losing interest in and was not adding to. In fact, she gave away several pieces to friends. Barbara also had a collection of gold cigarette boxes made of several types of gold, most of them inlaid with diamonds. These she would use as ordinary cigarette boxes strewn all over the apartment. Basile, who was ultimately responsible for the rest of the domestic staff, was always worried that someone, staff or guest, might slip one of these boxes in their pocket and retire in South America. In 1986 it was reported in the press that five of these boxes were sold at Sotheby's for £131,500 to pay off some of her debts.

Barbara's other great collection which was kept in Paris was her collection of jewellery. This she loved with an almost physical sensuality. The value of each piece was not the point. It was the beauty, the rarity and the historical background of the jewels which made her collection so interesting. She had jewellery which had belonged to Catherine the Great and Marie Antoinette. Pearls were her favourite and she had strings of white ones, yellow ones and black ones which were so large, and so perfectly matched that most people could not believe they were real. Her string of white ones, she said, had taken over twenty years to collect so that they matched in colour, texture and size; their size was that of cherries. Her emerald necklace, which had belonged to Catherine the Great, included a central stone which was over an inch in diameter. All the stones were translucent with the minimum of flaws – unique in emeralds even of smaller size. The necklace could also be worn as a tiara. For someone who hardly went out at all and who did not often dress up, one might feel it was a waste to have so much grand jewellery. Not so. Barbara indulged herself all the time with her jewellery. She looked at it, touched it and wore it as part of her daily attire. Jewellery gave her a great deal of pleasure because she knew so much about the subject. She could talk about it on equal terms with the experts. She could tell at a glance where a particular piece came from and who had mounted the stone. She

27

knew all there was to know about the cut, the shape, the design, the quality of a stone. Jewellers valued her as a customer, not just because of the vast sums she spent, but because they appreciated her knowledge.

In September, soon after she and Jimmy returned from the Far East, Barbara began to give her usual round of dinner parties for her Paris friends who were all pleased to be able to enjoy Herminie's magnificent meals once more. Barbara, who always gave credit where credit was due, would often, after the guests had gone, go into the kitchen in her evening attire to shake Herminie's hand and compliment her on the meal, and would often stay chatting for ten minutes or more. Barbara was familiar with some of the patois expressions of Herminie's southern birthplace, such as 'Boo Deeou', a derivation of '*Bon Dieu*'(My God). Herminie was quite naturally thrilled with Barbara's visits and praise, with being treated as an equal – as Barbara treated all her employees. Maria, the temperamental chambermaid, happened to witness this particular visit of Barbara's to the kitchen. She saw an animated conversation, both women laughing and gesticulating, and stormed into the kitchen in a fit of jealous rage. She ranted and raved about how hard she worked and how Madame never took any notice. She slated Hélène for driving a wedge between herself and Madame. She could not stand it in this house one minute longer. She was walking out and did not even want what was due her in wages; she couldn't stand to spend even one more night under this roof. She came into my office and raved like a lunatic. She clearly expected me to beg her to stay; she had the backing of Silvia and felt in a strong position. I took matters into my own hands and immediately obtained a replacement from an agency. I thought I had got rid of a troublesome person but this was not the end of the story. We heard that Maria was off work for some months from illness – was that, perhaps, the explanation for the dark circles beneath her eyes? She regretted her outburst like the person who killed the goose that laid the golden eggs. She went to Silvia and asked her to get her post back. Silvia pleaded with Barbara to take her back but Barbara had been disgusted and horrified at Maria's outburst and would not hear of it.

We managed very adequately with Janine from a temporary agency for the next three weeks or so until Barbara left for her winter stay at Sumiya, Cuernavaca. Unfortunately Janine was not able to stay – she was idle while her employer was in Australia for

28

six months, but unlike Barbara's employees, she did not get paid during this period of enforced unemployment. I therefore set out to find someone to replace Maria and I thought it was an ideal time to recruit a new person who would have a good long period to get used to the team and the routine so that she would be fully trained by the time Barbara returned to Paris. I found an ideal Breton girl called Nina – very modest, dedicated and hard-working. Further-more, she was well liked by the others because instead of being a know-all, she just laughed at their jokes and did her work well. I was extremely pleased with Nina. She never had to be told anything twice. She showed intelligence, yet she did not show any sign of the arrogance or confidence of clever people. I couldn't believe my luck. Nina became a valuable part of the team. I wrote to Barbara saying that she would be well pleased with the new maid, although I hoped that Nina would lose her shyness. When Barbara returned, she did not have an opportunity to see Nina personally but she did ask me if everything was all right with the new maid. I told her that it was. I detected some reservation on the subject. On the fifth day, Barbara told me to get rid of Nina, without having seen her. I was extremely surprised and upset. Hélène had to explain to me that it was Silvia's right to hire staff. She had persuaded Barbara that she would be able to find someone more suitable.

Barbara's return after a period away always caused a flurry of preparation. She always brought each one of us a gift, such as trinkets of Mexican silver or Japanese lacquered boxes. The buying of gifts for her various household staff and friends was a major occupation for Barbara. Being a generous giver, she enjoyed choosing things that would provide pleasure. I would say that this was the most enjoyable constant activity in her life. She never took her domestic staff on her travels, which meant that she had a full complement of staff at each of her three homes. Upon arrival each time she would have remembered each one with a personal gift. She did not believe in giving money, although that is probably what they would have preferred. Sometimes she would give money as well, but the gift itself was the personal touch. She would always make the choice herself although very often she would ask my advice since I was closer to the staff.

Before going to Sidi Hosni in Tangier one summer, she decided to give cashmere twin-sets to the female staff there. They were the current fashion in Paris, but they had to be the genuine article from

England. First there was the difficulty of finding out the various sizes of the staff, then to translate them into English sizes. Barbara sent me to London where, to my dismay, I did not readily find larger sizes available. To complicate matters further, I had to find a shop which was willing to make a shipment to Paris on approval. Barbara was fussy about choosing the colours herself. She had definite ideas about what colours would suit whom. When the girls were all given their cashmere twin-sets, I could see that it was not what *they* would have chosen. However, we all of us felt grateful for the thought and consideration we knew went into Barbara's gifts.

Sometimes Barbara's present-giving had an edge to it. For example, at Sidi Hosni we had a Moroccan sentry called Mohammed who guarded the door. He was an elderly man, still lean, with an upright bearing who stood at the door with a rifle. The only unsightly part of him was his face which he would shave only every few days. Barbara did not like his unshaven appearance and I asked him many times to please shave every day – to no avail. He would put on a pitiful look and reply: 'I can't afford it.' He collected a handsome salary and we knew him to be a scrounger. I kept him supplied with razor blades. That had no effect. Mohammed was just a lazy scruff. Barbara kept him out of loyalty; he had been with her for many years and was good at giving Barbara the hard luck story. One summer on her arrival, Barbara gave her usual expensive presents to everyone. Mohammed had a safety razor, beautifully wrapped. When he saw what it was, he was visibly disappointed. And he did not shave any more often thereafter.

Every once in a while Barbara would ask me to take staff out for a 'good time'. On one occasion she wanted me to take them to see *The Three Sisters* by Chekhov which Barbara adored reading. She innocently assumed that her French servants would enjoy seeing that play. Another time, she was told that they were showing the English film, *Carry on Nurse*. She had seen it in London and remembered laughing herself silly over it. The reason was that she had been in English hospitals and saw the humour in this type of send up. The film ended with a pompous person having a daffodil in his bottom, instead of a thermometer. I took them all to see the film, which not only loses a great deal in the translation, but whose humour is confined to the English. I did not find it funny as I had never lived in England. Herminie would say on such occasions, 'Couldn't you persuade Madame just to give us the money?'

30

Present-giving reached its climax in Paris just before Christmas when Barbara would remember all her friends and employees. Her godchildren, whom she never saw, were all remembered in a handsome way. Most of her friends would drop heavy hints and Barbara would choose to pick them up or to ignore them, depending on how fond she was of them at the time. So much did she like giving, that normally she would give a second present ostensibly from her boyfriend/husband of the day.

In the run-up to Christmas the suppliers of Paris would outdo each other to catch Barbara's eye. Large bouquets of her favourite flowers would arrive with elaborate verses or syrupy flattery. If, for example, Barbara decided to shop at just one store that season, she might very well buy dozens of brooches, cuff-links, gold cigarette lighters, and so on, amounting to several hundreds of thousands of dollars. The bills would always be padded out. Not only because of the commissions that were paid to her friends, but because Barbara refused to challenge a bill, bargain for a fairer price or ask for a discount for a large order.

The only occasions the suppliers had difficulty with Barbara's bills would be when Graham Mattison left a bill unpaid. All bills over $10,000 had to be sent to him for clearance. Naturally, whenever possible the bills would be subdivided into totals of less than that amount. What Graham was hoping was that Barbara would be forced to return the goods and that in the long run she would learn not to be so generous and extravagant. It was not a successful ploy, for Barbara was wilful, had no sense of value and she preferred not to know that her fortune could not sustain such heavy spending. Graham used to put the fear of God in me. He made it seem as though it were my fault that Barbara spent over $4 million in one year when she bought no new house, no new car, no new jewellery. She had no grasp of accountancy, but it was not from lack of intelligence, it was that she could not face all the sordid goings-on in the real world of her 'friends', her own shortcomings, the disappointments and failures in her life.

This hypocrisy, which Barbara wanted above all else to ignore, sickened me. I did not know how to cope with it. I had been brought up to respect honesty and integrity and in my youthful intolerance I was so revolted and horrified that within six weeks of being in Barbara's immediate and constant company, I told her as diplomatically as I knew how that I couldn't take it and had made up my mind to give in my notice. I broached the subject at my

31

morning session when I would go into Barbara's large bedroom, and sit at the foot of her huge bed, on a delicate stool covered with hand-made lace and Thai silk. There we would deal with all matters. When sober, Barbara had a crystal clear plan of her activities. That day she was stone-cold sober and I blurted out clumsily my wish to leave as the job was not what I had anticipated. She listened to me with attention, her large blue eyes never leaving my face. She replied in the most affectionate and motherly fashion. She managed to worm out of me my difficulty in accepting all these people who made money out of her. I didn't say 'friends', or mention any names, but she understood. She said, 'Come over here and sit by me,' patting her bed. I went and sat there. She took my hand and gave me her philosophy. 'You're young. You judge people as you'd like them to be. You will learn to accept them as they are because you can't change them. There is some good in everyone. Who can say they live without prejudice?' She then told me how fond she was of me, how she relied on me and how lost she would be without me. I was of course very flattered even though I had heard her use the very same endearing terms to others. I somehow felt protective of her. I saw that she not only allowed herself to be cheated, she encouraged it. Her whole attitude to life was to forget the hurtful points, to pretend that ugliness did not exist, to imagine a world of fantasy. With money, this is almost possible. But, by the same token, this kind of money will give rise to the worst type of corruption. I found myself in a dreadful whirlpool which, for the moment, I decided to hang on to.

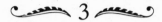

3

Peeling off the Mask

Very often my friends would ask, 'What does a person as rich as Barbara Hutton *do* with her time?' It was as if a vast amount of money was an obstacle to normal behaviour, as if there were more hours in a day for the rich. Or perhaps it is difficult for the average person to imagine a woman who has no job and no domestic responsibilities. The mind boggles at the idea of doing exactly as one pleases with no practical financial limits or the constraints of a timetable imposed by a job or a family. I can remember playing a game in high school which went, 'What would you do if you won a $1 million?' I remember someone saying, 'I'd have a double helping of everything at the best restaurant in town.' Someone in England said, 'If I won the pools I would educate all my friends.' I wouldn't say that Barbara's life consisted of doing exactly as she pleased. The majority of the time she was trapped by what was expected of her in the same way as a housewife is trapped by her duties and routine.

In Paris, where Barbara spent every spring and some part of every autumn, and where I now established my main office, there was little time to cover all the appointments which had to be met. Every season, there would be the choosing and fittings for the new wardrobe. During the years I spent with Barbara, she bought exclusively from the House of Lanvin, out of friendship for Silvia de Castellane. Silvia was employed by Lanvin on a commission basis and Barbara bought a lot more than she needed in order to let Silvia earn as much as possible. Barbara would say to me that Silvia had more than her fair share of financial burden, what with a brother who was an alcoholic, her children and household (she was at the time without a husband). People would say that it would have been simpler for Barbara just to give Silvia the money rather than having to spend huge amounts on clothes that she rarely wore. In addition to her own wardrobe, Barbara would order clothes from Lanvin for others, such as Silvia, her daughters and daughters-in-law, and special friends like the pianist Joan Moore (now the Countess Drogheda) who would come to Paris every season and pick the clothes she wanted, mainly for her public performances.

Lanvin's designer at the time was the Spaniard Antonio Castillo who was a friend of Silvia's and was often a guest at Barbara's dinner parties. He was a very handsome, middle-aged man and a most amusing and jovial person; if he was in the right mood he would give us a burlesque take-off of a female Flamenco dancer – it would be both an excellent mime and very comical. Every year, Castillo's collection was designed with Barbara's taste in mind. He had to make sure that she, Lanvin's most valuable client, should approve and be tempted by the new models. Thus some of the designs would always include Oriental features. If a particular number pleased Barbara, she might order one in blue cotton, another in Thai silk, a third with a bow at the back, and a fourth in pink for a friend. Before anyone else had an inkling of what was in the new collection, Barbara would be shown a portfolio from which she would indicate those numbers she wished to see. Within a few days, Lanvin would arrange for three or four mannequins to come to the apartment and model the dresses, usually in Barbara's bedroom. It would in effect be a private showing. Barbara had persuaded Lanvin to employ the daughter of her Swiss chauffeur, Fernand, as a model. She was naturally included amongst the mannequins who came to the apartment.

They used to use my bathroom as a changing room: it was ideal because it had mirrored walls from ceiling to floor. I attended the showing but I couldn't help thinking that it was rather sad that the mannequins who were mainly from working-class backgrounds, would never be able to afford the dresses they modelled and in which they looked so elegant.

After Barbara had made her choice, there would be several fittings at the apartment attended by two very deferential ladies, one a fitter and the other the seamstress. Barbara would give both women expensive presents, such as a brooch or a bracelet from Cartier. They were always very grateful and on the occasions when Barbara had been drinking and the fitting session was difficult because Barbara was unable to stand up, these ladies would deal with the situation with a great deal of tact and patience as well as affection. It might seem odd that I should mention gratitude at receiving an expensive gift, but my observations of the people around Barbara were that they always expected more. If she were to give a mink coat to a friend, it would most likely prompt the remark, 'But so-and-so got a sable.' Of course, these comments were never made in front of Barbara, but they were, nevertheless, made out of her earshot. It was so bad that I never expected people to be pleased with what Barbara gave them. Thus the two ladies from Lanvin stand out in my memory as being so gracious and sincerely thrilled at Barbara's gestures of appreciation. It was unusual.

The business of buying clothes and going through the fitting sessions was a dead bore for Barbara. She did not need the clothes; she did not really want them; but she submitted to the convention as something *de rigueur* – a chore, a duty to her friends. She once said to me that she thought of it in the same vein as going to the dentist. Indeed, that was another unpleasant task which awaited her in Paris. Barbara's teeth required constant attention. In the autumn of 1959 she went to the dentist every day for five weeks. The main purpose was the capping of all her upper teeth. However, the fundamental problem was that she had been suffering from malnutrition for so many years (she was constantly dieting) that it finally affected her teeth. She was loath to part with them and suffered the agonies of trying to save them. All her money did not save her from the dentist's chair.

Barbara also spent a lot of time in Paris fulfilling her social obligations, playing the role of society hostess. She invited old friends, such as the Windsors, Ingrid Bergman or Douglas Fairbanks Jr, whom she would normally not see at her other homes. Friends of Barbara's from all over the world would time their visits to Paris to coincide with hers. Barbara hardly ever went out to other people's dinner parties. Most people could not compete with her dinner table, with its ancient Venetian glass, museum-piece porcelain plates, exquisite flower arrangements – not to mention the excellence of the cuisine – and besides she much preferred her own territory. The accepted procedure would be to ring Barbara with an invitation; she would say, 'Why don't you come *here* for dinner on Friday?' and everybody would be happy. The polite person would send a dozen Baccarat roses before the dinner.

Barbara only enjoyed this formal role for a short time. Sophisticated and refined social activities were natural to her and she enjoyed catching up on the latest gossip and jokes. But she did not

35

really enjoy this kind of life: Barbara was not at heart a conventional person; she was happiest flouting conventions. Although she spent a great deal of money on couture clothes, it was really out of a sense of obligation, as something required of someone with her wealth. In fact, she loved to wear exactly what she wanted – the idea of constantly 'dressing for the occasion' got her down; she preferred to go barefoot than to wear stilletos.

Whereas people in society tend to be clannish and competitive, Barbara's mind spread across the frontiers and she needed to do her own thing. The formality of twenty-four people seated round her oblong dining table on Louis XV chairs became insufferable after a while; and, after a few weeks in Paris, she would start talking wistfully about her other homes in Tangier and Cuernavaca. Or else she would be planning a trip to the Far East, again with eager anticipation. Even in her teens she had expressed her desire to adopt a Chinese child. She considered the Chinese race the most beautiful on earth, both physically and intellectually. She often said that to me and at first I thought it was a way of flattering me, a special manner of showing affection at which she was particularly adept. However, I have since discovered many sources to confirm the sincerity and genuineness of her affinity to the Orient.

A good example of Barbara's strong streak of individuality and informality was her collection of saris, both ancient and modern; they were the envy of her Indian friends. Nor did she collect them to keep them in a cupboard. She wore them on formal occasions, as naturally as any Indian woman. When Cecil Beaton came for a photographic session in Tangier, Barbara wore her Catherine the Great emeralds and her favourite sari of light green silk with gold thread. Some of Barbara's closest friends criticized this wearing of oriental clothes as 'crazy'. Silvia would say, 'The woman is mad.' They could not imagine someone with so much money wishing to wear anything but French creations by the grandest couturiers. The Duchess of Windsor, for one, would only wear clothes that would be envied by her contemporaries. Barbara, however, preferred individuality.

She had also invented a kind of lounging pyjamas reminiscent of Vietnamese costume, which she had made specially for her in Paris. It may not be such a coincidence that her seventh and last husband was of Vietnamese ancestry. These lounging pyjamas consisted of a flowing silk tunic top, long sleeved with a narrow mandarin collar, fastened diagonally across the right below the shoulder and down the right side under the arm, leaving slits down both sides. The slightly flared A-line tunic reached to mid-calf, and under it was a pair of loose white satin slacks. The top was usually in a soft print, with a wide edging of the same material at the bottom of the slacks. The whole effect was soft and graceful. She owned dozens of these outfits. She first wore them at the Lido when she spent the season in Venice in her early twenties. They never dated. She wore them often over her bathing suit and at informal occasions during warm days in Cuernavaca or Tangier. These oriental lounging pyjamas were one thing Barbara would never give away to anybody. Whereas she freely gave her designer clothes to all and sundry, mostly to her staff, she was most possessive of these, her own exclusive creation. She never took any notice of hints about giving some old ones away when she ordered a new batch. And on one occasion, I remember her Indian friend, Leila Matkar (later Mrs David Lean), asking her for permission to have a copy made for herself. The request was refused summarily, in a manner I had rarely heard Barbara adopt. Similarly, her magnificent collection of saris was kept neatly stacked, each one separated from the next by a piece of silk and kept in a special cupboard in the Paris apartment. These, too, she never gave away in spite of her many Indian friends to whom she was very generous in other ways. Some of these Indian ladies would complain to me, 'What could Barbara possibly do with all these saris?' They would lament with covetousness. In fact Barbara treated her saris like her jewellery. She would sometimes ask Hélène to bring her some of her favourite saris and admire them, comment on them and touch them, just as I had seen her display and admire her jewels. The difference was that she would often give away her jewels, but never her saris!

Inevitably when working for Barbara Hutton, life depended on two things: dealing with her current lover and whether, or not, she was drinking. The person that I witnessed full-circle was Lloyd Franklin. Lloyd and I were close friends, and later I married his best friend. When Lloyd first entered Barbara's life, he was a nobody with no background, no education, no breeding, no style. Within a year, Barbara had turned him into a gentleman. By the time he and Barbara separated, he was well established in upper-class English society. Barbara had transformed Lloyd in very much the same way as Professor Higgins had transformed Eliza Doolittle. Unlike many of those who surrounded Barbara, Lloyd was never grabby. I can vouch for that because he had to come to me with his bills or if he needed cash. He made a superhuman effort to get along with Barbara's friends, some of whom were not particularly pleasant to him, calling him an upstart within his earshot. Instead of being jealous of the hangers-on he told me he felt they were unfortunate – like circus people who perform in various ways for a hand-out. The only time I detected any anger from Lloyd was when Barbara's 'friends' were encouraging her to drink. He did try very hard to make her drink less.

When it became apparent in his third year with Barbara that she was looking for someone else, he graciously stepped aside with more dignity than anyone I had seen. He relinquished the property that Barbara had given him in Tangier, saying he would take the future 'as it comes'. In fact he made a very happy marriage and became a stockbroker in his father-in-law's firm. He and his wife, Penny, bought a summer house in Tangier, keeping on friendly terms with Barbara. Unfortunately, this happy existence was short-lived. Lloyd and Penny, by now pregnant with their second child, were driving back from a New Year's party and, near Rabat, their car collided with a lorry. Lloyd was killed instantly; Penny died a few days later in hospital. The Maserati he was driving had been a gift from Barbara. Lloyd was thirty-one years old.

Husbands and lovers were, however, easier to deal with than Barbara's drinking. Her drink problem was a paradox. Her father was an alcoholic and died as a result of his addiction. She had spent her youth a complete teetotaller and even though she loved France, had many close French friends, such as Silvia de Castellane and her set, and enjoyed French social life, she never touched an alcoholic drink until she was in her mid-thirties when she sipped a glass of champagne at a wedding. From then on, alcohol became a major issue in her life. Some people believe that one is predestined to alcoholism; that it is in one's genetic make-up at birth. Barbara explained it as another curse she inherited from her father. When I started working for Barbara, I was told that she had just come out of such a bad period of drinking that she had been close to death because she had lost so much weight, for she never ate anything when she drank, nor did she get any sleep.

Everything that Barbara did depended on whether she was drinking or not. When she was sober, she held rigid rules and followed a strict routine. The prevailing mood was one of efficiency. We had to be careful not to make too much noise. When sober, Barbara was inclined to read quietly in her bedroom for long periods, in particular after lunch. Naturally, we would all wonder how long that would last, for when Barbara was drinking, the world would be turned upside down. The first signs would immediately be communicated as if by lightning. The signal might be a buzz for Basile to bring her a glass of champagne. It was like a starting pistol. Another sign was if we heard Japanese music coming from Barbara's room. She would play the same record over and over until it drove everybody crazy. Sometimes a drinking bout would start at a dinner party. Everybody there would freeze in mid-mouthful.

If Barbara was drinking we never knew what would be happening next – whether or not, for example, she would carry on with a planned dinner party. If she did have a dinner party while she was drinking, she would speak to one person only and ignore the rest. It could become embarrassing because the others would not know whether to start eating or not. Barbara usually ate very little, but normally she would give the signal, as hostess, for the guests to eat. On other occasions the dinner party would be prepared (the flowers alone sometimes cost over $1,000), all the guests would be there, dressed in their finery (to please Barbara who loved to see people dressed up) and Barbara would be drinking hard in her bedroom, not allowing her guests to start dinner because she herself was not hungry. Herminie would be having a fit about her spoiled meal. The guests would be looking at each other in embarrassment. But, worst of all, Barbara sometimes came out all dishevelled, her hair all over the place, her nightie half on and half off, barely able to walk and, if in an angry mood, she would hurl abuse at her guests. Her 'friends' would never answer back. Anyone with any self respect would never accept another invitation again.

When drunk, Barbara had a habit of giving away her jewels. Her staff would always put back the gift where it belonged and never mention the incident. But that was not the case with most of her 'friends'. Thus, she gave away some of her most valuable pieces to people she barely knew. There was an incredible atmosphere of jealousy among Barbara's hangers-on. What someone else managed to get out of Barbara when she was drunk was the subject of deep suspicion and criticism.

It was impossible to lead a normal life when Barbara was drinking and the difficulty was that we never knew when she would start, or when she would stop. During a drinking bout she was rarely sober for more than four days at a time, and though her degree of inebriation varied, it usually became steadily worse until her body could take no more, when she would – at last – stop.

The effect on all of us during such bouts was a feeling of sickness. My stomach would sink and stay sunk. Hélène would be prey to diarrhoea. The uncertainty of our lives was what made things so bad. Although drink usually made her sad, if Barbara was drinking gin she would become very angry, striking anyone who refused to do her bidding. Usually, Hélène was the recipient of such blows when she tried to take the drink away.

Perhaps the most difficult aspect of life to accept when Barbara was drinking was the fact that she did not sleep – which meant that no one slept. She wanted company day and night. She would usually be very maudlin, crying and talking about the mother she never had. She would also tell fairy stories about little foxes. Having to sit up with her night after night, always with that interminable Japanese music in the background, was the worst possible torture. Many times I pulled out a suitcase to go to a hotel just for a night's sleep. Hélène would beg me not to leave her, so I never went. She was a hundred times more of a nervous wreck than I was, and I always felt I couldn't let her down. Sometimes, though, Barbara would call her friends on the phone and she would talk to them for hours on end. Sometimes she would call her friends in Honolulu or Tokyo. Wherever it was, she would hold them at the other end of the phone and those who hung up had to consider they were no longer friends. That is one way that Barbara managed to lose many of her real friends, for people with jobs cannot afford too many sleepless nights. These night-long phone calls, however, gave me no respite. There was no international direct dialling in those days and all calls had to go through the operator, and Barbara, of course, was not about to start doing that for herself!

So what was Barbara Hutton really like? The usual press descriptions never bore much resemblance to the real person. People who knew Barbara knew her through her various homes, and the ambience of each was different – which was reflected in Barbara's behaviour and social life. For example people who knew her only from the rigid, formal ways of upper-class Parisian life would have found it difficult to recognize the Barbara of Sumiya, her winter home in Mexico.

Even people who apparently knew her well could only see glimpses of certain moods, moods which might fluctuate wildly. For example, Barbara was to all her friends extremely charming

40

and ultra well-mannered, whatever she thought of them. If she was fed up with them she certainly would not give any evidence of it. She would make excuses for not answering their messages, for not taking their calls, for not inviting them to dinner. The person being given the cold treatment would usually blame someone else for the ostracism – 'Barbara assured me that she loved me yesterday and that she wanted to see me very soon; it must be her boyfriend who is not allowing her to take any calls.' Yet nothing unpleasant was ever expressed to the person concerned. Once Barbara had decided she did not wish to see someone, she could forget them altogether in a totally unsentimental way.

From all accounts, Barbara's life in early adulthood was a socially dazzling one. She was courted and sought-after. Notwithstanding the disasters of her first two marriages, she was still the darling of the European aristocracy, be they impoverished or rich and powerful. In London, at the age of nineteen, Barbara was presented at Court to King George V and Queen Mary. She found the rituals and traditions very impressive. She was invited to parties at Buckingham Palace and elsewhere which included Edward, the Prince of Wales (later the Duke of Windsor). Barbara enjoyed dancing with him but even in those days she felt very little respect for him as a person. She criticized his habits of drinking too much and his lack of interest in all but gossip and frivolities. At that time, London also played host to another American, Wallis Simpson, whose romance with the Prince of Wales was just starting, and some of the anti-American criticisms expressed in the British press rubbed off on Barbara.

For the sake of objectivity, I researched while writing this book into what other people who had met Barbara said about her. The columnist Art Buchwald wrote in the *Herald Tribune* in 1953 that far from being the spoiled brat depicted in the American press, he was surprised to find her to be a very sympathetic person. Earl Blackwell of Blackwell's Celebrity Service (a company which used to compile information about the comings and goings of celebrities) said Barbara was one of the most refined ladies he had ever met. There are many quotes from David Niven in his autobiographies and from his interviews. He first met Barbara in 1932, long before he became an actor. He remembered her as a very pretty girl with tiny feet and with a sparkling and happy disposition. He was her guest at the Hôtel Pierre and she invited him to stay as long as he wished, not only all expenses paid but he was to receive very

41

generous gifts from his hostess as, he noted, did all her friends be they women or men, romantically attached or otherwise. Niven said she had looks, intelligence and wealth, with an amazing lack of self-esteem. It might have been the reason for her frightening generosity which lasted all her life and which she directed at people who were unknown, unconnected, unsuccessful – they were just people she happened to like. Some women relate to people, showing they care by feeding them, making a comfortable home for them. Barbara lavished money and presents, that was the way she showed her love and friendship.

Douglas Fairbanks Jr, who had known her since her coming-out party and whose house, Westridge, Barbara and Cary Grant rented, recalled that Barbara was full of fun and mischief. He believed that she lived in a fairytale world and that most of the time she did not live in the real world.

Jimmy Douglas, Barbara's companion from 1957 to 1959 has also made public statements on what Barbara was really like. They had gone on a trip to the Far East soon after they met and immediately after Barbara's health had reached its lowest ebb. After what he had heard and read about her, he was amazed to find her to be a person who enjoyed life to the full. She loved having fun and he discovered the person that the public ignored or had never seen. The real Barbara Hutton, he found, '. . . was quite remarkable, infinitely interesting, with great personality and imagination'. The other Barbara Hutton was an invention of the press.

Dudley Walker, originally Cary Grant's butler, was hired by Barbara to look after her son Lance. She had recognized in Walker a reliable and trustworthy person and she wanted him to look after all Lance's needs, financial as well as domestic. Walker found Barbara to be the ideal employer. She never questioned any accounts, she always paid promptly so that Walker was willing to advance his own money to pay Lance's bills, for like his mother, Lance had no idea on how to keep to a budget. Though she rarely saw him, Barbara never forgot Walker at Christmas, and he is on record as saying that she was as generous to him as to her own friends. I would agree with him – Barbara was not only generous, but thoughtful and considerate of her employees.

Not only did she always give her staff presents on her return from a stay elsewhere – she gave me the most beautiful pearl necklace when she returned from her trip to the Far East with Jimmy Douglas and she had only seen me at that very brief interview arranged by Graham Mattison – but she gave presents for no special reason.

One evening when Barbara went to the kitchen to thank Herminie, as was her custom, for an excellent meal, the subject turned somehow to travel. Herminie said that she had never left France in her life and that she had always dreamed about Greece. The next day Barbara asked me to organize a trip to Greece for Herminie as soon as it was convenient. She said that I could accompany her if I wished, or arrange for someone else to go with her. In the event, I did not have the time and Herminie preferred to go alone. The most convenient time was the summer when Barbara was in Tangier. Herminie was completely undaunted by anything: flying for the first time, being in tremendous heat or having to keep up with people half her age. She was as eager as a puppy. She came back full of enthusiastic stories although her arms and lips were covered with heat blisters. One of the stories she told me, 'Can you imagine, Mademoiselle, a specially-organized trip in Athens where we had to walk up a hill to look at a house that did not even have a roof!'

Barbara had an obsessive nature, for her it was all or nothing, whether it applied to people or to things or to activities. She had passions for certain pastimes. In her younger days she had a craze for tennis. She never became a very good player, but she would practise every day with professionals. She personally supervised the building of the tennis courts at her pre-war London home, Winfield House. She wanted to talk and live the tennis life. She worshipped the champions and many came into her life more or less permanently. She dated former champion Budge Patty quite seriously for a time because she loved the way he played tennis. Her faithful and long-suffering friend, Bill Robertson, was once a top doubles player. She had admired the skill and grace of Baron Gottfried von Cramm from the time she was barely twenty; she worshipped him through several husbands until she made him her sixth when she was forty-two. Even after this marriage ended, she still entertained some of von Cramm's close friends.

Early in 1960, just before going to join Barbara at Cuernavaca for the first time, I had instructions to meet a certain Dr Heinrich Kleinschrot arriving in Paris from Hamburg, to have him stay at the apartment and arrange for him to fly to Mexico City with me. Dr Kleinschrot was a small, wizened old man, rather quiet with very good manners. Little did I suspect when I first set eyes on him that he would prove a most entertaining travelling companion on

43

the long journey from Paris to Mexico City. I discovered that he had been the captain of the German Davis Cup team and he was full of interesting stories about the tennis world, past and present. He was obviously of the old guard. He deplored the fact that contemporary tennis players were no longer from the upper class. He said it was difficult to work with players who did not have the breeding or the self-discipline. I became interested in tennis myself thanks to him. From then on, he arranged for me to have a pass to the players' enclosure at the Stadium Roland Garros in Paris. The thrill of my life was once to sit next to Rod Laver who was very relaxed as he said to me in his lovely Australian twang, 'Yes, I think I'll try for the grand slam again this year.'

By the time I knew Barbara, she had emerged from the tennis craze, though there was still some evidence of it such as many photos of her in tennis attire, and people from the tennis world popping in and out of her life. Instead, I saw Barbara going through a jigsaw puzzle craze. It was difficult to drag her away from her puzzle. She did not treat it as a pleasant way of passing time; she took it as a personal challenge. She could look for a piece for fifteen or twenty minutes before trying to see if it would fit the space. And if Barbara was interested in something, everybody had to be interested in it. She was giving jigsaw puzzles to everyone she knew and she took offence if she found out that we did something else with our free time. But just as quickly as it had become an obsession, it disappeared and was forgotten, but I was not allowed to throw any of the old puzzles away. They had all to be kept as if they would be used the next day. But they were never used again, which was a pity because Barbara was quite calm and serene when doing her jigsaws. She then went crazy about Monopoly and we had to play all night with her.

After that she went through a period of wanting to play parlour games like charades, word games, guessing games and one particular game which was rather eerie. It had to do with thought transference. One person would be asked to leave the room while the rest of us would decide what it was we wanted him or her to do; for example someone would have to walk across the room, touch a certain person on the arm and then sit on the floor. The person would come back into the room and one of us would take him by the hand and ask him to close his eyes and make his mind a complete blank. Lloyd, who was best at this game, would close his eyes and concentrate on sending the other person images of what he had to

44

do. The whole operation would sometimes take more than half an hour during which we would all sit immobile, not daring to breathe.

Sometimes we would sit around after dinner and someone would come up with a joke and this would set off a session of joke-telling. Barbara enjoyed jokes and she would tell some herself with great glee. She was very good at mimicking accents, particularly the British cockney accent and the southern American accent. One of her favourite English jokes was about a drunk who, in the middle of the night, went banging on the pub door. He could not understand why they wouldn't let him in for a drink. He was making so much noise that the publican shouted for him to shut up from an upstairs bedroom window. The drunk went on making a racket, pleading, 'Please guv, let me in, I just want an 'arf an' 'arf,' whereupon the publican throws a bucket of liquid on the drunk and says, ''ere's your 'arf an' 'arf. 'Arf mine and 'arf the missus.'

Her favourite southern American joke was about a congregation in church on Sunday. One of the ladies says to her friend, 'Who dat good-lookin' gen'man over der?' Her friend answers, 'Wha ah do believe it's the Right Reverent Cunnigham with the gold-rimmed testicles on his nose.' One remark which always made Barbara shriek with laughter was something that her Aunt Marjorie Merriweather Post said to her just before Barbara was married for the first time. 'Barbara when you are married, always sleep in a bed with a board at the foot of it, so your husband can brace himself against it.' It was not meant as a joke, but as sound advice. If only Aunt Marjorie knew how much laughter it provided!

Barbara's sense of fun showed itself in other ways. She liked people who were amusing, whatever their background. And one of her favourite tricks at parties was to poke fun at pompous asses, as she called them. That is why she got along so well with her cousin Jimmy Donahue; they could let their hair down and cavort with anyone who gave them a laugh. At one time, in New York, they befriended a former prostitute who had become rich as a brothel-keeper. Jimmy used to say that it was the best west of Cairo. Jimmy would tease the ex-prostitute, 'Who are you going to leave your money to? You can't take it with you.' She would answer, 'I'll take it with me . . . You just wait and see.' Sure enough, when she died, her will had been drawn up in such a way that every penny left was to be put into the most elaborate mausoleum for her. Barbara enjoyed being with people with talent but not money. She was

45

fascinated by people who had a murky past, who had an unusual accent, who had achieved something noteworthy but not respectable. She could easily find herself on equal terms with them and spend an evening larking about, joking and laughing.

She also enjoyed going to a smart party wearing cheap jewellery from a Woolworth store and announcing that they were family heirlooms. Some people were not sure whether or not she was serious. She enjoyed doing this even in her middle years: it was her way of deflating the snobs and the pompous.

Most people on first meeting Barbara Hutton, including myself, remarked on her delicate and dainty appearance. She was of average height, yet her feet were tiny and her hands were narrow and very beautiful. No one could fail to notice her large light-blue eyes which radiated fragility, gentleness and sensitivity. There was an impression of helplessness which usually elicited a feeling of protection. Although she knew a great deal about many subjects, she never appeared a know-all. Although she knew what she wanted, she hated to assert herself. She wanted to be the one who could make possible a dream journey to the Far East, but she needed a loved one to share what she enjoyed. She had both intellectual and cultural confidence, but none emotionally. She married so she could be the wife of So-and-So. He would have all the status she could possibly offer him – his own fortune, a title, the trappings of a wealthy man such as polo ponies and sports cars – so that she could be the wife of a *somebody*. She abhorred the idea of her loved one being branded a gigolo, a kept-man or Mr Barbara Hutton. She belonged to the generation where a woman relied on her husband for her status – to be better than your husband was something to be avoided at all costs. How very ironic that Barbara, who was in a position to be somebody in her own right, preferred to be in someone's shadow.

Kind, generous, thoughtful, wishing ill to no one: these were Barbara's qualities. At the same time she was capricious, fickle and inconstant. She was a person of extremes and she had no knowledge of moderation. She had a streak of the Scarlett O'Hara in that she wanted everything immediately and hang the consequences. That trait prevented her from making rational use of her money. It led her straight into the most disastrous of marriages. By her own admission, she was quirky and immature and found it almost impossible to compromise. In 1938, Barbara gave an interview to a respected American journalist, Adela Rogers St John. Miss Rogers

46

wrote that she went to the interview believing that Barbara Hutton was useless and stupid. She resented her millions and the way she lived and played. After the interview, which lasted an hour, Miss Rogers wrote that she had 'found her gracious, intelligent and mellow. She didn't have our problems, but she had some of her own.'

What did Barbara want out of life? Was she driven by an inexorable quest for the perfect mate? She was, but no more and no less than any of us who are sensitive and vulnerable. She needed love and she needed beauty. She found some of each in her life. Her attitude to sex was a modern one. She had few hang-ups about sex and she certainly did not get married in order to have sex legally. Sex, to Barbara, was available and desirable but her need for it was not out of the ordinary. When she started to take drugs she had no more need for sex, but a lot more need for love. The love she needed could not be obtained from sex.

Barbara's whole life was to reach out to people – to do something for them in order to be loved. That was the reason why she was never allowed to see any of her 'fan mail' which consisted of a very few abusive letters and a massive volume of begging letters. Some of these letters would be from cranks, mad scientists with fantastic projects to change the world, people who wanted to fulfil their fantasies and needed financial backing in order to do so. Many, however, were genuine, I am sure: letters from people who were desperately poor. Barbara would have given everything she owned to any of these strangers, and she would have cried real tears for them all as well.

You could see the delight with which she showered things on people. She had no thought for herself, she wanted to make them happy. Barbara knew that Lloyd was self-conscious about his protruding ears. He thought they made him look ridiculous in a hat and he liked the idea of wearing a bowler. To make him happy, Barbara sent him to a plastic surgeon to have his ears pinned back.

Barbara was reluctant to give herself any credit for her generosity. It was Hélène, a patriotic Frenchwoman, who insisted on sewing on to Barbara's lapels the sliver of red ribbon indicating the merit of Chevalier de la Légion d'Honneur. The French government had conferred this honour on Barbara for her enormous donations in cash and in furniture, without which it would have been difficult to achieve the restoration of the Versailles Palace. I think that Barbara was inwardly proud of this honour but if anyone mentioned it, she invariably said that she did not really deserve it, it was thanks to Grandpa Woolworth, and changed the subject.

Was Barbara Hutton an unhappy person? I do not believe she was any more unhappy than the average person. Barbara remarked that unfortunately when she was not smiling, the corners of her mouth drooped, which was true. The shape of Barbara's mouth gave her a look of disappointment. And certainly throughout her life, she did not believe she achieved anything; in this respect she was unfulfilled and it added to her poor self-image.

Another assumption about Barbara was that her successive marriages meant she suffered untold heartache when each one in turn ended in divorce. Only the Reventlow divorce with its custody battle involved any acrimony. In all the other cases, it was a question of having grown tired of her partner. The magic had gone, other men looked more attractive. In her usual generous way, she would ask the person concerned to remove himself for a generous fee. Barbara's husbands were not breadwinners, rather they were expensive playmates. Money allowed her to indulge these whims.

Was Barbara's wealth a source of unhappiness? She would often say that without money she'd be much *more* unhappy. Would she have been happier if she never had any money to start with and had to earn a living? Or if she had to stick with a husband because he was the breadwinner? It is impossible to conjecture, for she would have been another person. Barbara's wealth afforded many joys and experiences to her and her friends. It is argued that because she could afford just about everything, she became jaded; because she was pursued for her money she was disillusioned. These assumptions are doubtless at least partially true, but there is disillusionment in ordinary lives. Marital breakdown, alcoholism, drug-taking and suicide are not confined to millionaires. I am personally convinced that money for Barbara Hutton was a contributory factor towards her happiness, not the contrary.

If her money did not make Barbara unhappy, her childhood experiences certainly made it difficult for her to form lasting relationships. At an early age she had learnt what it was to be unwanted. Imagine seeing all the other girls going home for Christmas and realizing you would have to stay behind because none of your family had remembered you. What an experience!

She expressed her sadness and grief in poetry. At school she wrote about her loneliness in secret, not sharing it with anybody. The loss of her mother, her unfortunate relationship with her father, people spitting at her in the street when she was a teenager, these events led her to write poetry to express the sadness of her soul. She wrote not only about life and love, but about subjects such as big business, unfairness in the distribution of riches, the plight of women, the beauty of Chinese literature, jade, suffering. Whatever the subject, she only wrote when she felt sad. She was always very shy of showing her work. She had been used to writing in secret; it was like crying in secret. The poems represented her very private feelings and disappointment. It was only the prodding of Morley Kennerley, a close friend who worked for the publishers Faber & Faber, that persuaded her to have a private limited edition published for her close friends. The first volume entitled *The Enchanted* contains seventy-nine poems and was published when Barbara was twenty-one. Later came a collection of poems about China entitled *Peking Pictures* which were set to music at the suggestion of Lawrence Tibbett, a leading singer at the Metropolitan Opera. *The Wayfarer*, a collection of forty poems, appeared in 1957. It included poems about Tangier, always a place that fascinated her, Thebes and ancient Greece and, as always, the ephemeral qualities of love.

This poem about Egypt was written by Barbara when she was twenty-one:

> Here is no tomorrow
> No years, nor yesterday
> Here is there Forever –
> No Time, and no today.
>
> Here there is no death,
> No falsehood, and no fear.
> Here is light eternal –
> Radiant and clear!

4

The Woolworth Heritage

Surrounded by the luxury of Barbara's way of life, I always found it difficult to realize that her grandfather, Frank Winfield Woolworth, started life in 1852 on a modest dairy farm in Rodman, Upper New York State. Frank, the elder of the two sons of John and Fanny Woolworth, found he did not enjoy farm life and at the age of eighteen decided to strike out on his own to find something else. Although his parents would have preferred him to continue on the farm and perhaps to improve and enlarge it, Frank was determined to leave, even though he did not know exactly what direction he would eventually follow.

Having no particular or obvious talent, Frank Woolworth took a job at $3.50 per week as a clerk in a general store in Watertown, near Lake Ontario, and joined an evening class in business and accounting. He soon became indispensable to his bosses who were extremely impressed by his ideas on salesmanship and marketing. His first promotion was from clerk to window display manager. Somehow, Frank had a way of arranging a display which would make people flock in and buy. There are pictures in existence taken around 1876 of the window displays which seem to have revolutionized people's shopping habits. Frank had the idea of starting a 'five-cent counter' where various items were put together, all costing five cents. The venture proved so profitable that it became a permanent feature of the store. Other stores began losing custom as a result of Frank's new ideas and his reputation was spreading to stores in the neighbouring towns.

In 1879, at the age of twenty-seven, Frank Woolworth received a loan of $300 from his bosses and opened his own shop in Utica, New York, a larger town 100 miles away. He called his store 'The

Great Five Cents Store' after his successful five-cent counter. In the meantime he had married a young Canadian seamstress, Jennie Creighton, who was to provide great support and companionship in his long career until, towards the end of her life, she suffered from acute senility.

Four months after opening his own business in Utica, Frank moved to Lancaster, Pennsylvania, over 400 miles away, and opened 'The Woolworth's Five and Ten Cents Store'. Within five years he owned a chain of twenty-five stores in five States with a turnover of over $1 million per year. These stores could be described as the forerunners of the supermarket, offering a wide range of goods at low, fixed prices, in contrast to the more usual specialist shops. They were also designed to be fun to browse in and take children to.

In twenty years Frank increased the turnover tenfold to $10 million and by 1917 the turnover was $100 million per year from 1,000 stores. By that time Woolworth was a household name throughout the United States where eventually he had a chain of over 2,000 stores. The next step was obviously to set up stores based on the original principles overseas. It was not long before the F. W. Woolworth logo, in its distinct red and gold lettering, became an integral part of high streets in Britain and most European countries, as well as Mexico, Canada, and the West Indies.

The American press regarded Frank Woolworth as a shining example of the spirit of American enterprise. His rise from modest beginnings to vast wealth was the embodiment of the American dream. Frank Woolworth, however, was not the average American. He was exceptional in many ways. He had a capacity for hard work, fuelled by excellent health and the belief in the Protestant work ethic which equated hard work with virtue. He also had a very keen feel for business in all forms (display, retail, marketing, accounts) which he had originally picked up at evening class. Few top businessmen have all these talents, they obviously have some but areas of weakness are dealt with by a group of trustworthy and talented advisors. Not only did Woolworth have all the necessary abilities, he personally kept in touch with each aspect of the business even when he was head of a large empire. He was a deeply Christian man who truly believed in humanitarian values, and frequently referred to his employees as his family.

He did not live to see the great Depression when the low salaries paid to the salesgirls in his stores became an industrial issue and pictures of picketing employees made front-page news. Woolworth, I am sure, would have been very upset at this scene. He sincerely believed that he offered training to women which allowed them to have a better job than in a factory or as domestic servants. He felt that he was elevating the industrial status of women. He wanted to give women an opportunity to better themselves and he believed that they were grateful for it.

If this colossus of a man, Frank Woolworth, had any weakness, it was his feeling of inadequacy vis-à-vis the established members of the upper class. He felt very strongly that millionaires who had inherited wealth or social position were superior to self-made millionaires like himself. However rich or successful he became, he would still be a *parvenu* who started life modestly and had not been educated at the best schools and universities, and whose wife had made her living making other people's clothes before she married. Some self-made millionaires take pride in the fact that they made it on their own; Woolworth, however, was a man who secretly longed to be part of the real nobility. Perhaps this feeling was inherited by his grand-daughter Barbara, who made a habit of seeking titles. Since he felt his pedigree was not up to scratch, Woolworth set out to outdo the upper class at their own game. He actively set out to woo their approval, especially so that his three daughters would be accepted in that society. Despite the admiration and recognition unreservedly bestowed on him he wanted more, he wanted acceptance among the established upper class.

Social acceptance and marriage into a good family are, however, transitory. Frank Woolworth also wished to leave tangible marks for future generations: he was obsessed with the need to create bigger and better buildings. Like other industrial giants he needed the security of bricks and mortar which guarantees a sort of immortality. He loved buildings in general and had the urge to create new buildings; he needed to have a hand in moulding his environment.

Woolworth and his family moved to New York City from Utica, in 1895, when his three daughters, Helena, Edna and Jessie, were seventeen, twelve and nine respectively. He bought a 'brownstone', a solid, terraced house, on Quincy Street in Brooklyn, a quiet and respectable area. Five years later, as his prosperity grew, he moved with his family to the Hotel Savoy in the centre of fashionable Manhattan while he built his own four-storey mansion on Fifth Avenue at 80th Street. The 36-room house was designed by the well-known architect, P. H. Gilbert, who, under Woolworth's watchful instructions, produced a magnificent town house to rival those of the Vanderbilts and the Carnegies. The interior furnishing left nothing to be desired in taste. Woolworth, as usual, personally supervised all purchases, many of which came from Europe. Once in the new house he proceeded to give glittering parties. The guest lists included not only the most interesting members of society, but also the leading members of industry and commerce, as well as American and foreign dignitaries. Barbara's Aunt Jessie, the youngest Woolworth daughter (and the only one I knew personally), would speak nostalgically of those days when she often went dancing six times a week. She told me that hers was the last generation to have a carefree youth and she regretted not having realized it at the time.

No sooner were they installed on Fifth Avenue than Woolworth bought a row of four houses in the same street which he had demolished in order to rebuild them. Woolworth needed one of the houses for his servants and one each for his daughters to occupy as and when they married. This particular venture received much publicity in the press, who were unaware that they had something even grander to witness.

Woolworth's most spectacular building venture was the Woolworth Building at Park Place and Broadway. It was completed in 1913 under Woolworth's personal supervision, as always. The architect of the 66-storey building was Cass Gilbert (no relation to P. H.), who was later to design the Treasury Annex and the Supreme Court Building in Washington DC His distinct neo-classical style became a characteristic of the nation's capital. The Woolworth Building cost $13.5 million to build and it was the tallest building (792 feet) in the world for seventeen years until the Chrysler Building was built in 1930. The Woolworth Building, lacily ornamented in modified Gothic and regarded as the best designed of early skyscrapers, was opened by President Woodrow Wilson and all America shared and identified in its glory. For Woolworth this was the pinnacle of his achievements, a tangible witness to his successful career.

Frank Woolworth's final building venture was at Glen Cove, on the North Shore of Long Island, where many of the millionaires had their country residences. Of all the millionaires' palaces on the North Shore, Woolworth's Winfield Hall was to be the grandest: it was quite specifically built to impress. Winfield Hall was a marble palace and its fifty-six rooms were filled with furniture that had belonged to European royalty. The circular driveway was a mile long and twenty-four full-time gardeners kept the formal gardens in good trim. The grand staircase was the most costly ever built – $2 million. The ceilings were trimmed in 14-carat gold leaf. Hundreds of guests were entertained in these lavish surroundings which included a summer pavilion, a swimming pool, tennis courts, greenhouses, fountains, arched pillars, and a carriage house. Woolworth had paid $9 million by the time it was finished. Unfortunately he was to enjoy it for only two years. He died of septic poisoning, having refused to see a dentist, at the age of sixty-seven.

5

The Making of a Millionairess

Frank and Jennie Woolworth had three daughters and no sons. Normally, empire builders are eager to perpetuate their name. Barbara was proud that her grandfather delighted in his daughters, apparently not regretting his lack of sons. He was an indulgent father who brought his children up to respect self-expression, in the same way that he felt his female employees had a right to a life outside their domestic duties. He impressed on his daughters the idea that they should fulfil their natural talents and inclinations as he believed this was what made people happy. Happiness was all he required his daughters to achieve. All things told, the Woolworth girls had a remarkably normal childhood among the hard-working middle-class. By the time Woolworth reached his phenomenal wealth and fame, the girls were already grown-up. They did not receive millionaire treatment as children.

The eldest daughter, Helena, was sensible and well-balanced. Being the eldest, she had the most developed sense of responsibility of the three. She fitted naturally into the accepted way of life of her father's position. She was the only one of the sisters to marry within her social station. Her husband, Charles E. F. McCann, was a brilliant young attorney who was also from a rich and influential family. Helena lived her life surrounded by luxury but not by publicity. The family was listed in the *Social Register*, owned yachts and a private railway carriage and socialized with their own kind. Their three children all attended top schools and universities and were instilled with the idea of their responsibility to the community. The McCann children continued their family's role as pillars of the social set. Their kind of privileged life never made the pages of tabloid newspapers.

The youngest Woolworth daughter was Jessie. She grew up with an artistic penchant and from an early age gave signs of being unconventional. She and Helena were opposites. Helena conformed and found comfort, self-respect and security in the tried and trodden paths. Jessie liked to dress up and in her youth always spent all her money. No wonder Barbara was close to her Aunt Jessie! Jessie found the usual society boys boring and when she married in 1912 it was to a charming but penniless Irishman called James Paul Donahue. He had no education, was not trained to do anything in particular and had not been able to keep a job for more than a few weeks at a time. Jessie was not looking for a meal ticket and she fell for the blarney. Her father was strongly opposed to this match and until the very last minute tried to dissuade Jessie from making this painfully obviously disastrous union. It was too late to bring her to heel; he had never tried to before.

As he was unable to change Jessie's mind, Woolworth did the next best thing in his role as father-in-law, he gave Donahue a job, believing that any sensible man would want to earn his keep. Under Woolworth's watchful but kindly eye, Donahue very soon proved to be completely unsuited for any kind of work whatsoever. He was incompetent, unwilling to learn and most of the time he did not even turn up. What he did enjoy doing was drinking and gambling, running up enormous debts which Jessie had to honour in order not to run the risk of being the laughing stock of New York society. Her own very generous allowance soon became insufficient to cover the trail of gambling losses left by her husband. When Barbara mentioned them, even *she* found them outrageous and unacceptable. Jessie had to ask her father to pay the debts, which he always did promptly in order to stop any gossip. Frank Woolworth always accepted that the problems of his children were *his* problems. He never hesitated to sign a cheque for any of his daughters and he never said 'I told you so.'

Before her marriage, Jessie was madly in love with Donahue, but once married, she found nothing but misery and humiliation. The source of her greatest marital unhappiness was that Donahue became involved in homosexual affairs, which Woolworth paid large sums to have hushed up. At the time, the truth did not leak out but it was obvious that Jessie had chosen a 'work-shy fortune-hunter' – a favourite term of Woolworth's to describe many of the young men who came courting his daughters. No doubt Woolworth would have had to continue financing Donahue's ever-mounting debts or else it might have turned out to be an expensive divorce if Donahue, a Catholic, were to have accepted that solution. Donahue, however, pre-empted matters by taking a dose of poison during a gambling session. He was forty-four years old and as soon as he had taken the poison he decided it was a mistake. He did not want to die. The doctors did their utmost to save him; no expense was spared. But, four days later, he died.

For Jessie, the whole experience of marriage had been a nightmare. She sold up all the property they had shared and bought a huge duplex on Fifth Avenue where she lived for the rest of her life. She thought she could forget, but she had two living reminders in her sons Woolworth (Wooly) and James (Jimmy) – reminders indeed, for they were to make her almost as unhappy as their father before them. It was a case of like father, like sons. When Jimmy died of an overdose, it was Jessie who found his body.

Edna, Barbara's mother, was the middle daughter. Her temperament was artistic and musical which might have explained her moodiness. She was easily reduced to tears and her parents were particularly indulgent of her. It was perhaps her shyness which made her fall in love, at the age of eighteen, with a broker named Franklyn Laws Hutton, a Yale graduate with no visible attraction or charm. Both Franklyn and his brother married women with looks, brains and fortunes. Coincidence? If they were going to marry, it might as well be women with such advantages. Marriage, however, prevented neither of them womanizing on a scandalous scale. Although Hutton had a profession, he was not really a good catch for Edna, and her parents vigorously objected to having him as a son-in-law. In spite of Edna's entreaties, her parents insisted that she was too young to marry. They demanded that she postpone her engagement, hoping that she would find someone else in the meantime. They accelerated their social life, giving parties which included 'a better type' of suitor. Many bachelors were interested in Edna. Not only was she good-looking, but her father's reputation as the most successful of the day's tycoons attracted the young men of breeding whose family coffers needed replenishing. Furthermore, the Woolworth girls were anything but boring or stuffy. In spite of a popularity which many girls would have exploited to feed their vanity, shy young Edna remained true to her Frank and to please her parents she waited until she was twenty-four before she married him. Most of the stories that Barbara told me about her mother's younger days were no doubt embellished. In Barbara's mind, her mother was perfect. When Barbara spoke about her disastrous marriage to Gottfried von Cramm after waiting eighteen years to marry him, she compared it to her mother who waited six years for someone who was not worth it.

Edna finally married Franklyn Hutton in 1907. He was neither amusing nor dashing, but seemed attractive to her, being older and busy with his brokerage firm. As was Woolworth's way, once his daughter's marriage was inevitable he gave it his backing. In spite of what he had said in the past, he told the press at the wedding that at least Hutton was not a foreign fortune-hunter or a work-shy aristocrat. That might have been true, but Hutton proved to have other traits which were guaranteed to turn the marriage sour: he was a heavy drinker and a womanizer.

Edna's happiness at being married was short-lived. As soon as Hutton had his wife's allowance at his disposal, he increased his indulgences, leaving Edna at home. People have speculated as to whether Hutton was an out-and-out fortune-hunter or if he cared for Edna at the beginning and then allowed himself to go the way of all flesh. Barbara's opinion of him was very definite; she was unable to forgive her father on any point. It was a subject she only mentioned when drunk, and then her bitterness and hatred would come pouring out. The first time that she did so, I was totally bewildered, terrified and at a loss as to what to do. I did not know that so many tears could exist in one small body. But no amount of tears could wash away the hurt.

Barbara was born five years after the marriage, on 14 November 1912. I am sure that the unhappy Edna passed some of her melancholy to her little daughter in that crucial early period in a child's life. Hutton was openly flaunting his mistresses and the press would report his night-life activities. Woolworth gave him severe warnings, and each time Hutton reduced his galavanting to a more discreet level for a while. Edna suffered more and more from bouts of depression and her feeble reproaches only met with drunken temper. Edna did not mind his drinking as much as learning about his affairs from the newspapers. That would cause bouts of depression which would last several weeks at a time.

In 1913 Hutton became deeply infatuated with a Swedish actress, Monica von Fursten. He was seen regularly in public with her. Edna was distraught, because she realized that this liaison was more serious than any previous one. She threatened to leave him and begged her father to help her in this situation. This time Woolworth threatened legal action and Hutton promised to give up his mistress. The following week Edna saw a photograph in the evening paper of her husband and Monica von Fursten at a night club and she took a lethal dose of poison. This was the end of her suffering on earth but tragically it was Barbara, aged four, who discovered her mother dead on her bed wearing her prettiest nightgown. The memory was to haunt Barbara's life; I believe it formed the basis of her insecure personality. The official explanation of Edna's death, given in great detail, was that she had succumbed to an ear infection, resulting in suffocation. It cost Woolworth a small fortune to hush up the true story, to persuade the police not to disclose the discovery of the poison and to destroy any files containing evidence. Woolworth also paid to prevent the authorities from conducting an autopsy.

Although Barbara's grandparents and aunts did their best to take an interest in this tragic child, the decisions taken then resulted in Barbara believing all her life that she was unwanted. Immediately after her mother's death, Barbara went to live with her grandparents at Winfield Hall, Long Island. This lasted until Grandpa Woolworth's death, two years later. She would speak about that time as a spooky period. The enormous house was intimidating to the bewildered little girl who could not quite grasp why her mother had gone. There was no one person to look after her and her grandmother was a victim of advanced senility. Barbara remembered Grandma Woolworth rocking in her chair, making strange noises, completely unaware of her surroundings and unable to relate to people.

Frank Woolworth's will left everything to his incapacitated wife who outlived him by five years. When Jennie Woolworth died, the estate was left to the three heirs: her two surviving daughters, Helena and Jessie, and Edna's share went to her only child, Barbara. Barbara's inheritance in 1924, at the age of twelve, was $28 million, to be held in trust and administered by her father until she came of age at twenty-one. No one in the family talked about this inheritance to Barbara, in case it would affect her character. It did. As a result of being kept in ignorance of her wealth, Barbara went through life with absolutely no idea of the value of money, much less how to manage it. Barbara said that she gradually became aware of her potential wealth from the newspapers, and from whispered conversations. At first she did not connect this fact with the cold and resentful attitudes of other children towards her.

After her grandfather's death, Barbara first went to live in Burlingame, California, with Aunt Grace, her father's sister. It was here that Barbara first discovered Oriental *objets d'art*. It was a happy period spent in a cheerful atmosphere with dogs and a pony. Barbara had private tutors and a group of friends her own age. Aunt Grace was affectionate, bubbly, and cultured. Barbara rarely saw her father who was busy with a variety of mistresses as well as the very successful brokerage firm he ran with his older brother, E. F. (Ned) Hutton. Although Barbara remembered missing her father on the rare occasions that she saw him he was cold and ill-tempered. Even at that age, Barbara was unable to feel any rapport with him.

Another unsettling factor was that Barbara had no steady or permanent person to look after her. Kind though Aunt Grace was, she was a socialite who was not taken with child-minding. Franklyn Hutton hired and fired a series of women at long distance, leaving Barbara to grow up with little direction. That is, until Germaine Toquet (Tiki) entered her life. Tiki was French and a sweet person. She was a kind, warm presence, but had no idea about how to raise a child.

When Barbara was eleven, Aunt Grace married and moved to the East Coast. Before packing up, she enrolled Barbara in a nearby boarding school, Miss Shinn's School for Girls. She took Tiki with her as part of her household. It was at school that Barbara experienced the worst kind of rejection, something she was to mention often in later life. The other girls went home for Christmas, but Barbara had to stay at the school for no one had invited her to join them. All her relatives lived on the East Coast. When Franklyn Hutton realized how inconvenient it was to have Barbara so far from reach, he transferred her to another fashionable school for girls, Miss Porter's School, in Farmington, Connecticut. At least, she was now invited to spend the school holidays with her family: Aunt Helena on Long Island, her father and step-mother in New York City and South Carolina, but mainly Aunt Jessie in Manhattan and Palm Beach. Barbara enjoyed the company of her cousins, Jessie's sons, Wooly and Jimmy. She eventually persuaded them that she would rather live with them and go to day school in Manhattan. She was enrolled at Miss Hewitt's School when she was fourteen, while she was living with Aunt Jessie. Barbara did not take to scholastic life. She was to say later that she learned

60

absolutely nothing at school. Perhaps this is why she never expected any academic achievement from her own son.

Franklyn Hutton had married again after a period of bachelor life. His wife was a blowsy divorcée called Irene Curley who was a working girl. Barbara disapproved of her taste in dress, but she had to admit that her father had improved with Irene who tried very hard to provide the family background that Barbara had missed. When Barbara decided at seventeen that she wanted her own apartment in New York, Irene persuaded Franklyn (who remained in charge of Barbara's inheritance up to her twenty-first birthday) to petition the court to release the money. Franklyn did this reluctantly for he, being an investment broker, was generally opposed to spending and felt that Barbara was far too lavish with her money. In spite of now occupying her own 26-room duplex apartment on Fifth Avenue, Barbara was a shy and withdrawn teenager, with little self-confidence and a fair amount of melancholy. Her spare time was spent writing poetry while slowly she entered into the social life of an adult heiress.

One relative who managed to inject some joy in Barbara's life was her aunt-by-marriage Marjorie Merriweather Post who at the age of twenty-six inherited $250 million. The inheritance came from her father, C. W. Post, a self-made multi-millionaire who manufactured Postum, Wheaties and other successful brand-name foods. Aunt Marjorie was living proof that a woman could inherit a fortune and enjoy life to the full. She took charge of her fortune and rode it with a full throttle. She married in turn Edward Close (a New England socialite), E. F. Hutton (Franklyn Hutton's older brother and partner in business), Joseph Davies (US Ambassador to the Soviet Union) and Herbert May (a wealthy Pittsburgh businessman). Aunt Marjorie had the foresight not to antagonize the public during the Depression, something that Barbara should have emulated to save her much subsequent heartache. When Aunt Marjorie took delivery of her $1 million super-yacht in 1929, the most luxurious owned by a private individual, she did so part-way across the Atlantic so as not to attract the attention of the press. Aunt Marjorie had a good financial brain and she multiplied her assets by good business dealings, at the same time engaging in massive philanthropic work. She created the most lavish living pattern of modern times, maintaining three enormous estates with between thirty-five and sixty staff each. She retained three full-time pilots for her private plane. She was a regal party-giver and befriended

61

royalty from many countries. Unlike Barbara, Aunt Marjorie was not haunted by the unfairness of her wealth. She used it to full advantage without inhibition. Barbara was extremely fond of Aunt Marjorie and throughout her life she continued to visit her, especially at Mar-a-Lago, her sumptuous palace in Palm Beach.

The first memorable event in Barbara's teenage life was a trip to Europe in 1929. It was the beginning of a full social life, of courtship and a wave of spending. The following year saw Barbara Hutton's début. *Time* magazine said, 'Barbara Hutton is a serial story, exciting, enviable, absurd, romantic, unreal.' She had just bought a private pullman train, like the one owned by Doris Duke, one of her friends.

Barbara's coming-out ball on the evening of 21 December 1930 was held at the Ritz-Carlton Hotel in New York. It was the most spectacular and outstanding formal ball that that generation could remember. There were over a thousand guests, including Doris Duke, and Louise Van Alen who was to be Barbara's first husband's first wife. Twenty-five years later, those friends of Barbara's who had attended this social event, such as Silvia de Castellane and Douglas Fairbanks Jr, still talked about it with awe. Trees and tropical flowers had been flown in from the West Coast and Florida. Champagne flowed like water, thousands of bottles were drunk even though Prohibition was still in force – and would be for another three years. Maurice Chevalier entertained the guests and Rudy Vallee and his band provided some of the music. There were three other orchestras, each with a special style, including a Russian group (a foretaste of things to come, perhaps). The press was naturally out in full force to cover the event, snapping every guest going into the ballroom. This event was probably the major cause of the subsequent anti-Hutton demonstrations staged by the unemployed and the poorly-paid Woolworth salesgirls. Barbara told me once that her coming-out party had been no fun for her. She was caught up with what she thought were her social obligations. She had attended her friends' coming-out parties for lack of anything else to do. In her more mature years, Barbara shrugged off these conventions as 'silly things we do when we are young'.

At the age of twenty-one Barbara inherited $42,077,328.53. She had experienced several years of a frustrating and unfortunate relationship with a father who was always drunk and somehow resentful of her. When she came into her fortune, she gave him $5 million for managing her inheritance, and added $1,250,000 to her then-husband's coffers. Thereafter she proceeded to use her money with unparalleled abandon. She was determined to use her money to bring her the happiness she sought. Unfortunately for her, the timing of her inheritance coincided with the severe economic depression suffered by the United States and, indeed, the rest of the developed world. The cost of her coming-out party – $50,000 for one evening of fun for the wealthy – was just the kind of publicity that was to damn her in the American press and in American public opinion. Barbara at that time failed to see why people should comment on how *she* spent *her* money. Indeed, her Aunt Jessie was able to lose $50,000 at the roulette table in one night but no one commented on it except her accountant. Cousin Jimmy would throw away $50,000 for the sake of a practical joke, again without being reproached in the press.

Barbara was, and continued to be, personally blamed for people's plight in times of adversity. Unemployed Americans made her responsible for their lack of work; employed Americans made her responsible for their low wages. In the 1930s the average American was very insular, in fact almost xenophobic. The tabloid press would fan this emotion with pictures of Barbara in company with foreigners. If these foreigners were titled, it created an even greater hatred. The American way of life is based on having broken away from a society that allowed privileges by right of birth. Barbara was very hurt by all this condemnation and rejection and she dealt with it by ignoring it and leading the very life that earned her all the public hatred. The journalist Elsa Maxwell expressed it in an article, '. . . Barbara Hutton is seen by Americans as a spoiled snob who buys foreign gigolos'.

Barbara herself regretted that things went so badly between herself and her country of origin. It did not help her low self-esteem. Barbara once said to me, 'Perhaps I was of service to my country at a time when they needed a scapegoat, but I was so ignorant of what was going on. I had no idea what it was like to be poor. I could only see from inside my car people shaking their fists at me. No one explained why.'

Never one to tackle life's serious or unpleasant issues, Barbara allowed herself to be courted by the handsome and eligible young men of the world's aristocratic classes. In the 1930s she was not only fabulously wealthy but she had the radiance and glamour of youth and could also converse intelligently. The rich and fashionable from all over the world would be seen in the summer at

Biarritz, on the Côte d'Azur, in Venice. Why should not Barbara Hutton be among them? Palm Beach, San Francisco, Hawaii and trips to the Far East were also part of Barbara's itinerary. I have seen in the press that the unhappy Woolworth heiress travelled the world in search for happiness, dragging her belongings from hotel to hotel and never finding roots. The idea that Barbara was forced to be on the move is nonsense. Most wealthy people find the world a very small place.

Nor did Barbara feel she was unlucky, even at times of ill health. On the contrary, she often remarked on how very lucky her life was, thanks to Grandpa Woolworth. Whenever she read that money had made her unhappy, she would always laugh and say how much *more* unhappy she would have been with no money. When asked what she would have done if she had had no money, she always said that she would probably have been a dancer, for she loved to dance and it would have been a beautiful occupation with refined and spiritual qualities. She obviously had a romantic idea of the life of a dancer. When people remarked on her failed marriages and her bouts of ill health, she would reply that thanks to Grandpa Woolworth she was able to get rid of people she did not like and to have the doctors and clinics of her choosing. No, Barbara Hutton never felt unlucky because she was rich. But it did make her feel guilty and insecure. All her life she felt a need to apologize for, and even to repudiate, her wealth. How many times have I heard her say, 'Don't thank me, thank Grandpa Woolworth.'

Money was not, of course, the sole cause of Barbara's problems. Her aunt, Marjorie Merriweather Post, and many of her friends who were much wealthier than Barbara, came to terms with their wealth and enjoyed their lives. It was the loss of her mother that was the root of Barbara's problems. Psychologists tell us that maternal deprivation occurs when an infant or young child is prevented from forming a warm, intimate and continuous relationship with his or her mother or a permanent mother substitute. Such deprivation, such as death of mother during early childhood, often develops into psychiatric illness in adult life, most usually depression. In Barbara's case, the deprivation she felt at the loss of her mother, aggravated subsequently by social neglect, manifested itself in anxiety, excessive need for love, and ultimately a thirst for drink and drugs. I am convinced that it was this early experience that produced in Barbara the sense of abandonment, the feelings of emptiness and her inability to maintain intimate human relations.

Frequently, according to psychologists, adults who have suffered from maternal deprivation '. . . lack a sense of direction, have a nameless feeling of longing, describe themselves as hollow shells washed up on barren shores'. These were almost the exact words which Barbara used to describe herself in the poems she wrote when feeling sad. As she said to me more than once, 'I never knew my mother, but I've missed her all my life.'

6

The Entourage

Riche homme ne sait qui ami lui est.
Thirteenth-century French proverb

They say that you know a person by his friends. When I knew Barbara Hutton she was in her late forties and her best years were already behind her. I remember an article about her at the time entitled 'Barbara Hutton: Her Future is in Her Past'. There was some truth in it. She had had a facelift and plastic surgery to reduce the size of her breasts; she had accepted that there was no such person as Prince Charming and there was an air of resignation in her expression. Most of all, her drink problem made it difficult for her to enjoy the social life that she had commanded in her younger days. She had been friends with royalty, international dignitaries, people at the top of their professions. Now, it was too big an effort to live up to such people and she found it easier to surround herself with fawning parasites; they were easier to deal with because it was no effort to talk down to them. When she was drinking she usually wanted to talk at length either face to face or over the telephone – and often in the middle of the night. Little by little Barbara had tried the patience of and then finally alienated all those who had their own activities, professions or lives. Most of those who were left were the dregs, and so Barbara's contacts consisted mainly of people who were dependent upon her financially – all in some way or other on her payroll or hoping to get something from her. Some earned their money honestly and usefully; others were merely spongers.

Barbara's last prolonged relationship with a person-in-his-own-right was with Prince Henri de la Tour d'Auvergne-Lauraguais, a handsome, refined bachelor from one of France's most respected families. He had a job as an international stockbroker, was a member of the French show-jumping team and had all the family and social obligations that his position demanded. Any woman would have fallen for this Prince, indeed he was probably the most popular and eligible bachelor of the French aristocracy. He had studied and worked in the United States and that gave him an attractive informality quite different to the rigidity of most French noblemen. When Barbara met him in 1950, her marriage to Prince Igor Troubetzkoy was on the decline and this was exactly the challenge that gave Barbara the desire to pursue this handsome Frenchman. It was very unlikely that she could land him as a husband but that made him more desirable. It was a stroke of luck that he was also immediately attracted to Barbara, the elder by eight years, the legend, a sophisticated woman of the world who spoke French as perfectly as he spoke English. They were seen together publicly in the United States, in Paris, in Deauville, on the Côte d'Azur, Barbara, as usual paying scant regard to the feelings of her current husband. But this time it was not just an excuse to get out of a marriage. For Barbara her relationship with Henri was more than just a new love affair; it was a meeting of minds, a shared sense of humour, a similar mix of cultures. The physical attraction was a bonus which kept them for a time in a magical world of their own. It was just what Barbara wanted: a fairy-tale come true shutting out reality with all its responsibilities.

Passion, some believe, can only exist because it is doomed. When cold reality started to emerge, Barbara had to admit that she was all too aware of the difference in their ages. To reporters who asked if she was divorcing Prince Troubetzkoy to marry Henri, she would say that this escort of hers was only a youngster. Barbara became impatient about the fact that Henri had to travel for his business, that he had family obligations from which she was excluded. His family totally disapproved of his dalliance with a four-times married American and their contempt for her type of woman was thinly veiled. Disappointment led Barbara to the comfort of drink. She was seen at restaurants and parties unable to sit up, or lying under the table. Barbara believed that Henri did seriously contemplate marriage with her, but by the time she made an issue of it, he found excuses based on family responsibility. He explained that he was duty-bound to produce heirs; Barbara had lost her ovaries in a Swiss clinic. Friends of Barbara's refused to believe that he ever had matrimonial intentions. The truth was that Henri de la Tour d'Auvergne-Lauraguais enjoyed painting the town red, he was known to escort Hollywood beauties and he was still sowing his wild oats. Like most Frenchmen, he was perfectly able to have a passionate affair without believing it would last forever. Henri had had his fling with the fabulous Barbara Hutton and he was ready to bow out gracefully. Barbara, on the other hand, was not prepared to let him off the hook. She clung on, she drank more and in her desperation only managed to push him further away. He began to despise her and was driven to losing his temper when he would insult her, making disparaging remarks about her performance in bed. One day in Paris, it finally dawned on Barbara that it was over; she was devastated; she decided to end it all and slashed both her wrists. Tiki, Barbara's governess, told me the story of that evening.

Barbara burst into Tiki's room, blood pouring from her wrists and her face bathed in tears. 'Look what I've done!' she sobbed, showing her bare arms. 'I've just spoken to Henri and he slammed the phone down. He never wants to see me again.' Tiki immediately called Hélène who administered direct pressure on the wounds until the ambulance arrived. Fortunately, there had been no publicity. Barbara never referred to this episode and henceforth made a habit of wearing several bracelets on both arms in order to hide the scars.

Tiki and Hélène both believed that the suicide attempt was only a cry of anguish, otherwise why did she run to Tiki? Apart from this desperate gesture, the end of the affair with Henri was the beginning of a drinking bout which lasted several years with hardly any respite. During that period Barbara did many calamitous things including marrying Porfirio Rubirosa.

As for Prince Henri, he did eventually settle down. Some ten years after the end of his affair with Barbara he married Patricia Galvin, a member of the American Olympic showjumping team. They met in Tokyo where Henri was representing France in the same event.

Silvia de Castellane was the closest and longest-standing of Barbara's all too numerous friends. Silvia had been born Silvia de Rivas, the very beautiful daughter of a Spanish nobleman. At a young age Silvia had the confidence of one who was familiar with the European aristocracy and their activities and utterly sure of her attractiveness to the opposite sex. A few years older than Barbara, the two became friends when Barbara went to Europe in 1931.

Barbara was only eighteen years old, and three years off her majority when she would personally come into that part of the Woolworth fortune which would have been her mother's. Even though her father was in charge of her inheritance and keeping her on a generous budget, Barbara was already showing signs of lavish spending. She displayed a taste for buying expensive jewellery; she was constantly asking her father for large advances. Still, at eighteen she was no more than a shy and awkward kid who was looking for the big time. Silvia was able to offer her an entrée to all the right drawing-rooms. Biarritz in the summer was the chic watering place of the rich and titled. Silvia and Barbara became friends; they needed each other. One had the connections, the other had the money. What a combination for a good time! Silvia's father had been ruined financially in the Depression and Silvia needed a rich and generous friend. She could not have found a better one. With Silvia there was her brother, Felipe Castilleja de Guzman, heir to a title of Marquis. That summer in Biarritz Silvia and Barbara embarked on a long relationship.

The first factor that drew Barbara and Silvia together was Prince Alexis Mdivani, who later became Barbara's husband. Alexis and Silvia were in love with each other but neither of them could consider marriage. Silvia's family would not allow her to marry a sham prince whose Georgian background was somewhat dubious. Alexis needed to marry someone very rich. Silvia suggested her friend Barbara but Alexis had already set his sights on another American heiress, Louise Van Alen, who had promised to share her fortune with him. It was nothing unusual for Alexis to love Silvia, conduct a courtship with Barbara and marry Louise.

As for Silvia, she was duly married off to Count Henri de Castellane, a charming young man from one of the best French noble families who had the misfortune to die young.

At the time I knew Barbara, Silvia and her whole family were kept in luxury by Barbara as they had been for thirty years. Graham Mattison would try and find ways to stop the increasing burden of that family. It included not only Silvia but her five children, a servant and Silvia's brother, Felipe, who was by now a senile alcoholic who had done nothing with his life but drink at the expense of others. Not only did each member of the family receive a generous allowance, but Silvia's was increased by her commission on Barbara's numerous purchases at Lanvin. When Barbara bought her apartment in Paris in 1958, she bought a similar one for Silvia in the same street.

On the evening Barbara returned from Japan with Jimmy Douglas after Tiki, her companion, had died in her absence, I handed Barbara the four pieces of jewellery that I had found in Tiki's night-table. The nicest was a ruby and diamond ring. 'This,' Barbara said, 'I shall give to Silvia.' She then asked me to call Hélène so that each of us could choose one of the other objects to keep as a souvenir of Tiki. I asked Hélène to choose first. She decided on a brooch in the shape of a basket of flowers with small emeralds and diamonds. When it came to my turn, there was a plain gold watch and a Venetian bracelet of rubies, sapphires and diamonds. I had been brought up always to choose the most modest. So I said I would take the watch. Barbara smiled and, taking my hand, said, 'Darling, let me advise you to take the bracelet. Not only is it worth a lot more but it is much more beautiful than the watch and it will look just right on your wrist. I can see that there is a lot you need to learn about jewellery.' She then asked me to call Silvia to ask her to come to lunch the following day and to tell her that she would be receiving a souvenir of Tiki. She handed me the ring and asked me to put it in a box and wrap it up as a present.

At times, though, she would pour out her indignation and dislike of Silvia to me, often with tears, and when she was drinking it would be with anger and frustration. On occasions Silvia would reciprocate and ignore Barbara. We all wondered why Barbara went on lavishing things on Silvia and her children. Perhaps it was because they were the closest she had to a family.

Barbara's generosity to Silvia and her family dated from the death of Silvia's first husband, Henri de Castellane. Silvia was left with very little money and three small children, the youngest only a baby. Barbara took it upon herself to keep the family in the style to which they had not been accustomed. A second marriage to a very old and rich Frenchman made Silvia the Duchess of Talleyrand Valençay. The marriage ended in divorce before the Duke could leave her his fortune and his famous château in the Loire Valley. Barbara continued to take a very important financial interest in Silvia's children, giving Cordelia the most spectacular coming-out party of the season in Paris.

Silvia then fell in love with a handsome fortune-hunter, an Austrian bearing the name of Baron Posch-Pastor. Barbara always said that with a name like that, he *had* to be phoney. She warned Silvia from making the mistake of marrying him. Silvia only saw the truth after he had begotten two daughters, thus adding to

Barbara's financial responsibility. They named the youngest daughter Barbara. Considering that Barbara did not like children, she felt an inordinate sense of responsibility towards them. On days when Barbara felt particularly bitter towards Silvia, she would say that she could easily cut Silvia off, but what of the children? At the time, Silvia had no other means of support.

Silvia's next interest was a married man, Kilian Hennessey of the cognac family. They were both, by that time, grandparents several times over. Nevertheless, credit must be given to Silvia's beauty and power of attraction for she managed to get Kilian to break with his family in order to marry her. At that point, Barbara would often come out with bitter words. Silvia would not include Barbara in her social functions because she could not run the risk of having Barbara in a drunken state. The betrayal, as it seemed to Barbara, was a sad thing for us to see; for she probably needed Silvia more than Silvia needed her.

When Silvia's children were young and Barbara was in Paris she would usually invite the smaller ones to tea on a Sunday afternoon. It would always be a rather dreary affair; Barbara was easily irritated by the children's natural restlessness. She made an effort to fuss over them, but it *was* an effort.

She did, however, take a greater interest in Silvia's sons when they were grown up and starting to go out with girls. In particular, Barbara had a soft spot for Henri, the younger son who was dark, good-looking and shy. He was vulnerable and sensitive and Barbara felt protective towards him. He did not have a brilliant mind and his studies were not spectacularly successful, but he got himself a job in a bank and tried hard. Barbara would ring him at work and ask him to come over to keep her company – she never understood that people who had jobs could not do as they pleased. Henri started to go out with Isabella di Rovasenda who was the daughter of Madame Antenor Patino, the Bolivian tin magnate. Isabella was an attractive slim blonde girl, somewhat cold and unresponsive. The courtship was encouraged by both families. Henri, inexperienced and somewhat immature, was probably not ready for marriage. He had, however, already made the fateful steps towards the altar and he could not escape. Barbara did not like Isabella. That was to be expected, for she disliked Isabella's mother and no one could be good enough for Henri. Barbara wanted Henri to stay single and just have a good time.

Barbara asked me to find out about obtaining some attractive call-girls for Henri and to organize something. I was puzzled and embarrassed. I did not know if she had meant an orgy, or a series of 'dates'. I was completely ignorant of these things. I neither protested nor asked for an explanation of these simple instructions. First of all, one did not question Barbara's wishes and also I was unwilling to display my ignorance and lack of *savoir-vivre*. There is nothing in the Paris telephone book under '*Bordel*'. As far as I knew, a man looking for a prostitute only had to stop one in the street. Rue St Denis was relatively cheap and very crowded both with client and commodity. I remembered how once, as a student, I had gone with some Danish classmates to watch the goings on in rue St Denis. We parked in front of one of the hotels at the cheap end of the street. I thought it all very wicked and was amazed to see that the clients did not wear raincoats with upturned collars hiding their faces. On the contrary, the transactions seemed very open and simple. The thing that amused my Danish friends most was seeing one client going in the hotel with a prostitute and coming out nine and a half minutes later. 'And that included walking up the stairs and coming down again!' one of them exclaimed.

No, that kind of woman would not do for Henri. I also knew that the Bois de Boulogne was full of prostitutes at night. But how could I drive up to one and arrange a meeting? She might be violent; there were ugly stories about what happened in the Bois. Some people did not even drive through the Bois at night because of stories of white slavery, pimps in the bushes and Mafia operations. Finally, I remembered that the most classy prostitutes had their patches around the church of La Madeleine. They were the most expensive, wearing fur coats and accepting American Express cards. I agonized in search of a solution, and feeling utterly defeated shared my troubles with Hélène, at the same time dreading her moral indignation. 'Why don't you ask Max? That's part of his job,' she said in a very matter-of-fact way.

Why had I not thought of it myself? Max was the hall porter and general factotum at the Ritz Hotel. Although I did not know that Max did this kind of thing specifically, he was a most versatile and efficient person. A man in his mid-sixties, heavily built with a gammy leg and wearing thick glasses, he was like an expert private detective and spoke like Jean Gabin. He knew everything there was to know about Paris and he knew all the goings on under the surface. He had worked at the Ritz since before the war and he knew the intimate business of all the residents. He had attended Barbara's first wedding at the Ritz. On that occasion he was in charge of dealing with the gate-crashers. Even though Barbara no longer lived at the Ritz, I still depended on Max to arrange things at the airport customs where he knew the senior staff. Max could expedite the luggage, and he could find ways of delivering valuables from one country to another in spite of restrictions. He had become indispensable to the late Prince Aly Khan who had helped Max with his son's education. During the summer holidays Aly Khan invited Max's son to one of his properties and treated him as his own son. Max was visibly moved whenever he spoke about it.

When I told him that I had to find some call-girls for Henri de Castellane, he said, 'Don't worry, petite, I'll arrange it. You shouldn't be mixed up in this. I'll take care of it.' 'Do you have to do that in your job?' I asked, wide-eyed. 'Not me personally,' he replied. 'It is usually the night porter who deals with this.' Some time later I asked Max if he had arranged things for Henri. Max did not answer, but I gathered from Barbara that it had not been the hilarious time she had intended. Henri went ahead and married Isabella. They had two children and then got divorced.

Barbara's relationships with her numerous godchildren were excellent – probably because they were long-distance. For instance, her English friend whom she had originally met in Biarritz many years earlier, the pianist Joan Moore (Countess Drogheda), had one child, a son Derry, of whom Barbara was extremely fond and whom she helped during the war by inviting him, with his mother, to the United States in order to escape the blitz. She continued to give him an allowance and remembered him generously at Christmas.

But it was obvious that Barbara had a definite preference for her male godchildren. Perhaps she felt a rivalry or pangs of envy when it came to the girls. One of her female godchildren was the daughter of Jean and Morley Kennerley. Jean and Barbara had met each other in the days before either married. Their friendship had strengthened when Barbara went to live in London. Jean's husband, Morley, worked for the publishers Faber & Faber. It was he who later persuaded Barbara to publish privately her poems. He used to keep Barbara supplied with reading matter, often helping her obtain rare books that were out of print. Despite this, Barbara could be rather vicious about their daughter, Diana, and Silvia's beautiful and nubile daughter, Silvita. She would say odious things about them, but when it came to distributing presents, she would be, as always, very generous even to those she usually said she detested.

People were constantly being introduced into Barbara's circle and, as regularly, some would be weeded out. It was a bit like a merry-go-round. One of the newer members of the circle was David Carritt, the art expert who, at that time, worked for Christie's in London. He had been introduced to Barbara by one of her many homosexual hangers-on. Carritt was a quite brilliant wit who could always provide an evening's entertainment with his biting sense of humour and ability to pluck rhymes out of the air. He would make up limericks, sometimes cruel, but always very clever and amusing. Barbara admired this person who was able to entertain all her guests and furthermore was extremely well-connected in the London art world. He was reputed to be a brilliant dinner host, always mixing his guests in an appropriate manner, but never, so the gossip went, inviting anyone who could not further his career in some way.

Barbara invited him to Paris, then asked him to come to Tangier. He paid for his keep by keeping everyone amused. It did not take him long to realize that his hostess was a pushover and he persuaded her to sell one of her paintings, a Cézanne, that hung in the small salon in Paris. The deal dragged on for almost a year, at the end of which Barbara did not receive the amount she expected. She then had to wait for more than another year to get her money. When Graham Mattison expressed concern over such a flippant and disadvantageous sale, Barbara replied, 'You always say I buy too many things, this time I have sold something for a change.' People such as furniture dealers, decorators, and jewellers were always looking for an entrée. Barbara was the greatest of soft touches. Those who made it into her world were lucky indeed.

Another who did was André Denet, Barbara's salesman at Cartier. A charming man with impeccable manners, Monsieur Denet's success in his job was undoubtedly due to his ability to make his rich clients feel good in his company. Barbara would occasionally invite him to her dinner parties and even used the familiar 'tu' with him. He carried on an innocent flirtation with her, flattering to any middle-aged woman. (Barbara had a similar relationship with her furrier, also a handsome, witty and charming man.) Although Monsieur Denet had not received the best upbringing or education, he made the most of his circumstances. He married the daughter of a wealthy landowner whose dowry helped to house the couple in a handsome flat in the 16th Arrondissement. They had two boys who they sent to a Jesuit boarding-school, which in France was the best education that money could buy. They also had a little girl whom they tried hard not to spoil. She was sent to a strict convent school but not as a boarder.

Barbara was curious to see André's children and she asked him to bring them to tea one Sunday. On the day, Barbara changed her mind and did not feel up to playing hostess to three kids, so she asked me to entertain them while she stayed in bed. She wanted to have a look at the children and asked me to let them come into her bedroom for a few minutes after they had had their tea. The children were very well behaved and had obviously been thoroughly briefed on this 'command performance'. Monsieur Denet was also painfully aware that his relationship with this important client was based on fragile ground which could easily be ruined. After all, had she not gone to Van Cleef & Arpels, Cartier's great rivals, when he had to attend to the Duchess of Windsor instead of Barbara Hutton?

After the children had eaten their tea with faultless manners, I took them into Barbara's semi-darkened room. She lay in bed, her small figure swamped by lacy, frilly pillows. The three children entered on tiptoe, their eyes bulging and their throats dry. They were asked to approach which they did with some hesitation. She spoke to them in French, thus making them feel more at ease. She asked them about their schools, about what they hated doing, about their plans when they grow up. The children answered in polite monosyllables.

Then Barbara asked them to listen to some advice from her: 'Never, *ever*, listen to what grown-ups tell you, especially not your parents.' The children did not know what to make of this but when they came out of the room, they had broad smiles on their faces. They had something to tell their parents! This was typical of Barbara's mischief-making humour. Henceforth she had a good giggle with André who swore that his efforts in bringing up his children had been undermined in just one sentence.

But it had not been just a case of trouble-making fun on Barbara's part. She really did disapprove of strict upbringing for children, just as she disliked stuffy and pompous people. She sincerely believed in giving children as much freedom and enjoyment as possible, in spite of the rather disastrous results with her own son, which she conveniently blamed on the negative influence of his father. In her mind, love was equated with indulgence and freedom. This was perhaps because her own childhood had been blighted by the over-powering spectre of her grandfather and then by the restrictions imposed on her by her father. Cutting loose from such restrictions was her idea of happiness – that is what she wanted for all children.

Someone else who was an occasional guest at Barbara's dinner parties was Professor Robert de Gennes, her doctor in Paris. A very kindly yet sophisticated man, he had known Barbara since the 1930s. Professor de Gennes had an excellent reputation among the upper class in France which earned him the nickname of 'Le Petit Frère des Riches'. He adored Barbara and we suspected that he had been in love with her for a long time, to such an extent that he was really quite ineffective as a doctor. Anything she wanted, he would grant. If he gave her any advice he knew very well that she would take no notice, but he was never insistent; he wanted her to have anything she pleased. So she got prescriptions for sleeping pills whenever she wanted. He had lovely bedside manners and his visits would always be a pleasure. I was once invited to his house for dinner; he had children who were my age and I remember how very warm his relationship with his children was. I was quite amazed that such a famous and busy person would still have time to devote to his family. Professor de Gennes told me that in 1957 he paid a visit to Barbara at the Ritz and her body was so emaciated from lack of food and constant drinking that she was covered with blotches which he had seen previously only on dead bodies. He did not believe it possible for anyone to recover from such a state. Yet, Barbara recovered completely when she met Jimmy Douglas who gave her the will to live after her broken heart over Henri.

There were also, in Barbara's circle, some who were easily as wealthy as her, but who were still not averse to enjoying Barbara's generosity, even if they didn't abuse it. In 1934 Barbara visited India with her first husband Alexis Mdivani and saw again some of the Indian friends they had met in Europe, such as the Maharajahs of Kapurthala, Jaipur, Cooch Behar and Baroda. They were made to feel tremendously welcome and Alexis was pleased to be able to play polo once more. They were wined and dined at the palaces of these immensely rich families. They visited many of the various states, they joined tiger hunts and, all in all, had a splendid time. Barbara was not to return to India very often, but during that trip she made some of her most lasting friendships. Barbara felt for two of her Indian friends, Sita of Kapurthala and Leila Matkar, such deep feelings of friendship that they were like sisters to her.

Sita and Barbara were not to meet often, but they kept in close contact at all times. Barbara would regularly send parcels of necessities and small luxuries. I would have to shop for and dispatch foundation garments for the portly Maharanee. Table linens, kitchen utensils, sheets and pillow cases were all gratefully received in a household that was no longer as affluent as it had been, but had to keep up appearances. I would receive a shopping list from the Maharanee and she would always write me a charming letter of thanks when she received the parcel.

The other Indian friend of Barbara's became a close friend of mine in later years. Leila Matkar, a delightfully entertaining and intelligent woman with hair so long she could sit on it, met Barbara in 1934. At that time Leila was the wife of an older man, a high-ranking civil servant, to whom she had been married when she was thirteen. It was a disastrous marriage. After the birth of her two children, Mr Matkar no longer felt the need to communicate with his wife in any way. Leila was a sensitive and artistic person. She turned to music and the playing of the piano and the sitar. Her husband's rejection slowly sapped her spirit until, by the early 1950s, she was a total psychological wreck. Barbara gathered from Leila's letters that her health was dwindling and that she was just waiting to be delivered from her miserable life. Barbara took the initiative of arranging for Leila to go to the best private clinic in New York and to receive the best medical supervision. It took several years for Leila to become a normal human being again and regain her will to live. During that time, Barbara took care of everything, better even than she took care of herself.

Once fully recovered, Leila went home to India to resume her life as the dutiful wife of a government official. At a function given by the Indian Government, Leila met David Lean, the British film director who had always had a fascination for India and had come to investigate the possibility of making a film about Gandhi. At the time, David Lean had a very limited reputation in Britain. *Great Expectations* and *Brief Encounter* had earned him respect for his undoubted talents, but he was in no way, in 1953, the international figure in the film world that he later became.

The very first time he set eyes on Leila Matkar he fell madly in love with her and began his relentless pursuit of her in the face of all odds. Leila was quite naturally flattered by the attention of this tall and handsome Englishman who seemed to captivate most people with his sensitive and intelligent manner. It was not love at first sight for Leila and in any case there could be no separation from her husband and two children in her milieu. Leila's world accepted the practice of suttee, where a widow would be cremated with her dead husband. She attempted to tone down David's wooing so as not to cause a scandal. Her husband appeared totally indifferent as long as

77

it did not cause a social scandal. David could not stay in India indefinitely but absence made his heart grow fonder and when he returned to Europe, he could not forget Leila. His third marriage to actress Ann Todd was over and he made known his honourable intentions to Leila. She had lived in the United States and had known many Europeans, so she was in no way impervious to the modern ways of life. She quite naturally longed to be married to a person who loved her, as David seemed to. She compromised and decided to leave home when her daughter had a home of her own. Her son would stay with his father. David had to wait seven years to be united with Leila and during that time, his love grew stronger. When Leila's daughter married a pilot in Air India in 1959, Leila finally felt justified in leaving the husband who had rejected her. She knew that in making this decision of pursuing her own happiness, she was burning her boats. She was fully aware of the reputation she had earned of deserter of a good home, of joining a man who had already been married three times. She knew there could be no returning, but by now she had grown to love this man who was offering everything he possessed for the love of her.

Barbara had her part in persuading Leila to leave her cold and unfeeling husband. Could anyone expect Barbara to preach any other line, herself having married and left six husbands by that time? Normally, Barbara did not take to her friends' lovers. A possessive vein in her character made her dislike anyone that her friends happened to fall in love with. The usual consequence of this was that Barbara would ignore the other person; she would not invite them to her parties unless she could not decently help it, such as when the couple were married. Even then, she had ways of avoiding the person with whom she had to share the affection of her close friends. One notable exception was David Lean, whom Barbara accepted and approved of from the moment she met him in Paris. As a result she decided to do everything she could to reunite him with Leila. So she invited Leila to come and live at the Paris apartment until her divorce came through.

I was made responsible for Leila's well-being and comforts in Paris for over a year. During that time, David was working in London but he came to join Leila in Paris most week-ends. I would go with Barbara's Swiss chauffeur, Fernand, to meet David at Orly Airport and I would accompany him back to Orly when he returned to London. He was a delightful and interesting person to talk to, considerate and polite as only the English can be. One day,

78

he said that he was sure I had better things to do with my time, especially as there would sometimes be delays and long waits at Orly. He insisted that I let Fernand come on his own and that I drop the conventional politeness of meeting the plane myself. Leila was very careful not to be seen in public with David in order not to impede the progress of the divorce proceedings. The following week-end, I sent Fernand to meet David's plane from London. When David arrived at the apartment, he told us something which made me regret my decision not to meet the plane. Apparently he had arrived on the same plane as Gregory Peck (my favourite star) and had given him a lift into Paris. When I thought that I could have been in the same car with Gregory Peck, I could have kicked myself. David, however, had very few complimentary things to say about actors in general. He said, 'You haven't missed anything; Peck is really a very boring person.' I was not convinced.

One week-end David came to Paris with some work in his briefcase. He had to decide before Monday who to cast as the lead in his film *Lawrence of Arabia*. He had wanted a well-known star and had approached his two favourite actors, Alec Guinness and Marlon Brando, in that order. For some reason which now escapes me, it did not work out for either of them, although Alec Guinness took a smaller role in the film. I remember vividly the three of us sitting in the music room taking coffee after dinner. David had this pressing decision to make. He had with him pictures of several English actors, none of whom meant anything to me. By the end of the evening, David held up one of the pictures and said, 'This is the one.' It was a picture of Peter O'Toole. He was totally unknown outside Britain, and even there few people knew his face. David said that he had done some work on the stage, that he had had plastic surgery on his nose, and that he had promise as an actor. 'After this film,' David said, 'this man is going to be an international star. His name will be a household word. I hope he can take it.' And so, that's the way it happened. Another person who hit the international scene with this film was Omar Sharif, best known in Egypt as the husband of the country's leading actress. *Lawrence* launched Omar Sharif and it started David Lean on the road to fabulous success, recognition and wealth.

Soon after that momentous and significant evening, David and Leila got married in a civil ceremony at the Mairie of the 16th Arrondissement, with Barbara as their chief witness. Happiness radiated from the newly-weds. It was a beautiful day and I realized for the first time that one did not need to be very young or very innocent to experience being in love. On occasions such as this, when Barbara had to appear in public, with the press and cameras in full cry, we in the household dreaded the possibility of her drinking too much. We held our breath and kept our fingers crossed. On David and Leila's wedding day Barbara stayed sober and the whole day went without a hitch. The wedding breakfast was held at the Hôtel George V with twenty or so people. Barbara sat opposite the groom and next to the British actor Jack Hawkins. Leila had her new husband on her right and Marlon Brando, who happened to be visiting Paris, on her left. They decided to put me next to Marlon Brando, because he was going through an intensely Chinese period. It was my misfortune that he had just broken up with a Chinese girl.

My first meeting with Marlon Brando did not show him in a good light. He arrived late at the wedding breakfast, which was a rather formal, sit-down affair. Everything had to be held up until he arrived almost an hour late, and then he offered no apology. He seemed to be saying, 'You are lucky to have me here at all.' My American schooling had taught me to appreciate informality, but Brando proceeded to help himself to food from my plate without asking permission. I was offended by his presumption that he could do anything he pleased. He then gave me a lecture on Chinese philosophy. He had discovered Confucius and assumed that I had not. He wanted to enlighten me. David explained later that Brando was more intelligent that the average actor, which is why he liked to give the impression he knew something about most things.

After their marriage, the newly-weds went off to film *Lawrence* on location in Jordan and Spain, and I was not to see Leila for another ten years.

Another of Barbara's long-standing friends was the Countess Marina Luling Buschetti, a vivacious member of the Italian nobility. She had the olive complexion typical of the southern Mediterranean region, grey hair, thick glasses and her appearance in no way indicated that she had any money at all. She was what we would today call a workaholic, motivated by a kind of Christian *noblesse oblige*. Although she and Barbara did not see each other often, they had been friends since their younger days when Barbara used to spend an annual social season in Venice. Apart from both being very rich, they had hardly any traits in common. Barbara admired and envied Marina's sense of purpose, and Marina had an evangelical need to protect Barbara from all the frauds and cheats that surrounded her.

I was a guest more than once at Marina's villa – the Villa Maser, near Venice, recognized as the most perfect example of the work of the sixteenth-century architect, Andrea Palladio.

I was always given the guest bedroom on the second floor, the walls of which were covered with murals by Veronese – from the floor to the very high ceiling. The effect was anything but warm and inviting. The objects depicted in the murals were obscure and slightly menacing. I asked Marina what they represented and she answered in a matter-of-fact way, 'They are poetic allegories, of course.' She asked me to please put everything away out of sight before 10 am as the public would be coming through.

She told me at that time that whenever Barbara came to Villa Maser without a personal maid, she would make her bed and tidy her bedroom herself. She would never call one of the resident maids because she felt they had enough to do as it was. This was a point of disagreement between Marina and Barbara. Marina believed in extracting value for money from servants, suppliers and the like. She demanded the best but at the lowest price. I remember one visit by the Lulings when they stayed in the Paris apartment in Barbara's absence. They went through the whole apartment with a fine tooth-comb and made a written list of all the details that could be improved. This included the shape of the shower head in one of the guest suites. I was told that if any dust was found anywhere in Villa Maser, it meant instant dismissal for the person responsible.

I slept very badly in my Veronese room. The furniture in the room was stark and simple, obviously so as not to detract attention from the murals. Lying in bed, the murals looming over me, it was the perfect setting for nightmares. Luckily I am a deep sleeper without a vivid imagination. I had my meals with Valeria, Marina's personal assistant, but was allowed to join in the family activities which revolved around Diamante, Marina's daughter, and the numerous dogs.

The food at Villa Maser was very spartan, even at a big dinner party. Having suffered through the war, the Lulings were obsessed with what they considered waste. Barbara, who was never bothered about food herself, would be concerned about whether the servants were fed properly. Whenever Barbara stayed at Villa Maser, she was characteristically lavish with her presents on arrival and munificent with generous tips on departure. She had concern for each servant that she spoke to and remembered them individually. She made an effort to converse in Italian. Often she would arrive with a special present for a child because she remembered one of the maids mentioning that she had a young son. It was not surprising that the employees were envious of us who worked for Barbara rather than for the Lulings. When Valeria came to dinner in Paris once, Barbara gave her a pair of real black pearl earrings from Cartier. On my visits to Villa Maser, twice in succession I was given a gift of a nylon scarf with a print of the Villa which was the most popular item in their small gift shop. Valeria would tell me how lucky we were to work for Barbara even though we sometimes felt at the end of our tether during Barbara's drinking bouts.

The Lulings' feeling for Barbara was of deep friendship, tinged with a slight sense of condescension for this pitiful creature that everybody took for a ride. The Lulings, in spite of their great fortune, were pinch-penny. Being dynamic people, they expected everyone to bear their crosses in the same stoic manner they had chosen to bear theirs. At home, the Lulings were never beyond doing any chores themselves and they enjoyed showing others how a job 'should have been done'. They were, in fact, more like people who had known what it was like to be poor.

Although the Lulings' attitudes always served to remind me that Barbara was easy-going, undemanding, tolerant and kind, not to mention generous, I nevertheless admired them for their ability not to indulge themselves with the privilege and wealth which was theirs. They had a crusading mission to improve by their own toil the lot of the less fortunate. This sense of purpose in life was no doubt what Barbara lacked and what led her to waste her existence. Her lack of purpose was certainly a weakness and weakness breeds corruption. The hangers-on around Barbara were able to exploit this weakness, returning instead of friendship disappointment and disillusionment. The Lulings had no such hangers-on. I envied that.

That Barbara could sustain friendship with people such as the Lulings, made her usual circle of hangers-on seem even more shallow and hypocritical, and her encouragement of them quite inexplicable. Some, such as her old friend Bill Robertson and her 'minder' Colin Fraser, gave her loyalty and real friendship – whether she realized it or not. And her two escorts that I knew best – Jimmy Douglas and Lloyd Franklin – also brought her considerable happiness during the time of their relationships with her.

F. W. Woolworth (1852–1919): self-made millionaire and Barbara's maternal grandfather. On his widow's death Barbara received one-third of his fortune (*UPI/Bettmann*)

The family arrives in Paris for Barbara's marriage to 'Prince' Alexis Mdivani, 1933: (left to right) Wooly Donahue, Mrs Irene Hutton (Barbara's step-mother), Jimmy Donahue, Aunt Jessie Donahue, Barbara, Franklyn Hutton (*UPI/Bettmann*)

Barbara participates in a charity carnival in New York, 1932, revealing the figure about which her first husband made cruel gibes (*UPI/Bettmann*)

En route for the USA with Cocotte, a present from her fourth husband, Igor. Barbara wears her favourite pearls and diamond ring; the dog is not wearing her diamond collar (*UPI/Bettmann*)

Inset: Barbara's maids-in-waiting. Left to right: Herminie, Hélène and Jeanette. In Barbara's absence from Paris they enjoy a Sunday outing

Civil wedding of David Lean and his fourth wife, Leila Matkar, in Paris, summer 1960. Leila's closest friend, Barbara, is their witness (*The Associated Press*)

The Leans' wedding lunch at the fashionable Georges V Hotel in Paris. I am next to Marlon Brando, who in turn sits next to the bride

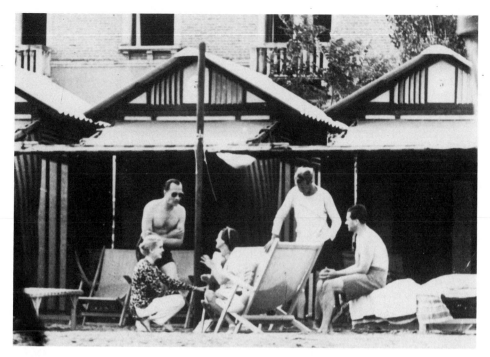

How the other half lives: at the Lido in Venice, 1937: Barbara and Kurt von Haugwitz-Reventlow and the Duke and Duchess of Windsor relax together. On the right is the Duke's equerry (*The Associated Press*)

Meanwhile, anti-Babs demonstrations are staged in New York by underpaid Woolworth salesgirls (*UPI/Bettmann*)

Even for travelling Barbara wears her most luxurious furs and huge diamonds, thus not disappointing the reporters who hound her wherever she goes (*UPI/Bettmann*)

London, 1936: Barbara and her second husband, Kurt von Haugwitz-Reventlow, with their son, Lance. Even at his christening Lance looked unhappy. Barbara seems to have fully recovered from the caesarean operation she elected to undergo because she felt it was neater than natural childbirth (*The Associated Press*)

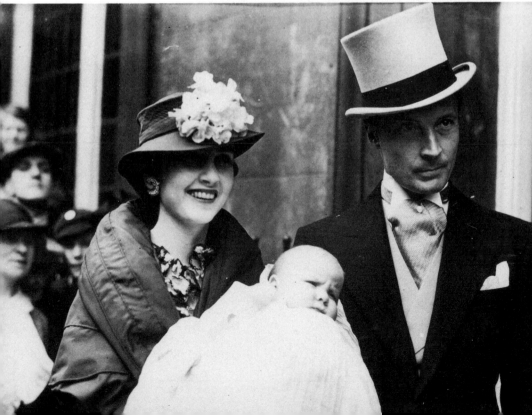

Winfield House in
Regent's Park, London,
donated by Barbara to the
US Government and today
used as the residence of the
American Ambassador
(*UPI/Bettmann*)

Schoolboy Lance spends his
summer with his mother in
Europe. Barbara relaxes in
her silk lounging outfit
(*UPI/Bettmann*)

1958: Barbara with
boyfriend Jimmy
Douglas. They return
from a trip to the Far
East during which
Barbara has added jade
rings to her collection of
jewellery (*Camera Press*)

1940: After two
unhappy marriages to
European, titled men,
Barbara takes up with
the all-American
golfer, Bobby Sweeney
(*UPI/Bettmann*)

Sadly for Barbara such people were exceptional. Instead, all those who really cared for Barbara, and that included two of her former husbands, had to watch, impotent and totally disenchanted, the scene of hangers-on, jockeying for position. It was revolting to witness the in-fighting behind Barbara's back, the grovelling in front of her. Barbara hated to face anything unpleasant. She found it easier to allow herself to be flattered even though she could see through it. Worst of all, her 'friends' would encourage her drinking because they knew that under the influence of alcohol her generosity would increase. Those who really cared for her fought a losing battle. Barbara did not want any spoil sports around her. If you told her the truth, she was liable to dismiss you as an employee or drop you as a friend. Not many chose to take that risk.

The underlying nature of Barbara Hutton was a search for affection and beauty and a life of refined activity. In her own way, she tried to create some beauty in her immediate surroundings. Her appreciation of those parts of the world that she visited regularly, also brought beauty to her life. As for affection, she was more often than not disappointed in it. By the time I knew Barbara, she was aware that for her, relationships were not likely to last. The next best thing was to take any pleasure for as long as it might exist. With very few exceptions, she was surrounded by weak and greedy people. Because Barbara did not really have the strength of character to stand up for what she really wanted, she created around her a world into which she preferred to retreat. She was happiest in her fantasy world. If she did succeed in some measure in finding beauty in life, it was in spite of the outside world she tried so desperately to avoid. She played the pretend game very well and probably fooled herself at times. More than anything else, she wished to shut out of her conscious mind all the sordid goings-on among her entourage, her own shortcomings, the disappointments and failures in her life. She often told me that she preferred to stay in her fairy-tale world.

7

Two Americans in Paris

Wallis Simpson, who became the Duchess of Windsor, is reputed to have coined the expression 'You can't be too rich or too thin.' If she did not originate the saying, she certainly used it often and probably believed it. Barbara Hutton, it would appear, should have believed in the same motto because of her much-publicized wealth and her obsession with being slim. The lives of these two American women were somewhat similar – they knew the same people, went to the same places at the same time of the year, had similar types of dwellings, entertained in the same way, valued the same *objets d'art*, had their Paris residences decorated by the same interior designer, Jensen, and even had the same salesman at Cartier – André Denet. Someone joked at the time that both women were like crumbs held together by dough. They were also connected by their relationships with one man, but that is where the similarity ended. Their temperament, aspirations and values were totally different.

At the time I worked for Barbara, she was on social though formal terms with the Windsors. They had previously been friendlier but that closeness had been broken by a scandal. However, because the Windsors lived in Paris for a good part of the year there were reciprocal invitations between them and Barbara.

I knew from the beginning that Barbara and Wallis had been quite close friends in their young days. Yet, from the start of my job I detected a coolness between the two women. I was to find out that this was due to the Jimmy Donahue affair which had ended with considerable bitterness on the part of Wallis. In spite of it, the relationship between Barbara and Wallis was superficially cordial. Although they maintained the appearance of friendship, a great deal of gossip and back-biting went on in our camp, as, I am sure, it did in theirs. Why the pretence of friendship? I wondered.

The Duchess would come to lunch at rue Octave Feuillet on her own, saying, 'I married the Duke forever, but not for lunch.' I thought at the time that she was like a mother who pursued her own interests while her child was at school. Sometimes Barbara would not be ready to receive her, so it was up to me to keep the Duchess company in the large salon. The minute she stepped inside the front door, her eyes would scan all the details around her and I am sure that she took a mental note of anything that she could criticize. I knew that, because she would comment on other people's tastes. The staff who worked for her told me that she was extremely meticulous and attended to every detail of the household personally. She would never delegate responsibility, only assign tasks under her supervision.

Sometimes the Duchess would look at what I was wearing, which always made me feel ill at ease. She herself was always dressed immaculately and never had a hair out of place. Not only was her dress in excellent taste, it was always in the most conventional taste. Whereas her husband enjoyed a certain eccentricity in his clothing, she never allowed herself any personal idiosyncracies. Barbara, on the other hand, with her love of Oriental dress, her saris and 'Vietnamese' pyjamas, was not shy of 'doing her own thing', of expressing her own personality. The Duchess, in contrast, relied only on the haute couture houses.

In our conversations, the Duchess would mention food and she greatly appreciated Herminie's excellent cuisine. Yet the Duchess never ate a great deal; she insisted on a very light lunch. Although she was clearly interested in food and certainly knew a great deal about it, she always exercised great self-discipline. She carried herself in a graceful way and the immediate impression she gave was one of authority and vitality. Apart from the fact that she could be rather intimidating, she was an excellent and witty conversationalist, talking with animation, her blue eyes sparkling. Everyone enjoyed her company.

The Duchess's secretary and I, of course, compared notes about our respective employers. I don't believe that any employer could have been more disliked by her staff than the Duchess of Windsor. She was harsh and demanding and paid notoriously low wages, on the assumption that it was an honour to serve herself and the Duke. Some of her staff may have felt privileged to work for a former reigning monarch, but most of them were dissatisfied and the turn-over of staff was rapid. One day when the Duke was waiting for his wife to say goodbye after a dinner party at Barbara's (he always wanted to leave early, something the Duchess disliked), he asked me what it was like to work for Barbara, and hinted that he would not be averse to having me join his staff, adding hastily that, of course, the Duchess took charge of such matters. I felt a slight thrill at the implied compliment, but told him that I was going to give up work shortly anyway. The Duchess was well-known for summarily dismissing a servant for the flimsiest of reasons. One of her gate-keepers had worked for the Windsors for eighteen years and on the day that his wife died, he asked for an extra day off. He was told that if he took it he need not return.

The Duchess was undoubtedly an excellent hostess. She was much concerned about the proper layout of the table and the right mix of guests. Barbara, on the other hand, just wanted her friends around her. The Duchess took infinite pains to see to every minute detail, and was an expert on protocol. I attended several events at the Windsors' home in the Bois de Bologne. The occasions there were always perfect; in every way a compliment to their guests. Her reputation as the best hostess in Paris was well-deserved. In this way she carried out perfectly her function of keeping the Duke entertained in the manner befitting a king. Yet, to her staff she never said a thank you, never passed on a compliment made by a guest. She was an unpopular tyrant who would try to short change people of their due payment or credit. The Duke was just as guilty of this fault. The staff knew that if they had to advance any money, they would never be reimbursed. Both the Duke and Duchess would promise large sums of money in their wills; some of the staff stayed on this account.

Unlike Barbara, the Duchess bought clothes from several couturiers and she would beat the prices down on the pretext that she would advertise the clothes she wore. She had a back-door shop where she sold her redundant clothes. Both she and the Duke were notorious for their stinginess, resorting to all sorts of shameless deceits to avoid paying bills. In the case of the Duke it was a pathological state induced by the loss of his throne and being an exile. But Barbara always maintained that with the Duchess it was due to her early poor beginnings and her later hard-heartedness. Barbara also believed that Wallis had a sense of having been cheated by life. At times she would sound bitter and implied that her husband had failed her, that he had not kept his promise. She had a way of denigrating him by reminding him that he had let her down *again*. People on her staff told me how she would reprimand the Duke like a harsh mother with a naughty child, not infrequently reducing him to tears. Paradoxically, this only caused him to cling more tightly to her.

Whereas Barbara always wanted to spoil her friends by lavishing presents on them, the Duke and Duchess led totally self-centered lives; there was no consideration for anything but the gratification of their own needs. The life they led was borne out of disappointment, frustration and unfulfilled expectations. For many years they had ardently hoped that King George VI would give them some worthy position within the British royal system. At every hint they received rebuke, rejection, refusal. What hurt the Duke most was the denial of the title 'Royal Highness' to the Duchess, thereby in essence denying her position as the wife of a royal son. This would normally entitle her to be addressed as 'Royal Highness' and to the curtsey. This slight on his wife became more and more intolerable to the Duke; it soured his personality. As King, he had often said that he wished he could live like an ordinary person. But when he had a chance to do just that, his reaction to the King's rejection was to cling even more to what he considered to be his birthright. What the Duke really wanted were the privileges accorded to him by his royal birth, with none of the disadvantages of the office. In his frustration, he insisted on referring to his wife as 'Her Royal Highness' and expected that ladies should curtsey and men bow to her. The entrance hall to their house in Paris was of such awesome grandeur that it could have been (I imagine) mistaken for Buckingham Palace. A red dispatch box was there as though in daily use. An immense banner representing the Royal Garter hung from the high ceiling and an enormous and ornate replica of the royal coat of arms was placed above the staircase in such a way that anyone ascending the stairs would be impressed with its majestic aura. The Windsors attempted to capture the respect which they considered their due, but which had been denied them.

At dinner parties, the Duke would drink too much, not from pleasure but from boredom. He made attempts at enlivening the crowd by putting on a kilt and playing the bagpipes, but he only bored the others who had to pretend that he could play the bagpipes. He enjoyed talking about the old days, but his conversation would never stray very far from his regrets. To the press, the

Abdication was the greatest love story of the century, in which the couple lived happily ever after. In private it was different. I felt at the time that if only they could turn their backs on those who had slammed the door in their faces, if only they could just enjoy life on their own terms, they might have had some happiness. On the surface, one might easily have imagined that their kind of life was a never-ending party. The public image of the Duke of Windsor was that of a revered hero, especially in the hearts and minds of his subjects. In his younger days he had been dashing, handsome and he could speak to anyone. He had the common touch; he had sympathy with the plight of the ordinary person which his father, George V, lacked. When, as the Prince of Wales and later King Edward VIII, the Duke made his official visits to various parts of the Commonwealth, he was an ambassador with charisma. The Empire was proud of his performance. During the Great Depression, he showed compassion with the condition of the miners. When he visited them in Wales, he promised that 'something must be done'. He was probably sincere but the public were unaware of what was behind the popular mask. A more realistic assessment of this popular figure appeared only much later, when the world had virtually forgotten him.

It was generally assumed that this excellent monarch, Edward VIII, had been corrupted by a 'scheming twice-divorced American'. In many British minds of the day, the word 'American' was the most damning in that epithet. My own impression of the ducal couple as I knew them in Paris in the 1960s had not been influenced by any previous knowledge or preconceptions. I had not lived through the Abdication crisis, nor had I yet set foot in Britain. I was seeing them simply as part of the social scene at Barbara Hutton's. I was instructed by Barbara to follow the expected British custom of curtseying to both the Duke and Duchess, to address them either as 'Your Royal Highness' or as 'Sir' and 'Ma'am', and never to speak to them until addressed by them. I found these formalities no more cumbersome than any other ritualistic greeting such as 'Good morning. How are you?' In either case, it is to break the ice, after which normal conversation ensues.

Inevitably I was to compare the two American women, Barbara and Wallis. The former had culture, breeding, consideration and generosity of spirit – all qualities that Wallis lacked. It would not be enough to say that Barbara was born to money and therefore had a better education or upbringing. In fact, Wallis had a better start in life; her education was more carefully planned and executed, her family more supportive. Although Wallis was the more successful of the two in terms of social skills and wit, she had a hardness and vulgarity which she did little to conceal. Her family background was not without social status and yet she smacked of the *nouveau riche*, with a certain insensitivity and hard edge lacking in the truly noble person. Still, she had a compelling personality which no photograph ever captured. She had a magnetism which invited attention and interest from anyone in her presence. It could be called charm, but I would not say she was charming.

The Duke was a totally different type of person. Whereas his wife had an abundance of vitality and confidence, he appeared to me to be a rather pathetic figure, generally melancholic and somehow lacking in dignity. Most of his biographers agree that he suffered from a personality deficiency which left him at the total mercy of his wife. That he utterly worshipped Wallis was obvious to anyone who saw them together. Wallis was the only person he had ever fully trusted and in whose company he felt completely secure. With everyone else he was guarded and cautious. His secretary told me that he was extremely secretive and kept a great many files under lock and key. His accounts were also kept in total privacy; he never delegated this work to anyone. According to those close to the Duke he was restless when the Duchess was not there. She was constantly in his thoughts and when she was present he watched her every movement, listened to her every word and responded to every inflection in her voice. He often said that nothing was too good for her. Those who never saw this total devotion for themselves find it difficult to believe that a person could be so besotted and for so long, wondering how it is possible for a man to be so completely dependent on a woman.

We are told by all the historic accounts that King George V and Queen Mary were cold and distant parents who ruled their children with fear. Their eldest son, David, was particularly sensitive and therefore suffered the most from this parental harshness. David was below average intelligence and had a weak nature. His biographers agree that had he not met Wallis Simpson, he would have used some other strong person to serve as his anchor and he would have clung to her in the same way as he did to Wallis. He seemed unable to stand as a person in his own right. The Duchess told some of her friends that before he met her, the Duke had only felt safe in the company of older married women, and that she, Wallis, was the first real physical experience the Duke had ever had. We could also see that there was an emotional need for someone to guide him, to tell him what to do and what to think.

In many ways the Windsors were made for each other. They needed each other and they complemented each other. However, whereas Wallis was the Duke's whole world, the Duke was unable to be Wallis's whole world. The Duke adored Wallis; Wallis was stuck with the Duke for better or worse. The Duke was happy as long as Wallis was happy and he knew that if she wasn't happy she would make him pay. Consequently, he did not make too many objections when, in the summer of 1950, Wallis, aged fifty-four, picked up Jimmy Donahue, aged thirty-four, to amuse her, even though he was a renowned homosexual and the Duke had an outspoken abhorrence of them. An abhorrence that went as far as publicly disparaging Noël Coward and Somerset Maugham, although he was not averse to accepting their lavish hospitality.

Jimmy was Barbara's first cousin, the younger son of her aunt Jessie. He had been at her side during the most important moments of her life, like an affectionate and amusing brother. He kept everyone entertained by his wisecracks and piano-playing and his outrageous frivolity and compulsive exhibitionism were forgiven by all who fell under his charm. Somehow, he got away with it, although at times his humour bordered on the cruel. He enjoyed taunting people; he could be diabolically wicked. In 1950 he inherited $15 million from a trust fund and he set out to play the most monumental practical joke – one that would surpass even his most outrageous ones. The Windsors were already acquainted with Jimmy's mother, Jessie Donahue, who had entertained them in Palm Beach. Jessie was part of the circle of rich Americans who provided the Windsors with the court they were denied in Britain. Wallis was immediately attracted to Jimmy. He loved staying up all night just like herself. He was a perfect playmate for Wallis whose husband always wanted to leave when the party was only just warming up. Now, Wallis no longer demanded that the Duke stay up too. The Duke also found that he could tolerate this young American because Jimmy would pick up the bill as well as keep Wallis amused and entertained. This suited the Duke so well that he was able to overlook other things. So they soon became a regular threesome, with Jimmy in the role of court jester, though he really played host most of the time. During the whole episode, Barbara was constantly involved because both Wallis and Jimmy confided in her. Barbara was an unwilling accomplice. She enjoyed the mischief but at the same time had more respect for an ex-king than her cousin had.

Wallis was obviously very taken with Jimmy. They behaved like lovers, passing notes to each other at dinner parties where they sat apart. They giggled, held hands and gazed into each other's eyes. Sometimes the Duke was seen to have tears in his eyes as he watched these goings-on. He tried to warn Wallis about gossip and remind her of the observance of proprieties. She defended herself by pointing out that she was much older than Jimmy and that everyone knew Jimmy's sexual preferences, so how could anyone read into the situation anything improper.

From Jimmy's point of view, and to his friends and family, he was having the most colossal joke at the expense of the former King of England. Jimmy's mischief took him to this extreme act of iconoclasm. He told Barbara that by seducing Wallis he could say that he was 'the boy who took the girl who took the boy off the throne of Merry Old England'.

Wallis fell into the trap which was to make her endure the worst personal humiliation of her life. The Jimmy/Wallis affair was the only topic of conversation in the gossip columns, which christened her 'the Queen of the Fairies' across two continents. It was like the Abdication all over again. It looked so much like the real thing. Was it or was it not? Did they or did they not? True, they enjoyed the same lifestyle, hitting the night spots, they laughed at the same things. But it looked like more than 'just good friends'. It looked like love. Wallis had to have Jimmy along all the time. The Duke began to feel like a deceived husband. Whereas in the past he had been branded as the 'other man', he did not enjoy being the victim.

The Windsors' staff reported that the Duchess made no secret of her infatuation for Jimmy and even in public she became less and less discreet. Her secretary told me that under the spell of Jimmy Donahue she had not only barred her bedroom to her husband, but she had put up a sign directed at him saying 'Keep Out and Stay Out.' The Duke was even further reduced to the 'pathetic battered child' and Wallis 'his cold and angry nanny', to quote from the book called *The Windsor Story*.

Another aspect of Jimmy's prank was to introduce Wallis into the Roman Catholic faith. He was on close terms with both Cardinal Spellman of New York City and Monsignor Fulton Sheen, the charismatic priest who converted to the faith such well-known people as Clare Booth Luce and the violinist Fritz Kreisler. Prompted by Jimmy, Wallis had serious instruction for several years, and so deeply attached was she to Jimmy that she was prepared to convert to Roman Catholicism. What made her stop short was firstly her fundamental atheism and secondly the end of her affair with Jimmy. Had the prank been successful, it would have been a tremendous humiliation for a former English monarch who by law is forbidden to marry a Roman Catholic by virtue of his position as Defender of the Anglican Faith.

In November 1950 the Windsors were in Paris, the Duke to complete his autobiography for which he had received a considerable advance and which was already so overdue that two biographers were doing the work for him. Nevertheless his presence in Paris was imperative to conclude the necessary chapters. Wallis decided to leave him there and to take the *Queen Mary* with Jimmy to enjoy the New York social season. In Paris the Duke was unable to work, so distracted was he by her absence. He spent most of his days and nights making transatlantic phone calls to Wallis in New York. He hardly ever found her at home and she made no effort to answer his messages. This made him more frantic than ever and even less able to work on his book. To make things worse, people sent him news clippings of the Jimmy/Wallis goings-on that were making daily headlines. Less than a month after they parted, the Duke dropped his already vastly overdue commitment and sailed to New York to see for himself how much truth there was in the gossip. The newspapers were having a field day, some were announcing the break-up of the Windsors' marriage; they were all taking sides on the issue, just as they had at the time of the Abdication. On his arrival in New York, the Duke found a battery of pressmen in hue and cry, demanding the truth. The Duke made a statement that there was no truth in the rumour of estrangement between himself and the Duchess, that they were still very much in love. The Duchess was at the quayside to meet him and they kissed seven times for the benefit of the cameramen.

The Duke had always said 'As long as she's happy, I'm happy.' Well, she was happy now. Should he interfere just because people were gossiping? But the fact was that Wallis was exceeding the bounds of decorum. She was flaunting her relationship with Jimmy in a shameless manner and treating her husband with contempt before the gaze of society. For example, on 29 March 1953, the day of Queen Mary's funeral, which the Duke attended alone, Wallis was very conspicuously out at a night club with Jimmy, deliberately attracting attention. It was widely reported in the press, which is what she wanted. Jimmy had conspired with her to show exactly how little respect she had for the family that had treated her unfairly. This was only to result in giving more ammunition to the enemy. It was also to hurt the Duke very deeply for he had been brought up to value displays of duty and tradition. However estranged he and his mother had become, her death saddened him a great deal. Perhaps this incident, more than any other, prompted him to sail to New York to confront his wife. He had passed the point of accepting, of trying not to notice.

In her memoirs, Wallis glosses over the episode with Jimmy and after the break-up she never mentioned his name again. She never inquired after Jimmy even to Barbara. She never forgave him. Various biographers are tentative with their interpretation of the true relationship between Wallis and Jimmy. My knowledge of the subject comes from what Jimmy himself said in my presence, what the members of the Windsor household said and what Barbara told me Jimmy told her. The Windsor household staff were in no doubt that Wallis was in love with Jimmy and that it was a sexual relationship – chambermaids are sometimes the only people who really know the truth of such matters.

Jimmy, in his post-Wallis life, would talk a great deal about the affair – it was a favourite dinner-time topic of conversation. Without mincing his words, Jimmy would joke that she was so ugly that he could not have sex with her unless he first got drunk. According to Jimmy, she dreaded the idea of getting old, and he was able to make her forget this. Furthermore, I can imagine that a woman could be flattered at having stirred the heart of an attractive man who would not normally be touched by feminine charms. Jimmy also said that she resented the fact that the Duke had lost his throne. Naïvely she had believed his promise of making her Queen. She despised his weakness and boring ways. With Jimmy, she found revenge and enjoyed humiliating her husband – in public if necessary. Jimmy made matters worse for the Duke by telling tales to anyone who cared to listen. He revelled in the scandal which was of his own making. The problem for the Duke was compounded by the fact that not only was he totally dependent on his wife, but totally petrified of her.

Barbara told me that Jimmy's intention was to make Wallis leave the Duke, after which he, Jimmy, would have left her. In the meantime he was keeping himself highly amused although he was getting tired of Wallis. He completely lost all respect for both the Windsors and he allowed his insolence to show through. He was drinking a great deal and losing control over his temper. He was openly referring to Wallis as 'the old bag'.

The occasion of the final break-up of the four-year relationship happened when Jimmy lost his temper with Wallis and gave her such a hard kick on her leg that it drew blood. This injury hurt the Duke more than the recipient of the kick and, uncharacteristically, he lost his temper. The two men shouted at each other, Jimmy letting loose his biting rhetoric and putting the final boot into the Duke's self-respect. The Duke asked him to get out. This was the last act of this play, but it was not the end of Jimmy Donahue, nor was he the last lover that Wallis afforded herself. Jimmy made a lot of noise about his triumph on behalf of the homosexual fraternity. Wallis could hear the trail of gossip that Jimmy left everywhere and in her declining years she spoke of all her ex-suitors and ex-husbands with tenderness and sentiment – except Jimmy Donahue.

8

Sidi Hosni

Through my open door
I see amazing sights.
Such fair and foolish things
Such wonders and delights.

Barbara Hutton, *Sidi Hosni*

Sidi Hosni, Barbara's palace in Tangier, was the most fascinating and complex of her three residences – partly because it had an interesting history in its own right, and partly because it was an intricate part of the multi-faceted social context of Tangier. Tangier, a unique and fascinating port which had been the scene of international piracy, where Europeans of high birth settled to lead a life on the fringes of accepted social customs, was a hot-bed of intrigue, smuggling and riotous living. Because it had been a free port, it included an odd mixture of seedy and respectable people.

The city has an ancient, and equally colourful, history. A thriving Phoenician trading post a thousand years before the birth of Christ, it was successively invaded by the Carthaginians and the Romans. After the collapse of the Roman Empire in the fifth century AD, Tangier was taken over by the Vandals, Byzantines and Arabs, the latter ruling for seven centuries. From the fifteenth to the seventeeth centuries Tangier was governed by either Spain or Portugal. However, the fate of the port of Tangier was different from that of the country of which it is part – Morocco. Strategically situated only twenty-seven miles south of the southernmost tip of Spain, it became a British possession in 1662. Twenty-two years later Tangier was returned to Morocco but British trade and political influence still predominated. Morocco became a French protectorate in 1912 but Tangier enjoyed a special status and in 1923 it was officially recognized as an international city with a regime composed of representatives from Great Britain, France, Spain, Portugal, Italy, Belgium, Holland, Sweden and later the US. Spain was in sole charge during the Second World War. Tangier remained a free port in an international zone until 1956 when it was integrated with the newly independent Kingdom of Morocco. Even then, it remained an important port and trade centre. With this hetero-geneous and variegated background one can understand how this city became a spell-binding and glamorous setting for a great many visitors.

The town itself is built on the slopes of a chalky limestone hill. The old town, the Medina, enclosed by fifteenth-century ramparts is dominated by the Kasbah. The idea of having a palace in this particular area, steeped in romantic history, appealed to Barbara and when in 1946 a certain Maxwell Blake decided to sell his residence, the Palace of Sidi Hosni located right in the centre of the Kasbah, Barbara rushed to Tangier to make a bid for it. She would talk about this episode with some glee. She found upon her arrival at the Hotel El Minzah a delegation of experts representing Generalissimo Franco on some mission. It came to her knowledge that the mission they were on was the purchase of the palace of Sidi Hosni. They discussed it with her not knowing that she was in Tangier for the same purpose! Barbara became fascinated with the history of this rambling house on the Kasbah hill. From the outside the palace had plain white-washed walls topped with battlements. She found out that the property had been seven separate houses at one time and since then it had been used in various combinations for various purposes including a restaurant and a prison. In 1870 it became the property of Sidi Hosni, the Moslem holy man who left his name to the property and whose tomb lies under the building. Three generations later, in 1925, Sidi Hosni's descendants sold the property to Walter Harris, an English journalist attached to the London *Times*. Harris was one of the most colourful characters of the Tangier scene, very sociable and a polished raconteur. His stories, whether true or invented, live on in Tangier society. After Harris's death, Sidi Hosni was acquired in 1933 by Maxwell Blake, a respected American diplomat who was appointed Consul-General in 1910 and was Dean of the diplomatic corps by the time he retired in 1940. In that time Blake had enhanced the property with Moorish accoutrements. He imported artisans, in particular stone-masons, to transform the inner courtyards with carved designs bordered with engraved inscriptions from the Koran. Some six years after his retirement, Blake decided to return to Kansas City to be with his sons.

It was a difficult decision for Blake, because he adored Morocco and his house in the Kasbah was a labour of love. The improvements he had made were widely known and appreciated by connoisseurs of authentic Moroccan architecture and furnishings. Franco let it be known that he was prepared to pay a high price for this unparalleled property. Blake knew that Franco had authorized his representatives to make a bid. Blake was, for reasons of conscience, unhappy at the thought of the Spanish dictator occupying his house, although the price Franco was prepared to pay was extremely high. It was a fantastic stroke of luck for Blake that Barbara Hutton came upon the scene just when he was considering whether or not to accept Franco's bid. Not only was Barbara a fellow American, but she loved and valued the same Oriental art treasures. Lucky for Blake, too, that Barbara fell in love with the property and offered $100,000. The offer was accepted, the bargain struck, and both parties were more than satisfied.

With the house, Barbara inherited Blake's household staff which comprised seven loyal though unsophisticated Spanish servants and their families who lived in the immediate area. Barbara also inherited Blake's daughter and son-in-law, Ruth and Reginald Hopwood, who retained their residence at Sidi Hosni as caretakers when Barbara was not in Tangier. Not one to impose conditions on others, Barbara accepted the Hopwoods' presence but as time went by they became intruders in her life. Barbara felt an obligation to consult them on matters which were not their concern and eventually the Hopwoods were asked to leave Sidi Hosni. Although this had happened before my time, I knew Barbara's attitude to the Hopwoods was hostile. The servants were circumspect when referring to them, which seemed rather odd to me as the Hopwoods had been their employers for many years. My guess was that, as happened quite often with Barbara, she gave the Hopwoods *carte blanche*; they assumed, quite understandably, that they could please themselves – the budget seemed unlimited. At some point, they must have over-stepped the limit or done something which displeased Barbara and the whole atmosphere changed. Whenever Barbara spoke to me about Ruth, it was always in a sarcastic manner and she avoided having to meet or talk to her.

The staff that came with the house were more like a collection of good-humoured neighbours. The Spanish women were completely untrained and unskilled, though willing and helpful. The antiquated kitchen was dominated by the old grandmother who had not a clue about cooking but who guarded her position tenaciously. She was deaf and very old and it was no use asking her to do anything she had decided not to do. The others deferred to her. If Barbara wanted a good meal, or if she had guests, the food would be ordered from Guitta's Restaurant. This was a good, solid place run by a Gibraltarian Jew who was a good professional caterer. His daughter, Mercedes, a charming and able person, was just as professional. She had an affair with Barbara's chauffeur Jean, a handsome, married man from Luxemburg who had replaced Fernard when he retired, and this added link made her part of Barbara's staff.

As owner of Sidi Hosni, Barbara indulged in further improving the place with authentic furnishings. She ordered custom-designed furniture from the best artisans in Marrakesh and she filled the rooms with Moroccan antiques and leather-goods. Mosaic floor tiles in Arabic patterns were laid in all the courtyards. Silks and hand-embroidered brocades from central Morocco were used to upholster the sofas. One of the most striking items was a fifteenth-century Indian rug which was hung on the wall of one of the salons. It was filigreed with gold thread and encrusted with gem stones. She bought dozens of magnificent kaftans and many pieces of jewellery with Moroccan gems and motifs. She ordered many of these items from a small shop called 'Art Africain' run by an astute Swiss businessman, Jacques Robert, who knew the best sources of authentic furniture, furnishings, kaftans, leather-goods and jewellery. Although his shop was very small in size, he had no rivals. He was extremely knowledgeable, had a pleasant manner and you could trust him to be fair in his dealings. He became an invaluable friend to Barbara. A homosexual, he had come to Tangier to escape the restrictions of Swiss society and being a beachcomber at heart he had found the perfect place to settle.

When Barbara had finished refurbishing her palace of Sidi Hosni it was truly a setting from *One Thousand and One Nights*. Because it had been amalgamated from seven houses, it was a honeycomb of corridors, staircases, mezzanines, terraces. The spaces between the dwelling areas formed open or partially covered courtyards. The tiles on the walls were genuine seventeenth-century Moroccan work. The light came from above and from the south-east which overlooked the bay. From a big open terrace you could look down onto the city and beyond to the Mediterranean. There were several courtyards incorporating mature trees. In the central patio stood a huge fig tree whose branches shaded the entire area. We would have our coffee there and at times an over-ripe fig would hit us on the head or fall in our laps. Whenever this happened, Barbara would have a fit of the giggles because it reminded her of something a big bird might drop while flying overhead.

One of the most remarkable things about Sidi Hosni was that from the outside it did not look like a palace. The plain white exterior walls, with Mohammed the sentry guarding a heavy wooden door, stood in the midst of the noise and bustle of extreme poverty. Stepping out into the Kasbah, into the raucous and smelly street where open sewers ran, was a violent contrast to the tranquillity within the palace's walls. The streets were so narrow that even a small car could not drive through. Barbara's Rolls Royce had to park some five hundred yards away. Several of the narrow openings in the Kasbah had been widened to permit the Rolls to get that far. The Municipality of Tangier made this gesture to thank Barbara for all the good work she carried out in Tangier over the years.

These good works were, in fact, considerable. Barbara was feeding more than 100 people a day. She had set up kitchens for the poor, especially for the refugees from the interior who had been driven out of their native mountains by famine in the late 1940s. She had set up schools, encouraged trade and given business to the local traders. Anonymously, Barbara regularly sent large cheques to most of the charitable and philanthropic organizations in Tangier. She initiated a programme of grants to allow the poorer Moroccan children to attend the American School and she insisted that they improve their Arabic rather than their French, Spanish or English. It was also donations from her that maintained the Tangier Polo Club, the social focus of the European community. The people of Tangier were also well aware that the increasing number of Europeans who settled in their midst was largely due to Barbara's example. She made it fashionable to convert old Moorish property. It was an economic blessing and a welcome benefit to the locals.

The poverty of the Kasbah was a new, and not altogether welcome, experience for most visitors to Sidi Hosni, and those of us who accompanied Barbara through this desperately poor area when she had to walk from the door to her car would feel some

99

apprehension in the midst of so many people milling around her. She, however, never worried. She felt familiar with them. The relationship was warm and cordial. The children would wave and cheer; Barbara would blow them kisses and talk to them in simple Arabic.

The smells of the Kasbah also came as a shock, and it was sometimes amusing to observe the reactions of newcomers. But, in spite of the location of Sidi Hosni, the prevailing winds never carried the smells of the Kasbah inside the house. This was no doubt due to the high windowless walls. This also kept the noise out, except for the chant of the muezzin over the minaret's loudspeaker, calling the faithful to prayer. That loudspeaker, obviously electric, seemed to be the only concession to modern life in the Kasbah.

For Barbara, Sidi Hosni represented an escape into a fairy-tale – the Arabian Nights. For a couple of months every summer, she enjoyed living this fantasy. It was her nomadic visit to another world. She revelled in inviting belly dancers to entertain her guests. She enjoyed having her guests wear colourful kaftans. One summer she invited Prince William of Gloucester. He was a student at the time and was visiting North Africa in preparation for his future diplomatic career. He knew a great deal about Moroccan culture and appreciated the authenticity of Barbara's improvements to her palace. He also appreciated the belly dancers at one of her parties. On his last evening in Tangier Barbara gave a formal dinner in his honour. Inside each guest's serviette, she had hidden a silver 'hand of Fatima'. Fatima was the daughter of the Prophet Mohammed and the 'hand', which represents her soul, is a common Moroccan symbol of good luck.

On special occasions Barbara would also invite the 'Blue People' of the Atlas Mountains to perform their ceremonial dances. These nomadic Blue People, the popular name for the Tuaregs, really did have blue skin, which came from the blue dye of their clothes. They did not wash themselves in the sense that we understand the word; instead they scrubbed themselves occasionally with hot sand which would not remove the blue colouring on their skin. When they arrived in Tangier at Barbara's invitation, they came in bands of about forty or fifty mounted on camels and carrying loaded rifles. The camels, of course, had to be left outside in the Kasbah, leaving little room for the usual inhabitants. Furthermore, once the performance had been given, the Blue People were in no hurry to

100

return to the Atlas Mountains. They would hang around for days to everyone's discomfiture.

For ten years or so Barabara's life in Tangier remained very relaxed and informal. It was almost as if she were the guest of the Hopwoods and she didn't want to upset things. She used Sidi Hosni as a refuge, an escape, enjoying to the full the languor of the country. It was Jimmy Douglas's influence that persuaded Barbara to become a hostess and to launch herself into the centre of European society in Tangier. With his encouragement, Barbara began to mix with such expatriates as the Hon. David Herbert, the second son of the Earl of Pembroke, who had the connections if not the bank account.

David Herbert's family owned Wilton House in Wiltshire, one of the finest stately homes in England, and had connections with the English royal family. His sister was lady-in-waiting to the Queen Mother; Princess Alexandra and her husband, when on their honeymoon, were guests of David's in Tangier. He would regale his guests with stories about the royals. His very entertaining repertoire of anecdotes were told with biting wit. He would entertain us with stories about the antics of members of the English aristocracy. Although David himself explained his residence in Tangier as 'an easier place to indulge his artistic tastes', Barbara would say that he was an embarrassment to his family and they were very pleased to have him out of the way. Under a very smooth and charming exterior, David Herbert was an opinionated individual who enjoyed his position as leader of the European community in Tangier. He seemed to me to like whoever deferred to him and dislike anyone who threatened his position or treated him as an equal. He tried and more often than not succeeded in surrounding Barbara with 'his' people. Most of the time Barbara allowed him to manipulate her social preferences, for she was impressed by his royal connections, as were most of the other English-speaking people in Tangier. At times she would rebel and give him the cold shoulder for a while but, as she would say, 'Outside of Tangier I don't have to put up with him.' Someone remarked that David 'was merely a big bubble whom nobody had yet bothered to burst.' He was known locally as the 'Queen of the Mountain'.

It was David Herbert who introduced a new person onto Barbara's staff. Ira Belline was an eccentric White Russian who, at the age of eleven had escaped the Russian Revolution with her parents and a physically-disabled brother. They had settled in Paris where she became the mistress of the great actor, Louis Jouvet. For some years she was Charles Boyer's dresser and later became a theatrical costumier. Jouvet died during the war, and Ira emigrated to Tangier with her brother and two Americans. One of these Americans, Jay Hazelwood, opened a very successful bar/restaurant.

Ira and Barbara first met in Jacques Robert's shop where Ira worked part-time on a commission basis and already knew Barbara as the shop's most important client. Ira was also well liked and respected by the Europeans, including David Herbert. During a particularly bad period, Ira was reduced to telling fortunes with Tarot cards; she had learned as a small child how to read them. Although she did not believe in the cards, she decided to try her luck and found them a successful way to make a modest living and she also discovered that the cards never lie. She was very useful, willing and resourceful. It was no wonder that she was recommended when Barbara needed a local person to take the household responsibilities. For me, it became a most pleasant collaboration which continued until Ira's death – after we had both stopped working for Barbara. We complemented each other very well: she had the social experience that I lacked; I enjoyed the paperwork and the accounts which she did not; she treated me like a granddaughter and I was extremely grateful for her support. I admired her understanding of people and her complete honesty. Even though it was David Herbert who was her friend and introduced her to Barbara, once she was part of Sidi Hosni, she joined Barbara's camp and gave her total loyalty.

Ira was given the daunting task of training the household staff to a more sophisticated level. All the Spanish ladies in the staff were large, but the two youngest sisters, Toni and Pepa, were quite enormous, although they were very light on their feet and seemed to abound with energy. Toni, the elder of the two, was the major domo, aware of everyone's needs, but particularly conscious of Barbara's own requirements. Pepa was a giggly immature fun-loving girl, but Ira recognized her potential, and set out in that first winter to educate Pepa in the culinary arts, having first used all her diplomatic negotiating skills to persuade the grandmother to accept retirement on a good pension. Then Ira taught Pepa six or seven main dishes and an equal number of desserts. In Paris that winter I received accounts of Pepa's progress. In one of her letters, Ira wrote '. . . last night we entertained the British Consul and his wife. Pepa made a very good *oeuf en gelée* but the beef was a disaster . . .' Ira was enjoying the Professor Higgins role.

At the same time as becoming a good cook, Pepa fell in love, got married and became pregnant without any of us knowing. She kept it a secret as she did not want to lose her job. She was such a huge woman that no one suspected her of being pregnant. As Ira said, after the birth, 'How can you tell when a hippopotamus is pregnant?'

No one knew exactly how old Ira was but it was generally thought that she was not far from seventy. She was wiry and an insomniac. With all her extra duties, her tendency to asthma increased and her health deteriorated. Barbara asked me to arrange for Ira to go to the London Clinic to have a complete check-up. There she was found to have a tumour and she was operated on by a surgeon called 'Mr Butcher', which Ira thought very funny. She returned to Tangier but her asthma attacks increased in frequency and intensity. Not only had she become virtually indispensable to the running of Sidi Hosni, she was also the life and soul of the household. Barbara decided to give Ira the retirement that she would have wished for, in spite of the fact that she had only worked for Barbara for little more than two years. Ira had always dreamed of living on an orange farm near Marrakesh. Barbara asked me to go and find such an orange farm. This was a very pleasant trip for me. I found a large farm with some eighty orange trees where Ira was able to retire with her brother and her dogs. With the generous pension that Barbara accorded her, Ira had no more worries; she was even able to hire some farmers to harvest and market her oranges. Unfortunately, Ira only lived for five years on her farm, but they were five very happy and fulfilled years. Her friends dropped in on her and she was able to sit in the sun in the beautiful country surroundings.

After Ira left, there was a large void that was difficult to fill. Barbara met a quick-witted courier at the airport, called Ali. Tangier was full of 'slick guys' who were able to help in many small ways. For instance, the bureaucracy at the customs was unbeliev-ably inefficient, but the red-tape could be cut through by 'helpers' such as Ali, who always knew someone who had a cousin who worked for the customs. Ali worked at Tangier airport. He was good-looking, glib and spoke several languages. He had witnessed Barbara's comings and goings and his sharp eyes did not miss a trick.

He made his approach to Barbara by one day picking up a bag she had left behind and giving his name and phone number in case she needed anything done – anything at all. She was quite impressed by his clean handsome face and she was on the look-out for a jack-of-all trades who knew Tangier well. He also offered his 24-hours a day taxi service. Barbara gave him a job on the spot.

It was not long before Ali was running the entire household at Sidi Hosni. He was efficient and helpful – though somewhat arrogant. The girls did not like him at all. Until then all the staff except for Mohammed, the doorman, had been Spanish and the girls did not like being ordered about by a Moroccan young man. As many had previously, Ali became too smart for his own good. Things started to disappear – cash, clothes, cigarettes. We caught him in the act. He had lasted six weeks, but in that time I am sure he amassed more than he would normally have done in a year.

One of the delights of Tangier was the variety of interesting bars and restaurants each with a character of its own. The most famous bar in Tangier was Dean's Bar, frequented and patronized by David Herbert, thereby guaranteeing a certain clientèle both permanent and transient, behaving like the British abroad. The place itself was modest in size and décor but Dean was a character who was a legend in his own lifetime. He was dark-skinned and spoke with an upper-class English accent. He liked people to believe that he had been educated at Westminster but there were many theories about his antecedents. One was that he was of wealthy Jamaican lineage; another that he was the product of a liaison between a French-woman and a prominent Egyptian. He was accorded all the respect of an aristocrat by the Europeans in Tangier. Whatever his genetic background, his career started as the lover of a rich and titled English gentleman after which he became chief barman at the Hôtel Negresco, Nice. He moved on to Tangier to take over the bar at the Minzah, the best hotel in Tangier, but was sacked over some alleged dishonesty. In 1946 he opened his own bar which became very popular with sophisticated and artistic people. Dean had a fantastic wit and a cynical sense of humour which earned him many admirers who used his bar as a refuge, a gossip shop, a fashionable club and an information centre.

Another very popular spot was Jay's Parade Restaurant which featured at the entrance two beautiful birds, an owl and a snow-white cockatoo. Jay's fascination with birds was matched by his excellent cuisine served in cramped quarters where you would literally rub shoulders with people such as Tallulah Bankhead, Truman Capote and the like.

A bar enjoying a fashionable vogue in the years I visited Sidi Hosni was Les Liaisons, run by two young Americans. Mel Levy, the son of a New York millionaire, had enjoyed Tangier so much that he wanted to stay. He persuaded his father to finance a restaurant ('If I told him it was a bar, he wouldn't have let me have the money') and together with his lover Frank, they ran a successful bar in which Frank would play any requests on the piano. These two handsome bi-sexuals made ravages in many feminine hearts (including my own) and their bar was always packed.

There was also a bar called The Safari with the stuffed heads of wild animals on the walls. It was run by a charming English woman, Diana Walford. She, too, preferred this life to going back home.

For a taste of the local sights there was the Kutoubia Palace where the best and prettiest belly dancers would perform while you had a Moroccan meal sitting on velvet cushions. These belly dancers would sometimes be invited to dance at Barbara's more formal parties. Their dresses glittered with beads and brocades and the girls would also be available for the night. Usually, though, Barbara preferred to invite the belly dancers and musicians who performed in the streets for the local populations. Often such groups would include a young boy, dressed in a kaftan, with a marvellously flexible body and very graceful gestures. It was part of the Moroccan tradition to have boy dancers among the women.

Social life in Tangier revolved around David Herbert and the people and places he approved of. Everyone either fitted into it, or were excluded from it, although there were a few who hovered on the fringe and would sometimes be included and sometimes not. One such person was Mrs Marjorie Allen, an elderly widow of a British naval officer. A colourful and outgoing person, Mrs Allen had been reduced by her modest pension to circumstances below her expectations. In Tangier, she was able to afford a servant and a semblance of the old British colonial style. She lived with a shy and socially-awkward daughter, the two of them very reminiscent of the mother and daughter in Terence Rattigan's *Separate Tables*. The pair lived in the daily hope of being included in the social activities. If they did not receive an invitation to an important party they would be down-hearted for days.

One of David Herbert's long-time friends who often visited Tangier was the English society photographer and designer, Cecil

Beaton. Beaton wanted very much to photograph Barbara inside her Tangier palace, something no photographer had ever done before. Indeed he was curious to see the inside of the palace. In the summer of 1962, Beaton attempted to gain entry via David Herbert. Barbara did not wish to be rude to David so she told him to make arrangements with me. She then told me that under no circumstances would she have Beaton in her house and neither did she want him at her annual ball. I was put in an embarrassing situation, but one I had experienced before, because Barbara often found it easier to put the onus on me. I was known by the Moroccan press as 'the Chinese guard dog'. I received a call from Beaton saying that everything had been arranged between Barbara and David for him to do a photographic session at Sidi Hosni, and he only wanted to make sure of the day and time. I delayed my answer to check back with Barbara. She had a way of changing her mind, and I had learnt to keep all options open. Barbara repeated that she did not wish to have anything to do with Beaton; she was suspicious of anyone connected with the media. When I reported this to Beaton, he assured me that he would not use the photos in any way but for Barbara's own private enjoyment. She, on her side, was getting the same message from David and, on these conditions, she agreed. For the sitting, Barbara put on her famous emeralds and her favourite green and gold sari. She was photographed in black and white, strumming an ancient lute, in front of her famous jewelled carpet. All the pictures depicted Barbara in the context of her Moroccan palace. Some included Lloyd Franklin in casual dress. He had not intended to be in the pictures, but Barbara asked him to and the contrast of one person in formal attire, the other in open neck shirt and cotton trousers was comical. The story had the inevitable end – within two months the pictures were featured in all the major American magazines as the scoop of the season. I was very angry and suggested to Barbara that she sue Beaton. She preferred to do nothing, for it would only have resulted in more adverse publicity.

One day, before Beaton's visit, Barbara gave me a small metal case which was locked and for which she had lost the key. She told me that she did not think it contained anything in particular but she wanted me to take it to a locksmith to have it opened. I found a man in a filthy little alley and he tried various keys without success. He said he would have to drill it but that he didn't have the proper instrument. He would have to take it to his cousin who did have a drill. He asked me to come back in half an hour. This I did. When I returned, the lock had been broken and the box was on the side of the untidy bench alongside various bits and pieces. After paying him 800 Dirhams I walked out of the shop, stooping to negotiate the small entrance. I then paused to look inside the box and there, wrapped in two paper tissues, were the Catherine the Great emeralds estimated at $3 million. Barbara had forgotten that Hélène had packed them safely on their own. My blood ran cold, and I almost fainted at the thought of what might have happened.

The centre of social activity in Tangier was the polo club. The English contingency would go there to have tea and read *The Times* in a manner reminiscent of the British Raj in India. The place was faded and seedy but the symbolic worth remained, even for those who did not play polo. It was important to be seen there.

Barbara was very much the patroness of the polo club, not merely because her donations allowed the place to survive, but because her then boy-friend, Lloyd Franklin, was one of the leading polo players. She had given him a string of superb ponies and had built him a bungalow and stables on land adjoining the club. Lloyd had done his National Service in the Household Cavalry, so he took to polo like a duck to water. The regular players included an English doctor, Denis Little, who had exchanged a rather drab life in England for a more exotic one abroad. In Tangier he had found a delicious new young French wife and a job as the official vet to the Moroccan cavalry horses. This allowed him to play polo to his heart's content and to have an extremely pleasant existence as a respected member of the European élite. Another regular member of the polo team was Dr Spriet, a hard-working French doctor who ran the local hospital on a shoe-string and often had no time to have a meal, yet enjoyed playing polo so much that he would stretch his schedule to jump on a horse in between his numerous medical commitments. There was also a young American banker, Tom Seeley, who had done a degree in California, majoring in polo. Short, and slightly built, his horses were all enormous and from a distance the image one had of him was that of a large horse mounted by a broad smile. In Tangier one did not need to be rich to have horses or to play polo. The grooms' wages were very low. Similarly, with the mild climate, stables could be make-shift with canvas partitions. Because Lloyd had the best and fastest ponies, he would usually lead the field even though he was not necessarily the best player. In this sense, as in so many others, money makes a big difference.

It was, in fact, in Tangier that Barbara met Lloyd.

One evening in July 1960, David Herbert went to Dean's Bar and met there Frank Franklin, a young Englishman who had recently arrived in Tangier with nothing else but a charming demeanour, the clothes he stood up in and a guitar under his arm. This young man had left England behind and tried to make a living playing the guitar. He spent some months in Spain, learned the language and pushed off to try his luck in Tangier during the tourist season. Dean took Frank in because he was such a pleasant person and gave him a meal in return for some flamenco music and a few bawdy rugby songs. Frank soon became a friend of the British residents, a welcome diversion from all the old faces. David Herbert, in particular, took an intense fatherly interest in him. Some believed they were lovers.

When Barbara arrived that summer, depressed and alone, David suggested that he take her to Dean's Bar. She was already well into a long drinking bout, and she agreed. She sat listening to Franklin and in a drunken haze asked him to play 'I can't give you anything but love, baby', which she called her theme song. Franklin had a marvellous ear for music, which also made it easy for him to learn languages. He sang flamenco like a Spaniard and he was able to improvise to suit the scene. The next thing that happened is that Barbara asked him to come to her palace. Frank had very little to bring with him. Just his guitar. When Barbara awoke the following day, she said, 'Who is that in my bed?' She was told that she had said to him the night before, 'Come and live with me.' And that is exactly what he did. In spite of her loneliness, and her desperate need to replace Jimmy Douglas, Barbara would never have done that if she had been sober.

Frank Franklin was younger than Barbara's son. He was six foot one inch tall, fair haired, reasonably good-looking in a bland sort of way, and had an ear for music. Aside from these traits, he was culturally unformed, but he learned very quickly and had an easy disposition. After finishing his national service, Frank had a short stint at the London Dance Centre teaching ballroom dancing. He then joined a travel agency, working as a courier in Spain. While there, he went to classes to learn Spanish, have his voice trained and learn how to play flamenco guitar. After two years he left the travel agency to go freelance in entertaining tourists.

Barbara decided to take on this eager young man who was so dazzled at the luxury around him. At least she could form him in the image of her choice; he seemed to be willing to do anything; he was docile, and at least he was not a homosexual. She was, however, uneasy about his very modest background. His parents were of the very poor working-class and Frank had five brothers and sisters, all a good deal older than himself. He felt rather bitter that his parents had been unwilling to offer to improve his education. He was envious of those who had a good education. He was bright and ambitious and he felt England had nothing to offer him. He felt terribly lucky to have found himself in the midst of the rich and famous. When Frank found himself in Barbara's palace, he thought he was dreaming.

The first thing Barbara did with Frank was to change his name, declaring that it was ridiculous to be called Frank Franklin. She decided to call him Lloyd Franklin; it had a better ring. That summer, I accompanied Lloyd to London so that he could be fitted from head to foot with the best clothes money could buy. Luckily, he already had an idea of what good taste was and he had no trouble fitting into Barbara's idea of what she wanted her companion to look like.

Apart from ordering several dozen suits, shoes, silk pyjamas, and much monogrammed underwear, Lloyd was also to choose an entire kit necessary for his future string of polo ponies. He also decided, while in London, to look up his friends in the cavalry with a view to offering one of them the job of head groom at his future stables. He managed to find an excellent person in Peter Smith, who at the time was working in the royal mews polo stables at Windsor Castle, and whose father was on the household staff of the Queen Mother. Peter was made an offer he could not refuse, although I was surprised at how reluctant he was to leave England. He was not sure if he would enjoy a country where there was no English beer and he was suspicious of any country that did not play cricket.

On our return journey we stopped in Spain, where it did not take Peter and Lloyd long to choose six of the best polo ponies in the country. Those ponies were going to be the fastest things on four legs in Tangier. As a result, although Lloyd was the least experienced player, he would usually manage to reach the ball faster than anyone else.

Lloyd's ponies had to be stabled properly and Barbara bought him a site adjacent to the polo club for a bungalow and stable block. Lloyd had some grandiose ideas about what he wanted. He wanted a large block to resemble the royal stables, he wanted to call the place Combermere, after the English royal stables, and he wanted the Union Jack to fly over it. When eventually the stables were complete, in 1962, their official opening almost created an international incident. I had ordered the Union Jack from a tailor in Tangier who said he knew exactly what it looked like because he used to work in Gibraltar. On the day we were to unfurl it, it turned out to be not the Union Jack but the Royal Ensign. Nevertheless, we decided to hoist it up the flagpole, when we heard a siren and a motorcade of policemen arrived to tell us that it was a criminal offence to display any flag but the Moroccan flag unless it was at a diplomatic mission in which case both flags had to be displayed with the Moroccan one no lower than the other. The policemen were very agitated and we were afraid for a while that they would decide to prosecute, feeling that we had been disrespectful of the country's recent independence. But, fortunately, nothing further happened.

Peter Smith was perfect for his job. There was nothing he did not know about horses. He had a weakness for drink and was delighted to find that, unlike back home, there were no restrictions on when drinking could take place. The bars were open all day and all night. He found himself with more money than he ever had before and the drink was very cheap. He enjoyed the night life and soon after his arrival, he was drinking until 3 am every night. He would go to bed fully dressed and get up at 6.30 am to supervise the schooling of the ponies. He was responsible for six highly sensitive ponies, four of which had to be fit to play on any day. Sadly, in the end, Peter's drinking caused him to neglect his duties and he was given the sack.

Time and time again, I saw Barbara trying almost too hard to please people: on a trip to Paris, Lloyd mentioned that the tea did not taste the same as back home. We tried all brands and had packets sent from England. Still it was not the same. We tried boiling mineral water and installing a water softener. Eventually, Barbara asked for gallons of water to be flown from London.

One evening at the beginning of the summer season in 1961, Barbara said to Lloyd, 'Why don't you invite some of *your* friends to spend the summer in Tangier – people of your own age.' Barbara had with her in Tangier the usual retinue of hangers-on, plus a constant stream of people coming and going at her expense. She was very much aware that these were not the type of people whose company Lloyd enjoyed. She was also aware that some of her

110

friends did not really approve of him. He was not a conversation-alist; he had no sophistication. Lloyd had to think hard about any friends he had. It had been several years since he left England. His thoughts turned to his national service days. How great it would be if he could be with some of the troopers he used to know. He could play polo with them; they could challenge the Tangier team.

It was my task to try and find the whereabouts of his regiment. I had the help of the Home Office and other official departments. Within a week I had traced half a dozen of them and Lloyd called them up with his fantastic story. They all thought, at first, that he was joking. 'How would you like to have a holiday in Tangier, all expenses paid?' Three of them took him up on it. David Johnson who used to play the kettledrums on the great shire horse in the regimental band; Michael Davis who had a possessive girlfriend but managed to get her permission for two-weeks' absence; and Jeremy Eldridge who had just qualified as an architect. Lloyd remembered that Jeremy had originally taught him to play the guitar and that had started him on a promising career. Lloyd decided to commission Jeremy to design and supervise the building of his bungalow and stables.

All Tangier was in a state of excitement at the prospect of three ex-guardsmen arriving. The majority of men in Tangier wrongly hoped the new guys would be gay. Barbara herself fell for Michael Davis, the most handsome of the three, but she was to learn that he was not to be had even with all that she could offer. Michael could easily have taken Lloyd's place, and he knew it. But, somehow he felt revolted at the idea of making up to an older woman, however rich she might be. One evening, in an attempt to extricate himself from Barbara's advances, he said, 'You are old enough to be my mother.' She was shattered and sat up all night with her rejection and her champagne. The next day, she had regained her self-respect and told everyone that Michael had told her that she reminded him of his mother, the greatest compliment a woman could wish for.

Although Michael was really rather straight-laced, and had no intention of having an affair, he let himself be seduced by one of the British girls, daughter of one of the regular cocktail party crowd. The girl used to sneak into Michael's room which was just below Barbara's and by the time Michael had to go home he had started to acquire a taste for this new kind of life. We heard that he married very soon after his return.

Jeremy Eldridge, the young Yorkshire architect, had no hang-ups.

111

He was determined to enjoy the scene. He was separated from his wife and had been living with a girl back in London but that hardly bothered him. He took to the life like a duck to water. He played polo, joined the cocktail parties, and started on his job designing the stable/bungalow complex for Lloyd.

As for David Johnson, he was a shy, socially awkward person who felt totally bewildered by the scene in Tangier. Unfortunately for him on his first evening he became the subject of David Carritt's caustic wit. He left on the next flight back to London, having lasted just two days in Barbara's world.

Sometimes there would be an important guest in Tangier and it might be part of his programme to watch a polo match. Barbara would always be asked to present the winner's cup. One summer we were to be visited by King Hassan II of Morocco, an excellent horseman himself.

The exhibition match was scheduled for 4 pm one Saturday. All the preparations were made and everyone – players, guests, staff – waited and waited and waited. Not only had his Majesty not arrived at the polo club, but he had not even arrived in Tangier. By 6 pm it was rumoured that he had not even left Rabat. The King was notorious for rarely being on time, so no one at the polo club was surprised when the exhibition match had to be abandoned when it became too dark.

We were, however, visited by another young monarch, King Hussein of Jordan. This dynamic and modern monarch seemed to me to be so very different to King Hassan. Yet, they were roughly the same age and both educated in the West. King Hussein in England, at Harrow and Sandhurst, King Hassan in France. King Hussein came to the club on a private visit. I found him very open, informal and relaxed. He treated everyone as equals, had a natural, relaxed manner and made everyone feel at home. Barbara introduced the polo team to the King. Lloyd Franklin, when it was his turn, bowed and called him 'Your Royal Highness'. Barbara corrected him and reminded him that it was 'Your Majesty'. The King laughed and immediately changed the subject, asking if he might try one of the ponies. He wanted to have a go on the polo field. This was arranged and the whole episode was characterized by lively fun. It was obvious that here was a man's man and I could see that there was an easy rapport with the polo players, whatever their nationality. I was filled with admiration for this exceptional person who obviously was favoured with a fantastic personality.

112

Barbara, on the other hand, felt that he was too informal. She would have preferred more stiffness and convention. She expected some rituals and ceremony; she was disappointed.

One of the funniest sights I have ever witnessed was the polo team dressed as women at one of Barbara's parties. Dr Little came in a red polka-dot dress as flamenco dancer, his bald head covered with a black wig. Dr Spriet was dressed as a hospital matron. Tom Seeley came as Little Red Riding Hood and Lloyd came as a blonde courtesan – looking absolutely gorgeous.

This occurred at one of the many parties at Sidi Hosni where the men were asked to come dressed as women and vice versa. For a week prior to the party all the dressmakers and shoemakers in Tangier would be frantically busy making the costumes – all of them sworn to secrecy. It was of course hilarious seeing the men dressed as women, with false eyelashes, wigs and high heels. The gay men who enjoyed dressing up in drag were in their element. And throughout the evening we would have to behave in keeping with our dress, so the 'men' would ask the 'ladies' to dance and take the men's part. On these occasions Barbara would be the spectator. Her costume would always be that of a discreet and somewhat girlish boy, such as a page at the court of Henry VIII or principal boy in a pantomime. She never compromised her femininity. Her real role was to lend the stage for the comedy played by her guests. The servants would stand by and join in our laughter. This is the scene in which I remember Barbara at her happiest – laughing until tears ran down her cheeks.

There would also be masked parties. Somehow, people behave differently with a mask on. It is as if we think that no one can see us because our face is covered. When we couldn't think of anything else, we would hold a pyjama party where guests would come in night attire ranging from ordinary pyjamas to sexy negligées and some of the more outrageous men would come in women's undergarments and heavy make-up. At one such party, I remember that everyone got well inebriated and the men started to dance wildly with each other, doing a strip-tease at the same time. The whole evening ended up the next morning with several massive hangovers and clouded memories. This was as outrageous as it ever got; it could be compared to an evening of undergraduate fun. Then I would read accounts in the press about the parties, the orgies of sex and drugs that took place at Sidi Hosni – nothing but the invention of a fertile journalistic mind.

113

This kind of childish horseplay was, however, peculiar to Tangier. In Paris it would never have been contemplated. At Sumiya the cultural atmosphere would have forbidden such ribaldry and there were never enough people to make up a sizeable party at any one time, nor would we have found people to make the costumes.

Barbara always enjoyed having Moroccan guests at her parties but it was sometimes difficult to mix with them. At her formal summer ball she would include local dignitaries such as the Mayor of Tangier, some of the more outgoing members of the Moroccan royal family, and officers of the Moroccan forces – very colourful in their gold-braided uniforms. At a large party one could include different types of people with no difficulty, but at smaller parties barriers of language and culture become more obvious, which tends to make conversation stilted. At the time, Morocco had just acquired independence from the French and the leaders of the community had not yet found it easy to deal with their new authority; it made them very touchy and unsure. Another difficulty was that Moroccans were forbidden to take alcohol. Those who did enjoy a drink would disguise it in Coca-Cola, but when they did drink you could see they were self-conscious in the presence of friends who did not drink. Altogether the atmosphere would not be easy.

Although Barbara enjoyed seeing her friends at Sidi Hosni, at times she enjoyed having no friends around. When she spent a day at home, without entertaining anyone, she would go around the house as if to make sure that it was all real. Many of the tables, including the dining-table, were glass-topped and flowers would be arranged under the table in such a way that you could see them through the glass top. Barbara enjoyed arranging the flowers. She adored tuberoses which have a delicate scent similar to gardenias and there would always be a lot of marigolds in pots. If certain flowers were unavailable in Morocco, we would have regular shipments flown from Paris, either directly to Tangier or some-times we would have to send someone to pick up the delivery at Gibraltar. Flowers meant a great deal to Barbara; it would set her mood at times. For instance, she hated gladioli to such an extent that she could dislike someone who, in all innocence, sent her a bouquet of them. She also disliked flowers in glass vases, for she thought that the sight of the stems was ugly.

Another thing that Barbara enjoyed doing at Sidi Hosni was looking after her six bird cages. These cages were exceptionally beautiful in their workmanship. One was a replica of the Taj Mahal, another represented a mosque. In them there were some colourful birds of the parakeet family. They did not sing, nor were they out of the ordinary, but Barbara treated them as pets and we would clean the cages, put in the food and drink. It was a task she missed if for some reason she was unable to do it. The birds were the last thing she would say goodbye to before leaving Sidi Hosni at the end of the summer season.

The big event in Tangier, of course, was the Annual Ball which took on mythical proportions, and so did the gossip and grovelling for invitations.

My task for the Ball was dealing with the guests. First, of course, came the guest list and that would be the cause of quite a few disputes, as people jockeyed to receive an invitation. There would be a black market for the invitations and we had to number them to avoid counterfeits. David Herbert would be the self-appointed arbiter of who should be on the guest list and Barbara was, as always, much influenced by his advice. However, she also included her friends from around the world: Mexico, India, Japan, the USA, France, Italy, England. I would be responsible for finding them accommodation in the already crowded hotels. The jealousy of Barbara's friends was always at its worst before the ball; they would complain to me about their accommodation not being as good as someone else's. Their status-consciousness was easily bruised. They all wanted special treatment. Lady Kenmare, of the renowned La Fiorentina at St Jean Cap Ferrat, was a guest one summer. She arrived at the Hotel Minzah just as I was engaged with the manager. She had to wait a few minutes for her luggage to be taken upstairs. Because I did not drop everything to ensure that she was served immediately, she formally complained to Barbara of my rudeness and inefficiency. She felt that her position entitled her to better service. Barbara's guests, lodged in seven different hotels across Tangier, would call me if they did not like their toilet paper. One particular friend of Barbara's used to complain to me about the other guests wearing furs and jewellery given to them by Barbara when they *should* have been given to her.

I was responsible for all the guests' travel expenses and hotel bills. Most of them would take advantage of Barbara and order things from shops, putting the expenses on their hotel bills for me to pay. Their justification was that the others were doing it. They would send Barbara expensive flowers and Barbara would know that she was paying for them. Yet, curiously, Barbara wanted all this to happen. She resented it when I took issue with those bills. She could not do enough for her friends. Such was the nature of her generosity. I am convinced that she also wanted to forget that people were taking advantage of her – it was a painful fact that she preferred to blot out. My job was not to question, but to pay all the bills. The difficulty arose when someone fell out of favour with Barbara – then the payments had to stop for that person. At that point the source of money dried up. At times, I would not be told when this change in the friendship occurred and I would thus be put in a very invidious position. Dealing with the guests was a nightmare of a job.

The most important part of the preparations was, of course, the décor. This was left entirely to Barbara's American friend, the talented interior designer Dan Rudd. Most of the time Dan was one of the entourage based in Paris where he lived with his Swiss friend, Claude Eggiman. In Paris he was normally invited to everything because he was amiable, charming, good-looking and versatile, although he tended to be rather possessive of Barbara. At the Annual Ball he became a magician. The plain, bare, flat roofs of Sidi Hosni were a perfect stage for any decorative theme. Dan's ability and taste were universally recognized and the immediate impact of his work on the guests was to take their breath away. Every year there were different decorative styles, but tents were always erected just for the evening. These open tents were elegant, delicate and beautiful. Usually there would be one for Barbara to receive her guests – as a potentate would receive his vassals. Colourful cushions would be used as seats. Sometimes guests would position themselves next to her and it would be difficult to shift them. Barbara would then get up and circulate. Her role, which she played beautifully, was to welcome everyone. She would be at her most gracious and you could see that she enjoyed it. There would also be larger open tents for the guests to view any entertainment such as the belly dancers. At times the evenings could be chilly and as the hours passed the guests would find it comfortable to gather in small groups on the cushions.

The orchestras (there were normally three) would usually be flown in from Mexico or the Caribbean. Barbara did not favour big name bands; she preferred calypso or jazz for these occasions. Plane-loads of food and fresh flowers always arrived the day before. Waiters and waitresses would be hired for the evening to serve the food and drinks. They would all wear Moroccan dress.

116

Each year Dan's ingenuity seemed to surpass itself. Among his more memorable creations were some papier mâché animals covered with paillettes and spangles of various colours. They were almost life-size but they looked as delicate as Fabergé jewels. Another unforgettable sight was a pair of human statues, twelve feet high, completely covered with fresh flowers. As if these artificial ornaments were not sufficient to lend an atmosphere of Arabian magic, the dawn from the roofs of Sidi Hosni was like a delicate dream. The light descending on the still city was a poetic sight. It was particularly effective after the Ball when everyone had enjoyed themselves at a memorable occasion. Those of us who had worked for months towards the success of that day could at last relax and watch the sun come up. That image is graven in my memory as the encapsulation of my existence in Tangier; at my second Annual Ball I fell in love with my future husband.

Barbara always gave credit to those who had worked hard. She lavished well-deserved praise on Dan Rudd. She would always give us more than the recognition and praise we deserved. After the Ball she recompensed us with a generous bonus and to me she would give a Moroccan souvenir such as a jewel, a silver Hand of Fatima, a translation of a book of Arab poetry. And I would also receive the ball gown she had worn, for me to wear the following year.

The Ball was always held towards the end of Barbara's annual stay in Tangier. For me it was a good way to round off the season, as I left before the others to prepare the Paris household. Anything after that would have been an anticlimax.

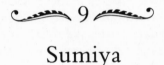

9

Sumiya

In the winter, Barbara would step into her own paradise near Cuernavaca in Mexico. The setting was truly magical. Cuernavaca (Spanish for bull horn) was dominated by the snow-capped Sierra Nevada and in full view of the lofty dormant volcanos Mount Popocatepetl (Aztec for smoking mountain) and Ixtaccihuatl (Aztec for white woman). The sight of these snow peaks, both more than 17,000 feet high, in a climate where orchids grow wild, is more than a poet could put into words. Cuernavaca, about forty miles south of Mexico City, was the ideal setting for Barbara's dream house for several reasons. It has a marvellous winter climate: because it is close to the equator the sun is almost directly overhead, but being at an altitude of almost 8,000 feet it is not too hot and the air is as crystal pure as in the Swiss Alps. The climate is dry and it is possible to acquire a deep tan without ever feeling too hot. Indeed, the evenings are chilly. There seemed to be a fragrance in the air, a peace and calm, that was truly out of this world. I cannot imagine a more perfect Shangri La.

Mexico was already popular in the early 1950s as a playground for rich Americans. Acapulco, the resort on the Pacific, was fast developing a skyline of skyscraper hotels built to accommodate wealthy honeymooners and business conventions. Barbara's attitude towards the Mexicans was anything but typically American. Instead of regarding Mexicans as somewhere below Blacks, she admired the Aztec civilization, about which she had read a great deal and of which she had a deeply romantic image. Her real introduction to Mexico came, however, through Merle Oberon.

In the 1950s Merle Oberon was still a big star. She had been launched in London by Sir Alexander Korda and had later become

Lady Korda. Her most memorable films were *Wuthering Heights* with Laurence Olivier, *A Song to Remember* in which she played Georges Sand in Chopin's life story, and *The Scarlet Pimpernel* with Leslie Howard. Merle divided her time between her three homes: Cuernavaca, Mexico City, and Bel Air.

Merle had bought a house in Cuernavaca which was a former jail and was reputed to be haunted. She left it looking like a cheap hut on the outside but inside the walls the area had been turned into a world of enchantment with a garden filled with flowers of every imaginable colour and description. Masses of blooms festooned the ancient stone walls around the swimming pool.

The very first time Barbara saw the setting of Merle's house, she became enchanted with the area. She was struck by the resemblance of Mount Popocatepetl to Mount Fuji in Japan, and immediately started to look for land on which to build a Japanese-style house. She soon found what she was looking for: a 30-acre plot in a tiny village called Paris just outside Cuernavaca. The land faced Mount Popocatepetl and Barbara bought it from a Mexican contractor. There were no roads for a radius of twenty miles. Paris itself resembled a small forgotten town in the Far West, the village street being just dry dust.

Here, in Cuernavaca, Barbara found she could relate to Aztec history – she tended to read into any Mexican cultural trait the greatness of the Aztec tradition. What is more, she had always been enamoured of all things Oriental and now she had an opportunity to build an Oriental house and, in fact, to make her fantasy world, where she felt most at home, come true.

Barbara's fifth husband, Baron Gottfried von Cramm, whom she married in 1955, had been jailed by the Nazis in Germany for being homosexual. As a result he was unable to obtain a visa to enter the US. The sentence, Barbara always maintained, was on political grounds for Gottfried and his family were known to be anti-Nazi. Now, because of the lack of visa, Barbara could not go with him to the places she usually visited in winter, and until then she had always made a point of spending Christmas with her Aunt Jessie and cousins Jimmy and Wooly in New York. The idea of a winter retreat in Mexico, where Gottfried would not have to suffer the ignominious reminder of his past, was an attractive one. However, by the time the house in Cuernavaca was completed in 1958, Gottfried von Cramm was no longer part of Barbara's life.

Albert Ely Ives, the architect Barbara chose to design her

Japanese-style house understood the Japanese soul completely and was an expert in Oriental art. He had designed several such houses in Hawaii where there is a wonderful mix of oriental races and where each culture is encouraged to flourish side by side. Barbara's choice of Ives was a good one, they formed an excellent partnership: the client wanting only the best, with no expense spared, which the architect was more than able to provide. Soon the house became the most talked about architectural project in Mexico. But it was typical of Barbara's sense of fun that she called this magnificent house, which eventually cost her $3.2 million, 'Sumiya' after a brothel in Kyoto. Every time she mentioned the name it would be with a smile and a twinkle in her eyes.

A Japanese landscape designer, Mario Oguri, was brought in to design the gardens which included landscaped terraces, a rock garden, a stream and a bamboo forest. In the end he stayed on to direct the team of fourteen Mexican gardeners maintaining the gardens.

The building materials started to arrive from Japan in 1955 – Barbara had insisted that only authentic Japanese materials be used. There was no road up to the site, but everyone within fifty miles of Mexico City was able to direct the crates arriving from Japan to Sumiya. Every tile, every lacquered board, every piece of furniture and linen, every stone and every plant in the garden was shipped directly from Yokohama. It was the most successful experiment in cultural transplanting. T. V. Smith wrote in *House Beautiful* in 1962 that this single house had had more influence than any number of missionaries.

Sumiya was beautifully sited, with slight rolling hills as part of the grounds. The house itself was a conglomeration of detached buildings linked by enchanting corridors, passageways and bridges over a fishpond. Water was, in fact, a feature of Sumiya's design; there were several waterfalls, as well as the fishpond. Despite the open-plan of the house, the inner courtyards were always cool during the heat of the day, while at night they insulated us from the cold. The guest house, where I stayed, was detached from the main house and situated at the far end of the swimming pool, next to the pool bar. Anyone staying in the guest house could lead a quite separate life from those in the main house.

The exterior wooden columns of the house were encased in decorative stone bases, in typical Oriental style. These decorative footings on the columns differed in their details – some were square and some had a cast-metal shoe. Barbara explained to me that originally the metal shoe had protected the wood from termites and prevented it splintering. Eventually, these careful refinements became valid for their own elegant simplicity. Barbara enjoyed the historical and poetic implications in Oriental design and appreciated the Orient as no one else I have ever known, of any nationality. She not only appreciated it, but she was vastly knowledgeable about it.

There are several ways of looking at this exquisite phenomenon of Sumiya. From an architectural and design point of view, it could be seen as a museum. The site chosen was ideal for an open-style Japanese house, all on one level. Most rooms contained seventeenth-century lacquered screens and oriental tables and chests. Upholstered pieces, for those more used to Western furnishings, were fitted around in an unobtrusive way so as not to distract attention. Although the classical Japanese design was never compromised, neither was comfort. The dining-table was set low to the floor with the traditional cushions, but for Westerners unused to sitting on the floor, there was a well in the floor beneath the table to provide leg-room.

One entered the main living room through a pair of antique doors decorated with peacocks and chrysanthemums. In the living room itself glass panels had been set into the outer walls. These panels, placed between bamboo posts and shaded by broad protecting eaves, gave the room the feeling of a pavilion open to the surrounding garden terraces and distant mountains. Throughout the house, the floors were covered with the traditional tatami mats, and the sliding doors were, of course, made of the traditional shoji paper. All the carpentry detailing, such as the lapped board ceiling and the silk-bound split-bamboo shades, was done by Japanese craftsmen working in the classical tradition.

Even the smallest details of the furnishing were handled with exquisite taste. There were lacquer boxes and trays on the tables. In the bathrooms we had seventeenth-century lacquered containers for cosmetics and jewellery. It felt much too good and expensive to use, but Barbara wanted us to behave as though we were, in fact, living in seventeenth-century Japan.

The atmosphere of Sumiya was one of serene simplicity, in spite of the expensive items all around us. Nothing seemed artificial or contrived. The lighting was diffused by wooden grills. Each guest room was planned around a particular theme. Here, Barbara allowed a deviation from authenticity – we all had comfortable beds with modern mattresses. Indeed, there was a certain amount of upholstered furniture, covered in Oriental silk, but blending perfectly with the antique furniture.

There was no road in the adjoining village of Paris and the path to Sumiya was a very rough dirt track which tore car tyres to shreds. Still, a made-up road would have been as incongruous in this setting as an item made of plastic. When you arrived at Sumiya you found yourself in front of an enormous gate in the traditional Japanese frame, with an old stone lantern decorating the central gravel path. The doors of the gate, when open, formed a frame for the view of Mount Popocatepetl.

Part of Sumiya included a building which housed a Kabuki-style theatre. At times Barbara would invite a Japanese troupe to perform. At other times films would be shown. In true Japanese fashion there were no chairs – just tatami mats and duvets for warmth when it became chilly in the evening. For those of us who were not used to sitting for hours on the hard floor, there were folding contraptions which served as supports against which we could lean to ease our aching backs. The theatre was conceived to further our cultural experience. However, it was not often used for the real thing and we used it mainly to show films which Bill Robertson would obtain from Hollywood. It was usually the only entertainment offered to us at Sumiya, although once a season Barbara, who never otherwise left the house during her stay, would take us to the Woolworth store in Cuernavaca – just for fun.

Life at Sumiya was different from anywhere else. The serenity and natural beauty of the landscape plus the pleasure of living in such an exquisite house led one to contemplation rather than activity. The sun was a delight every day. I did my work in my bathing suit next to the pool, with peacocks venturing timidly towards the possibility of titbits. They particularly liked peanuts, but their natural mistrust would not allow them to come close to humans. One of the challenges we had under the blue Mexican sky was to see how close we could get a peacock to come to us. The game required us to sit motionless on the ground with a bowl of peanuts. The peacock would be about ten to twelve feet away, knowing you held the peanuts. You would throw one peanut at a time in the path between the peacock and yourself, luring it towards you. Any overt or sudden movement would make it take flight. It never took less than twenty-five minutes to make it come up to you. Five feet was the closest I ever succeeded in getting a peacock

122

to come to me. Only Lloyd Franklin was able to get them to eat out of his hand; no one else had the patience or the ability to sit motionless for so long.

It was in Cuernavaca at the end of 1960 that Barbara decided to have Lloyd circumcized. She said it was cleaner. She had a very good doctor whom she trusted, and as there was little activity at Sumiya in the winter, it was the ideal time to do it. I had to give up my room to Lloyd after the operation because I had a double bed and he needed to stretch his 6 foot 1 inch frame for comfort. He boasted that the doctor had to take fourteen stitches. Lloyd decided to hold a formal burial of his foreskin. He laid it neatly in a small tin coffin, lined with velvet, and we buried it in the Japanese garden at the foot of a hill. A tree was then planted to commemorate the ceremony.

Working in these conditions took on a surreal expression. The household staff never hurried. The pace was leisurely and nothing seemed important enough to concentrate on. I never stayed longer than three weeks, so I could let things pile up until I returned to France. Barbara was lucky in having Bill Robertson, her American friend from the days of her tennis craze, to deal with the household arrangements. In this way, I was fortunate too, as I could rely on him to deal with everything. He was a good friend, with an ideal temperament, always cheerful and very considerate. In his youth, Bill had reached the quarter-finals of the US tennis championship. Apart from this achievement he had done very little else and desired very little else. Barbara would say that although he probably had had the talent to get to the top of the tennis world, he did not have the killer instinct necessary to get there – he was too decent. He was known now as the tennis partner of the stars: he often played, back home in Hollywood, with actors such as Gary Cooper and Charlton Heston. His quiet sense of humour kept us sane at times when we might have had hysterics. Bill was an excellent friend to me because he was understanding and sympathetic to women. He became part of Barbara's entourage in the 1940s when she lived in California. She bought him a property overlooking Beverley Hills and kept him on her payroll. Bill's passport described him as 'retired' before he reached his fortieth birthday! He was satisfied with the simple life of quiet comfort afforded him by Barbara. Of all the people who were permanently part of her court, Bill was the most faithful and sincere friend. He was available whenever Barbara needed him, although he made it very plain that he would rather stay in California, than join the party in Tangier, Paris or on a world tour.

When Barbara acquired Sumiya, she asked Bill to make the arrangements for her yearly winter stay. He could speak enough Spanish to get by. Each year his duties would start with the purchase of a new car in Beverley Hills, then he would set off in it to arrive at Sumiya a few weeks before Barbara. He was extremely popular with the staff who were young, unsophisticated Mexicans, but very hardworking. They were pleased to get a good salary all year round for six weeks' work.

At the time, I was extremely keen on tennis both as a player and a spectator. Bill gave me a custom-built tennis racket, and introduced me to René Lacoste who gave me a Lacoste tennis shirt. I would often ask Bill to tell me about all the tennis greats who had been my pin-ups in my high school days. He did not have much regard for most of them as people and he would laugh at my hero-worship.

The days revolved around the swimming pool as the natural focus and centre of the property. It was the first place to look for anyone you wanted. Yet we were not often in the pool for swimming purposes. A short dip would be the most we could bear for Barbara liked the pool to be heated to 90°F and it was like getting into a very hot bath. We would have liked to have turned the heat down to do some proper swimming but Barbara was very touchy on the subject. She enjoyed it at 90°F although she did not often go in and we never dared to turn the thermostat down unless she was drinking, when she never left her bedroom. Bill was the only person with the authority to touch the thermostat and he would sometimes give us a treat so we could do a few quick lengths.

In this unbelievably enchanting, yes perfect, setting, life was not always as ideal as one might expect. Depending on the guests present, time could hang heavy. Most of Barbara's friends were unable to appreciate the cultural implications which meant so much to her. It was absurd, I used to think, that Barbara never surrounded herself with people worthy of her. The answer, of course, was quite simply that she found it easier to be bored with sycophants; she did not have to make the effort of living up to them. What Barbara's friends enjoyed were the activities of cosmopolitan cities. They did not want to hear her eulogize Japanese culture. All they wanted to do was satisfy their curiosity about the house, so they could tell their friends back home what a ridiculous idea it was to have a Japanese house – and in Mexico of all places. After that they had had enough of Sumiya. Some even said they felt as if they were in prison. It was, to my mind, casting pearls to swine.

124

Barbara was a different person in Sumiya. It was here that she was at her most tranquil. She seemed to lock herself in another culture, another era, it was almost as if she were living Japanese culture. Naturally, we all had to wear kimonos. A big selection, beautifully embroidered in silk, hung in every bedroom. The servants also wore the Japanese uniform of white trousers and dark kimono jackets with the Japanese character for Sumiya on the back. We had to take our shoes off before entering a room and we ate off authentic antique Japanese plates. Apart from those observances, informality was the rule. There were no set times for meals, no routine, no clock watching. Here, more than anywhere else, we were at the mercy of Barbara's moods. If she wanted quiet, we had to stop talking because the stillness of the atmosphere and the paper walls and doors would carry the noise. If she was drinking, we had no escape. We would then be dependent on her usually tearful mood and would have to take turns in staying up all night with her. In Tangier and Paris there were many more of us to undertake this task. Here sometimes there were only two or three of us and it would be almost unendurable. A few days of this, plus the Japanese music she always played non-stop when she was drinking, and even Paradise could seem like hell.

The staff were charming. The most mature was Raoul, the major-domo-cum-chauffeur. He said very little but he had contacts with the suppliers and all the other servants treated him with respect. Barbara's personal chambermaid was a small lively girl called Inés, and then there were two houseboys, Luis and José, and two girls who were not always the same depending on Inés' decision every year. We found out years later that Raoul and Inés were married but never revealed the fact to anyone. They were quite right not to, for part of Barbara's interest in them was the feeling that they belonged to her. Had she known the true situation one, at least, of them would have been sacked.

One winter, during a lonely drinking bout, Barbara decided she loved José, the houseboy with a fresh and innocent face. She saw in him the beauty of the Aztec civilization. He was completely baffled at the poetry that she would read to him. He probably did not understand when she said that she wanted to take him with her to Europe and make him her escort. Bill and the rest of us began to worry about the scandal. The most worried person, of course, was Lloyd, who was never sure when he might be replaced. He must have remembered how Barbara had picked him up during a drinking bout when all he owned were the clothes he wore and a guitar. The main difference between himself and José was that José could speak no English. The whole José situation took on tremendous importance, for when Barbara was drinking anything could happen.

We never saw the kitchen staff and it would have been too much to expect them to prepare Japanese food. Barbara was always slimming and meals played no part in her life except in Paris, and then only as a social formality. Mexican food was not very palatable to most of us. Avocados were plentiful and prepared in many ways. Good meat was difficult to get and no one bothered to improve matters because the general trend was to have club-sandwiches, gazpacho, peanuts and potato crisps. Hamburgers were a luxury and the meat was always tough. What a contrast to the Paris scene! I was never able to convince Herminie of the truth about our meals at Sumiya. She could not envisage Barbara leading such a different life.

The local people who would drop in were Barbara's doctor and his wife, both extremely interesting and genuine. They would be invited to the ball in Tangier in the summer. Barbara would sometimes invite local artists, to encourage them in their work. I remember one sad-looking artist who came and stayed for several weeks. He made us little ash trays with his signature on the bottom and insisted that his name would one day be famous. One day Barbara said: 'Who is that in the swimming pool?' She had forgotten that she had invited him to stay for as long as he wished. She got Bill to make him leave.

One winter, Barbara decided to learn Spanish and invited a lady teacher to come in to give her lessons. As usual, Barbara was slimming and she asked the teacher to come in at lunch-time while the rest of us were eating. At the third lesson, the teacher, seeing all the wealth around her and having witnessed Barbara's tremendous generosity, decided to give Barbara a sob story. 'Madam,' she whined, 'I have ten little niños at home who are hungry. Madam doesn't know what it is to be hungry . . .' Whereupon Barbara flew into a rage and said: 'You don't know what you're talking about; I'm *always* hungry!' Then she threw the poor bewildered lady out!

I enjoyed most the times at Sumiya when there were no guests. There would just be Barbara, Bill Robertson, Colin Fraser and I. Both these fellows were tremendous company. Colin was a great story-teller and mimic and aside from his many uses he was the court jester. Given the right incentive and prodding, he could do a few 'acts' which would have us rolling on the floor, helpless with laughter. I enjoyed immensely the times Colin and I were 'on duty'. He was unofficially the indispensable jack-of-all-trades in the household, ready to provide any kind of service. The press described him as Barbara's latest suitor, the one who refused to marry her, and so on, but in fact he was a very private person who was not prepared to tie himself down to a job or sell his soul for a fortune. When he was available, he would be willing to do anything. But when he needed his freedom, he would disappear for as long as he wanted. He carried Barbara when she was unable to walk; he stayed up at night with her listening to her sad stories and making the right noises in reply. He was polite and friendly to all Barbara's friends, not always an easy task.

Colin was quite mysterious about his path from the beaches of Perth, Australia, to the drawing-rooms of Europe. What he wished to keep to himself, he kept to himself. At some point he found himself in the entourage of Noël Coward. Colin had many an amusing story about that crowd. He said that when he first came out of his modest neighbourhood, he was invited to a party at Coward's, whose name did not ring much of a bell with Colin who never tried to hide his lack of erudition. After dinner, the Master enjoyed having an audience. His guests would sit on the floor in a semi-circle at the Master's feet while he would tell them a story, enjoying the sound of his famous voice. At the end of the story, Colin recalled, there would be gentle appreciative applause. Colin was so impressed at Coward's story-telling ability that he ventured a compliment 'Hey, Noël you're a real beaut. You should try writing your stories!' Whereupon the Master turned to the bookshelves lining the wall behind him and gestured towards the rows of books while the guests had a good chuckle. My God, thought Colin, his face the colour of beetroot, this geezer must be famous!

Colin made inferences that Noël and his crowd indulged in scatology and enjoyed the humour surrounding it. I was never sure if he made up the stories or if there was any truth attached to them. Basically, Colin had a very moral and proper background. Even though Barbara had many people in her orbit who were anything but shy about their sexual inclinations, Colin preferred to keep mum.

The first time I went to Cuernavaca, it was Colin who showed

127

me around, at Barbara's request. We went to all the well-known night-clubs in Mexico City. The most spectacular bull fights I have ever seen were in the newly-built stadium there, the largest in the world. The first time Colin took me to that stadium for a bull fight, Inés recommended us to take an umbrella. I paid no attention to this advice as we had seats in the shade. What we did not realize was that the stadium's cheapest seats were those furthest back. Bottles were not allowed in the stadium so that men would bring their drinks in paper cups which they then filled with urine. They would then throw those missiles onto the people in the expensive seats below. That was part of the afternoon's entertainment for the poorer people. It was not long before one of those missiles hit me on the back of the head, drenching my long hair and the entire back of my sundress. Thanks to Colin, the whole episode and the hour's drive back to Sumiya turned into a hilarious joke and we laughed all the way home to Inés who said: 'I told you to take an umbrella!'

It was also Colin who nursed me through my first tequila experience in a Mexican bar. I found it exciting to learn the ritual of putting some salt on the back of my left hand, knocking it into my mouth and then downing in one gulp the small glass of tequila and then biting into a section of lime. Colin knew that I was not used to drinking and when he saw my enthusiasm for this new-found game, he tried to warn me to take it slowly. I paid no attention until I fell on the floor like a sack of potatoes and Colin had to pick me up unconscious. He nursed me through my first hangover, assuring me that I would live. I have been a teetotaller since that experience and Colin used to give a very funny version of that most important event in my life.

Colin was most at home in outdoor places, like the type of life he led in his native Perth where they would have beach picnics at Christmas. He loved Tangier with the two beaches, Mediterranean and Atlantic. He loved the bustling town full of intrigue and odd corners. Where Colin was, there was a continuous atmosphere of holiday and merry-making. He was the driving force, the life and soul of the drag parties which were fantastic fun for all involved in them. They were not the common drag parties associated with gays. These were like masquerade balls with a theme.

As Colin became more and more indispensable to Barbara, he changed from being a guest to being part of the household. The first time he came to Paris he was like a kid at Disneyland. Barbara had asked me to paint the town red with him. I showed him all the places he had heard about, Maxims, the Folies Bergères, the Eiffel Tower, the topless Lido girls. Everyday he wrote home to his Granny, who according to Colin was a 'beaut'. 'They'll never believe me,' he said. Even in the staid, socially-rigid atmosphere in Paris, Colin would manage to keep us in stitches. The first time he sat down at a fully laid formal dinner in Paris, he asked what the bowls of water with a floating slice of lemon were for. Everybody roared with laughter at this Australian who had never seen or heard of a finger-bowl. 'I thought it was for drinking,' he admitted. From then on, whenever Colin and I had a meal in the dining-room, we would solemnly raise our finger-bowls, touch them together in a toast and drink down the contents – just to see Basile cover his face with his gloved hand to stifle a guffaw.

Colin never complained about anything. At most, he would tighten his lips and give a meaningful smile. Whereas the rest of us would bitch and plot, Colin would make us laugh to relieve the tension. When he had had enough, he would do a bunk. Barbara understood it and was tolerant of it. The only trouble was that when he disappeared, we would not know where to reach him, how long he would be away or, indeed, if he would ever come back. That's the way he wanted it. We used to liken him to a tom cat who had to go when he had to go. The fact was that he was not on the payroll. What he got out of being part of the household was a very good life. He had no desire at the time to settle into a routine. You might say he was a professional escort. Barbara was generous to him, giving him large sums of spending money. He never asked for anything, unlike other people, he was never jealous and he honestly appreciated living a certain life into which he had not been born. He enjoyed drinking and having lots of laughs with people. He told me that he did not expect this kind of life to last for ever and he was making hay while the sun shone. He was quite wrong, for he lasted longer than anyone else in Barbara's favour. He never became greedy, he never got conceited.

Barbara never considered Colin as a possible suitor. If she had, he would have run a mile away. It was not because he was not good looking, quite the contrary. It was not because he did not seem interested; after all she married Gottfried von Cramm. Nor was it because Colin was not cultured or well-bred – witness Lloyd Franklin. It could be said that Barbara regarded Colin as a friend, bodyguard, male nurse during her last and sad decline. I have read that Marilyn Monroe had the same type of relationship with her masseur. A confidante who is a friend and who is reliable, amusing and faithful is worth more than a lover or a husband. Anyone would be lucky to have such a friend. Barbara was aware of Colin's good qualities from the start and luckily for her she was romantically involved with other people when Colin appeared on the scene. Otherwise, she might have decided to turn Colin into a permanent companion and that could have spoiled a remarkable and long-lasting friendship.

~~~~ 10 ~~~~

What Price Motherhood?

May God protect you in your flight
Throughout this long and loveless night.
May all His angels keep you warm
And wrapped in light until the dawn.
And may there rest upon your face
The peace and splendour of His Grace.
    Barbara Hutton, upon the birth of her son

Motherhood for Barbara was not the rewarding and fulfilling experience that many women enjoy. When Barbara fell in love at first sight with Count Kurt von Haugwitz-Reventlow in 1934, she saw him as the incarnation of the fairy-tale prince of her favourite novels. He was extremely handsome, tall, elegant and fair. He was the owner of a castle, within a village which bore his name, in Denmark. Here was a true nobleman, not a phoney aristocrat like her first husband, 'Prince' Alexis Mdivani. She was swept off her tiny feet by Kurt and she later said that with him she experienced the true meaning of passion for the first time in her life.

Within hours of obtaining a divorce from Alexis in Reno, Nevada, she plunged for the second time into marriage, letting her heart guide her as would be the pattern throughout her life.

When, within three months of her marriage, Barbara found that she was pregnant, her feelings were strangely mixed. Instead of feeling elated at this natural consequence of her love for Kurt, the prospect of providing an heir to the house of Reventlow did not bring her any joy. She herself described pregnancy as a cow-like process. It certainly was not worthy of the slim body she so carefully maintained with a harsh regime of dieting.

As her body thickened she grew more and more repulsed by the idea of childbirth. She told me that she felt like a person who had swallowed a watermelon, and in her fifth month she decided that she would not have a child the way the animals do. She told her gynaecologist that she wanted to be delivered by Caesarean section so that she would not have to endure the ignominy of natural delivery. The only acceptable method of birth to her was the idea of a neat incision from which a beautifully-formed baby would be lifted – all clean and rosy and smiling. She also vowed that she would never endure a pregnancy again. The sight of her swollen body disgusted her and she did her best to hide herself until she could display a slim figure again.

The date chosen for the Caesarean was 25 February 1936. The place was Barbara's rented London home in Hyde Park Gardens, where the dining-room was converted into an operating theatre. The surgeon was Mr C. S. Lane-Roberts, the most eminent English obstetrician of his day. He was assisted by a team of six. The operation went without a hitch. Still, on the following day there were complications arising from an internal infection and a rupture of a blood vessel. Barbara had to have an emergency operation to save her life. It was four days before she was out of danger and her health was impaired for a long time. It was several weeks before the new mother was allowed to have a look at her son, a beautiful blond baby who weighed 7lb 14oz at birth. Barbara felt that the surgeon had been careless during the Caesarean operation. In spite of the enormous medical bill caused by the birth and the emergency operation, Barbara donated $200,000 to the British Hospital Fund in appreciation for the excellent nursing care she received.

In later years Barbara was to deplore her lack of maternal instincts. She said that the only feeling she experienced for the baby was the awareness that it was totally helpless. She did not feel that he had been part of her, or that he existed because of her. He needed a name and she picked Lance after a hero out of a novel she had read, the title of which she promptly forgot. No doubt it was short for Lancelot. It sounded like a name for someone courageous and dashing which is what she hoped her son would grow up to be. In fact, it was a bad choice of name because Barbara spoke with an English accent and always pronounced the name 'Lawnce', whereas Lance himself always preferred the American version of 'Lance'.

At the time of Lance's birth, Barbara took on a reliable Scottish nurse, who was down-to-earth, sensible, reliable and frugal. Her name was Margaret Latimer but she was known as 'Sister', the term used for nurses in Britain. Even after Lance was grown-up she was to continue to play a large part in Barbara's life.

Before Lance could even be christened, Barbara received kidnap threats. This was ironic, because Barbara and Kurt had originally decided to make their home in London, believing it to be safer than France or the USA. One of the threats was followed up by Scotland Yard and resulted in a jail sentence for the unemployed would-be kidnapper. The security measures had to be increased and every precaution was taken to safeguard Lance. He was only allowed outdoors with Sister and two security men. Often he was wrapped in a blanket, like a parcel, and whisked away before anyone could spot him. The British press were unrelenting in their attention, and there would be a crowd outside the house most of the time.

Although Barbara and Kurt had lived in London since 1935, they had found no house they wanted to buy until in 1938 Barbara fell in love with the site of St Dunstan's Estate which had been used as a school for the disabled. It was a rather ugly Regency-style mansion occupying fourteen acres in the centre of Regent's Park. The building was over one hundred years old; one of the owners had been Lord Rothermere but it had been allowed to fall into a state of disrepair. Barbara commissioned a British firm of architects to raze the building and to rebuild it in Georgian style. She named it Winfield House in commemoration of her grandfather Woolworth's palace at Glen Cove where she had lived for a time after her mother's death. The conversion of the four-storey, sixty-room house cost £3 million. Lady Milbanke, a friend of Barbara's and a popular interior designer of the day, took charge of the interior of Winfield House. The property included a music room, a billiard room, tennis courts and swimming pool. Most of the furniture and carpets had belonged to French royalty. However, the most valuable items were a pair of Chinese Chien Lung vases and a sixteenth-century staircase brought from a French château. A staff of thirty-one was needed to run Winfield House.

Sadly, after all the work and expense, Barbara was to enjoy her house for only two years. Life with Kurt became unbearable. He had a cruel streak in him and she cringed at the way he treated her servants. He was very rigid and authoritarian which was repugnant to Barbara. When the first flush of passion abated, Barbara knew she had made a mistake. For Kurt also, the early promise of happiness had not materialized. He found it irritating to see his wife drink black coffee all day instead of having meals with him. He disapproved of her friends and activities. He expected a wife to do as she was told and found that, with Barbara, this approach did not work. The escape for Barbara was to allow other men to pay her court – which not unnaturally soured the marriage beyond redemption.

The beginning of Lance's haphazard and lonely life was fraught with a tug-of-war battle for his custody which lasted four years. Even after the settlement, the fight continued with charge and counter-charge, libel suits and writs, Kurt and Barbara each trying to prove the other an unfit parent. In fact, they could hardly have been further apart in their views of how Lance should be brought up. On one side, Kurt believed in strict discipline for Lance similar to his own training as a German soldier in the First World War. Kurt tolerated no breach of his strict rules and he disapproved of Lance staying away from school because of his asthma. Barbara, on the other hand, deplored the discipline imposed by Kurt. To make up for what she saw as unreasonable harshness, she indulged Lance with luxuries enjoyed by men years his senior, an unlimited amount of cash and no discipline.

Lance's holidays with his father could have been beneficial for a boy with no roots, for Kurt had married again, this time to Margaret (Peggy) Drayton, a member of the American Astor family. Peggy brought to the household her own daughter, Binky, who was roughly the same age as Lance. There was now a stable, happy family atmosphere which was by no means unpleasant. But Lance suffered from the contrasting sets of values in the homes of his two parents.

When Lance was with his father and step-mother it would be in Pasadena, California. When he was with his mother, it would be somewhere in Europe. The courts allowed Barbara to choose the school that Lance would attend. At nine years of age, Lance attended an elementary school for upper-class boys but only stayed two months because someone made a remark about his mother. He was then enrolled at St George's School in Newport, Rhode Island. It had the reputation of being the finest prep school on the East Coast, but the climate there aggravated his asthma. In 1950 he was transferred to a high school in Tucson, Arizona, where the air was warm and dry. All his school reports noted that Lance was a withdrawn boy who found it difficult to make friends, yet his marks were always good. Lance remembered his school days as being very unhappy. The other boys were cruel and punished him in a hundred ways for being asthmatic, for having bigger cars, more money, and a head-line hitting mother. The final hurt of Lance's school days was when his mother promised to attend his graduation and at the last moment couldn't face it. She, like Lance, dreaded the idea of a crowd of people looking at her. She was convinced, especially in the US, that she was the most hated woman in the world. Instead of going to his graduation as promised, she decided to drown her shame in champagne and order the latest Cadillac to be delivered to Lance the next day. It was not appreciated. He never forgave her. He was later to say 'When I needed my mother, she would send me another car.'

Not surprisingly, Lance became a taciturn and moody child. His parents had each tried to poison his mind against the other. The result was that he grew to hate his father. Barbara had devised a code so they could write nasty things about Kurt in secret. But it did not, for all that, result in any closeness between mother and son. Barbara and Lance were mutually disappointed in each other. Barbara seemed unable to be a consistent, loving mother however hard she tried – after all she herself was looking for a mother all her life. Lance was a living reminder of Kurt whom she hated and she knew that Kurt had done his best to turn Lance against her. Most of all she wanted a warm, affectionate son. She was looking for love herself and what she got instead was a son who was distant and hostile, largely due to her failure as a mother. After his fourteenth birthday, Lance chose never to see his father again, and refused to acknowledge any correspondence from him. He would have liked to have turned his back on his mother too, but he was tied to her by just one thing: money.

During Lance's childhood, the only constant person in his life was Sister Latimer. She, however, was not a warm or affectionate person. Lance's early childhood had been similar to his mother's. He did not have the continuous love of a mother and in later life he was to show signs of the same personality disorders. Pathetically, in his teens, he had desperately sought substitute parents which he found in Jack and Nina Kessler, the parents of his best friend Bruce. He called Nina 'Mom'. He also had a close relationship with George and Gracie Burns, the parents of his friend Ronnie at whose birthday party Lance was to meet his first wife, Jill St John. Whereas Barbara would lament the loss of her beloved mother, Lance's mother was very much alive, a fact of which the press reminded him all too often – with talk of her boyfriends, divorces, marriages – things he strongly diapproved of. The fact that Barbara was very generous to him only increased his guilt and alienated him from her the more. He could not stand the hoards of hangers-on around his mother, the succession of lovers and husbands, the frivolity of her life which his father had condemned. And when she started drinking, she completely lost her son's respect. He would refer to her as 'the lush'.

Barbara married Cary Grant when Lance was six years old and to all intents and purposes the marriage lasted barely two years. During that time Lance started to put down badly-needed roots. He was to cling to the Californian part of his childhood for the rest of his life. It was a natural choice for Lance who disliked the phoney aristocratic snobbery he was brought up in. This was the ideal setting for a forward-looking youngster and he embraced that way of life firmly for all the comfort he could get from it. He was in effect turning his back on his parents' way of life.

The press like to say that Cary Grant was the only step-father who cared for Lance, even that he was the only real father-figure in Lance's life. This image was manufactured by Grant's studio who were in charge of his public face. Periodically, pictures of Barbara, Cary and Lance would be taken and circulated to the media. It was done to counteract the 'Cash and Cary' label that had stuck to the couple. It was deemed detrimental to Cary's image that he should be thought of as a kept man.

Another reason for the 'Cary as a loving father to Lance' myth is that Cary himself said that he wished to have children. This was no doubt a sincere wish, as the future would prove. But there was, of course, more to it than that. The responsibility of a growing boy did not change Barbara's tendency to feel all or nothing towards people. She so hated Kurt that when she settled down in California with Cary, thus offering a home to Lance for the first time in his young life, she would boast about Cary being a marvellous father. She went so far as to have Lance's school clothes marked 'Lance Grant'. This provoked Kurt to take the matter up in the courts, although he knew it was just a childish way in which Barbara could spite him. In truth, Cary thought Lance an ungrateful, spoiled brat and was very resentful of the money spent on him. Cary's legendary parsimony made him turn away in disgust from what he called 'the hangers-on', Lance being one of them.

Having finished high school, Lance had but one idea in mind: to avoid any further purgatory of that kind. The boys that he knew were all going to college as a matter of course. Everyone encouraged Lance to give college a try as he had never found any subject difficult to grasp. He was obviously college material. Because of the pressure, Lance consented to joining a small junior college where he would have fewer people to cope with. He still found it difficult to fit into the social context of an institution, however small. He left after the first semester. Not only did he have no academic ambition, he could not feel at ease with people.

What Lance wanted to do was to prove his manhood. He very much suffered from the restrictions that asthma had put on him as a boy, when he was told that it would be better not to participate in sports. That made him feel diminished and inadequate. As he grew up, he veered towards dangerous and daunting activities. Before his twenty-first birthday he had taken up deep-sea diving, a difficult sport even for the non-asthmatic. He enjoyed fast cars, boats and airplanes – he considered these masculine activities.

When he dropped out of college he wished fervently to join the army. He took the test but was rejected because of his asthma. Lance had no alternative at that time but to live a millionaire's life – going to parties, dating attractive Hollywood actresses and generally drifting into a pointless existence. People who knew him at this time described him as deeply insecure and prone to unintentional arrogance and reserve. His temper would also flare at remarks about his mother.

In 1957 Lance celebrated his twenty-first birthday by opting to become an American citizen, thereby renouncing his right to the Danish title of Count Reventlow. There had never been any doubt as to his choice. He detested his father and what he stood for; he was contemptuous of the aristocrats his mother had as friends and husbands. He had become totally American; he identified with American culture which does not accept titles of any kind. Paradoxically, his mother who was born an American had opted for Danish nationality when she married Kurt. Subsequently, she travelled on a Danish passport until the end of her days. As for Kurt Reventlow, he settled in the US upon his second marriage and eventually became an American citizen.

In the year of his twenty-first birthday, Barbara gave Lance a magnificent property in Bel Air, the most exclusive section of Los Angeles. The house was set on a mountain top in Benedict Canyon from which on a clear day you could see San Diego, more than a hundred miles across the ocean. The house was a sprawling grey bungalow with a shingled roof and it cost Barbara a half a million dollars to have it built according to Lance's own design. There were unique features to the house which made it the envy of the movie stars who were his neighbours. It had an outdoor swimming pool which came right into the bar room. This made it ideal for parties at any time of the year. Another exclusive feature was that the whole house was wired up with hi-fi outlets so that not only could you hear music anywhere in the vast house, but you could control it from anywhere in the house. It was the first house to be so designed with hi-fi wiring and many people were quick to adopt this status symbol. Another status symbol which Lance initiated and which was copied was a waterfall with continuous cascades in the garden.

In this dream house, Lance lived somewhat like a recluse. He enjoyed cooking and had a reputation as a good amateur chef. He liked to give parties, but only for his close friends. Needless to say, the press was always kept at arm's length. After her marriage to Cary, Barbara had persuaded Cary's valet, Dudley Walker, to join her payroll. As Lance grew up, Dudley became his minder. Barbara knew Dudley was reliable, loyal and flexible. He had to be with Lance, over whose household he had complete charge. He often had to pay the bills out of his own pocket, but he knew that Barbara would reimburse him promptly and she was always generously appreciative of his services, giving him the same presents as she would her own household staff. Dudley took care of Lance's correspondence and accounts and reported to Barbara, who was thus able to keep in touch with Lance. It was probably Dudley who knew Lance best. He said that what Lance wanted above all was to be treated like everyone else. Lance had a phobia about being singled out as he had been all his life. He was careful with his money, did not spend much on clothes, disliked going out to night-clubs. His only extravagance was cars.

In 1957, when he became an American citizen and got his home in Bel Air, Lance decided to do something serious in motor racing. He was moderately successful in a few races in California in other people's cars. That was not enough of a challenge. His ambition was to build a new car which would be his own make and a totally American-made car which would challenge the long-term European supremacy in the field.

He put together a team of mechanics and converted part of his property into a workshop under the name of Reventlow Automobiles Inc. He spent his time building and experimenting with his new racing car, made with a Chevrolet Corvette engine, which he called the Scarab because it was shaped somewhat like the Egyptian beetle. The first Scarab cost him $210,000. He was to spend similar amounts on each of the five other versions of the Scarab. He entered two of his Scarabs in local races and won a fair number of them. He went on to win more important races such as the Sports Car Club of America at Riverside, California, in 1958. Later he won the Laguna Seca Road Race at Monterey. Success followed success and the future looked very promising. Lance received a great deal of publicity in the serious sports media. For the first time he was experiencing fame in his own right. Some people did not even know whose son he was! It was no doubt the happiest period of his life. He went further afield and won both the Governor's Cup and the Nassau Cup in the Bahamas. For the first time both events were won by an American car. This was to be the apex of his triumphs. Lance's confidence soared; the withdrawn man became expansive. He welcomed interviews.

Lance felt at that time that the Scarabs were ready to enter the international field. He resolved to prove that the American colours could dominate racing. He joined the European arena expecting his success to continue, but neither of the two Scarabs succeeded in qualifying for four out of five Grand Prix events. They only qualified for the Belgian Grand Prix and then failed to complete the course. It was a bitter humiliation and a blow to Lance's hopes. It was the end of his racing career. The only person to rejoice was Barbara who dreaded racing. She knew too many people who had killed themselves in fast cars.

What Lance wanted to prove, and failed, was that an American car could beat the European cars. All he managed to do was demonstrate European superiority. He had also managed to get himself into deep financial trouble. He could no longer afford to pay his team of mechanics. He was estranged from his mother and reluctant to ask her for money. Indeed Barbara and Lance only continued their relationship on a long-distance basis. When they did have to meet there was a chill so strong that it was not even possible to make small talk to cover the embarrassed silence.

It was about this time, the beginning of 1959, that Lance began to be seen with the ambitious, shrewd and energetic starlet, Jill St John, whom he met at his friend, Ronnie Burns', birthday party. Jill had started life as Jill Oppenheim, and when she met Lance she was married to Neil Dubin, a young manager in a linen supply company. However, from the day of the party on she paid single-minded attention to Lance. He did not mind in the least for she was beautiful and highly intelligent.

Jill moved in with Lance, and soon made herself indispensable. She educated herself in all matters concerning racing so that she could talk with ease with Lance and his mates. She then convinced him that she was so necessary to him that they ought to make it legal. Lance acquiesced on one condition: no children. His own childhood had been such that he would never impose it on another human being. When Barbara heard of the impending marriage through her Californian friends, she disapproved vehemently, although she wisely kept her feelings to herself. The reports she had received of Jill were very negative.

Jill and Lance, although surrounded by all the glitter of Hollywood, had a small wedding at the Mark Hopkins Hotel in San Francisco on 24 March 1960. Barbara had no intention of attending but she was at the time very deeply involved with Jimmy Douglas who persuaded her to 'do the right thing'. She did it for Jimmy, and joined the handful of guests for the short and simple ceremony. On her return to Paris, we had to endure a very miserable Barbara. The wedding had thrown her into a depression which triggered off a period of heavy drinking. She kept referring to Jill's 'piggy eyes' and 'grabby nature'.

The first time I met Lance was at Sumiya, in the winter of 1961. He and Jill were in Mexico on holiday and at Jill's insistence they came to see the house. Barbara felt ill at ease even before their arrival and took to her bed. Lance impressed me as a very good-looking and cultured young man. He was tall and fair with impeccable manners and a sophistication beyond his twenty-four years. Although he was very attractive, the most lasting impression was that he was unhappy and withdrawn – even brusque. I thought he looked like someone in a dentist's waiting-room. I never saw him relax and he very rarely smiled. The five days the couple stayed at Sumiya fortunately went by quickly and without incident because

Jill's idea was to 'have fun' and that meant going out to night-clubs and drinking. There was nothing for her at Sumiya, with only nature to contemplate. They borrowed the car and the chauffeur to visit the night-spots in Mexico City.

All expenses, of course, were sent to me to pay. Barbara also gave Jill a ruby bracelet worth $125,000 which Barbara had bought for herself but decided she disliked. So she gave it to Jill because she disliked her as well as the bracelet. Some reasoning! Lance was obviously relieved to go. So uncomfortable was he at being in his mother's presence that he was unable even to say goodbye. He arranged it so that they left while Barbara was still asleep. At least mother and son had managed to avoid each other by sleeping late and going out early to minimize any possible friction between them. They had hardly seen each other – by design on both sides.

Only a few months later, Jill and Lance came to Paris for a visit. They arrived with two dachshunds who became my responsibility. Jill had a way of kicking them with her pointed shoes when she was in a bad mood. This was very often because she was dissatisfied throughout her stay in Paris. She disliked the French, she complained about everything. We felt that she should have stayed in California. They occupied the room next to mine and I could hear her calling her friends complaining about everything French she could think of.

Why had they come? It became obvious that Jill wanted to save Lance from bankruptcy. He had decided to quit racing, certainly not because his mother had always implored him to do so, but because the Scarab had beaten him. There was no future in it and he had lost heart. Jill's idea was to put it to Barbara that she, Jill, could persuade Lance to give up racing if Barbara would pay Jill a handsome fee. A deal was struck between them and Graham Mattison. I do not know what the figure was, but I know that Barbara would have given away her whole fortune for Lance to give up racing. I never told her that I knew that Lance had already given up racing, and that there was no need to pay anything except what she wanted to give. If he had just said that he had certain debts to clear, however heavy they might have been, Barbara would have gladly paid up. I felt that there was no need for the moral blackmail. After arranging the transfer of funds, Jill and Lance did not waste any more time in Paris; ten days were enough. They had not stopped complaining about everything and everyone there.

Jill's two dogs did not want to go back. They had become fond of us.

Not long after their return to California, we heard rumours to the effect that the marriage would not last much longer. There was a total lack of communication between them. In the end the divorce became final in 1963 and Jill continued in her social and professional climb.

In November 1964, Lance married a second time. His new wife, an actress called Cheryl Holdridge, was nineteen years old and the daughter of a retired army officer living in California. She was tall and blond and could be described as the *ingénue* type. This time, the wedding was a grand affair in Hollywood, with the bride in a traditional long white dress. There were six hundred guests including many Hollywood notables, but Barbara stayed away. On this occasion she did not have someone near her to persuade her to do 'the right thing'.

Lance was unable to sustain a close and long-term relationship. He was very different from his mother, but in this respect they were similar. The honeymoon with Cheryl did not last long. Lance was happiest when not living with her. He acquired a new home in Aspen where he enjoyed the skiing. He spent more and more time there while Cheryl stayed in Bel Air. They talked a lot on the phone but only saw each other occasionally. Now that motor racing was a thing of the past, Lance enjoyed piloting his own plane, sailing his schooner which was moored in Hawaii, and skiing. He was a frustrated man, with no real purpose or enthusiasm. He often said that he was happiest in a pair of overalls working on his cars. In his thirties, he tried to recapture his bachelor days.

Cheryl was still his wife in 1972 when Lance took off with three friends in his single-engine plane. He let Philip Hooker take the controls although Philip was only a novice. Lance wanted to view a tract of land which he hoped to buy. High winds and a thunderstorm were forecast and the plane should never have taken off. The group chose to ignore the warnings and the plane crashed into a wooded mountainside near Aspen. All four were killed. Cheryl had to decide about the funeral and she chose to have it in Aspen where Lance was happiest. Barbara felt unable to attend. She had always avoided going to funerals and was not about to start now. Later, Lance's body was cremated and put in the family mausoleum at Woodlawn Cemetery, New York, where Barbara was to join him a few years later. In life, Barbara had not experienced the close bond between mother and child. After Lance died, she was tormented by feelings of guilt, reproaching herself into deep depression. Barbara's experience of motherhood had brought her very little happiness and no joy.

11

For Richer for Poorer

C'est la mer a boire que de lutter contre
un coeur de femme.
                    Richard de Fournival, thirteenth century

The main cause of Barbara's notoriety was her seven husbands.
Nowadays, when divorce is relatively easy in most western countries
multi-married people are no longer rarities, but forty years ago
even those who could afford to get divorced by paying the
unwanted spouse a large settlement, would generally be held back
by social pressure. I believe that acquiring foreign titles and then
paying-off their holders in relatively rapid succession was the main
reason for the public image of Barbara Hutton as a spoiled brat. In
this sense it was probably justified, for Barbara was a romantic and
easily fell in love with people – usually for the wrong reasons. When
she loved, she needed to take the person over completely and
immediately. She would then shower everything that money could
buy on them. Inevitably and without exception this ideal situation
contained the seeds of its own destruction. As soon as things started
going wrong, Barbara would look for the next ideal person to
replace the preceding one. Nevertheless, she both expected, and
wanted, to make it worthwhile for the fallen hero. The only way
she could express this was by a large cheque. The person in the
middle was Graham Mattison who was left to negotiate the terms;
in most cases he also drew up a pre-nuptial contract.

I never believed that, as some newspaper articles claimed,
Barbara went through life in one long search for the ideal mate.
Much more to the point was that she lived for the moment and
tomorrow would take care of itself. She wanted what she fancied,

144

now, with no thought for the consequences. With money, this becomes possible. What she fancied could be a piece of jewellery, a glass of champagne, a $1 million gift for someone – or a husband. This need for immediate satisfaction was a dominant feature of Barbara's character. Hélène used to blame Tiki for having brought Barbara up to believe that she could have anything her heart desired, that because of her money she was entitled to privileges with no obligations. The latter would be taken care of with money. I agreed with Hélène on this. Tiki was kindly, but ineffective. She was dazzled by money and always let it speak, so how could she possibly teach any values to her Barbara?

By the time that Barbara was old enough to be courted by young men, and there were many who fancied their chances with this shy but very attractive heiress, her character was formed and she was definitely not wife-material. There might have been a right man for Barbara, but she could never be the right woman for any man. She was too wilful and capricious, she was unable to compromise. She wanted the moon as well as the stars.

But why did Barbara feel the need to get married, and why so many times? My answer to this, having known her well, is that in the first instance she wanted to get away from her father whom she loathed consummately. She always blamed him for the death of her mother, and his drinking disgusted her so much that she never touched a drop until her mid-thirties. Then, when she was in her teens, he remarried. It was not so much that Barbara disliked her step-mother, as felt quite unable to respect her.

Although Barbara knew that when she was twenty-one she would inherit her fortune, and be free of her father, she was too impatient of the constraints and longed to be totally free to do exactly as she pleased. Five months before reaching her majority, Barbara leapt into a disastrous marriage with Alexis Mdivani, someone she was not in love with, but who would give her the title, however fake, of 'Princess'. She would be able to lead her very own life, do exactly as she pleased, be completely free with a husband to live happily ever after . . . just like the characters in her favourite novels. Apart from freedom Barbara thought she had found in Alexis someone to whom she could belong, a person who would show affection, protect her and be her admiring escort. In the wealthy international set being a Princess was a social asset as well. As Barbara said on her wedding day, 'It's going to be fun being a Princess.'

145

What kind of man was Barbara's first husband, the one who set the precedent for the successive divorce settlements? 'Prince' Alexis Mdivani was a Georgian whose father, Zakhari, had served as a colonel in the infantry of the last Tsar. There is no evidence that Zakhari had inherited the title of Prince, nor that he had been created one by the Tsar as a reward for his military exploits, as his children were later to claim. The family had not even been landowners. After the Revolution of 1917 the family took refuge in Paris, together with thousands of other White Russians. Alexis' mother, who was of Polish ancestry and who spoke better French than the rest of the family, queued up at the police station to apply for their refugee documents. There, she registered herself as Princess Mdivani. The children all adopted her idea, but Zakhari refused to be included in the deception, later saying, 'I am the only man who ever inherited a title from his children.' He was rightly proud of his military achievements for he was indeed much-decorated, though not ennobled.

'Prince' and 'Princess' Mdivani had three sons, Serge, David and Alexis, known as the 'marrying Mdivanis', and two daughters, Roussie and Nina. They capitalized on their cunning, unscrupulous and colourful ways. Their daring self-assurance bordered on the fraudulent. They got away with a great deal by sheer devastating charm. They were money-mad rogues and made no secret of it. They were prepared to go to any lengths to live like rich aristocrats without having to work in the accepted sense.

The brain behind the three brothers' social and marital successes was their sister Roussie who was a fascinating, attractive and persuasive woman. Young Barbara fell under her spell. Roussie's expertise on graceful living (all self-taught) was penetrating. She had managed to lure the Spanish painter, José Maria Sert, famous for his Waldorf Astoria murals, from his formidable and celebrated wife, Misia. Roussie not only married Sert but became Misia's best friend. It was Roussie who arranged for Alexis to make an excellent catch by marrying the shy and gentle Louise Van Alen, whose family was both enormously rich and extremely well-connected. Louise was related to the Astors and the Vanderbilts; one of her grandfathers was a general, the other an ambassador.

It was partly by accident and partly by design that Louise and Barbara both fell in love with Alexis. He was very dashing, and an excellent polo player. He was neither tall nor handsome in the classical sense, but he exuded sensuality. Louise, a childhood friend

Mexico, 1961.
Colin Fraser,
Barbara and me at
Sumiya, Barbara's
Oriental dream
house and winter
residence

A partial view of
Sumiya. The right
wing of the main
building houses
Barbara's bedroom
with a terrace
overlooking Mount
Popocatepetl

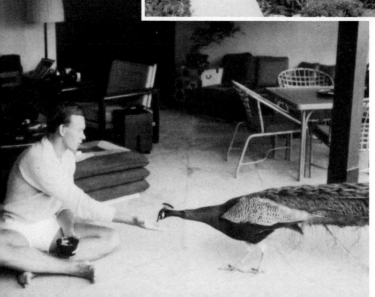

Ex-guardsman
trumpeter, Lloyd
Franklin, having
sat motionless for
twenty minutes,
succeeds in getting
a peacock to eat
out of his hand at
Sumiya

Top row left: An informal evening at the Kasbah. Left to right: Peter Smith (sitting), Jeremy Eldridge, me, friend of Bill Robertson, Bill Robertson, Bob Lebus
Top row centre: Ceremonial dance by the Blue People from the Atlas Mountains. Watching (left to right) are: Barbara, wearing rubies, Graham Mattison (sitting), Silvia de Castellane, Silvia's daughter, Cordelia (standing)
Top row right: Barbara in her emerald tiara and yellow pearls. The belly dancer is from the Koutubia Palace

Centre row left: Dressing up at Sidi Hosni: Ira Belline (left) and the Hon. David Herbert
Centre: An evening at the Paris Lido with Jeremy Eldridge, Lloyd Franklin's old regimental buddy
Centre right: The Tangier polo team (left to right) Dr Denis Little, Tom Seeley, Dr Spriet and Lloyd Franklin
Bottom: Annual ball at Sidi Hosni, summer 1961: some of the decorations organized by Dan Rudd

Tangier, 1962: A photographic session with Cecil Beaton. Lloyd Franklin, by now Barbara's confidant and lover, strolls in on the act (*Camera Press*)

Barbara arriving at the Metropolitan Opera House, New York, in December 1933, with husband no. 1, Alexis Mdivani (*UPI/Bettmann*)

Summer 1935 in Venice. Barbara is flanked by husband no. 2, Kurt von Haugwitz-Reventlow (left), and Jimmy Donahue (*The Associated Press*)

Marriage to husband no. 3, Cary Grant, in California, 10 July 1942 (*The Associated Press*)

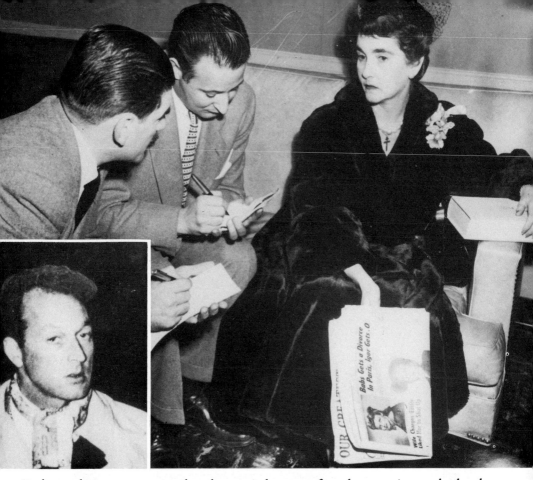

Barbara admits to newsmen that the magic has gone from her marriage to husband no. 4, Prince Igor Troubetzkoy (*inset*) (*The Associated Press*)

The smooth, suave continental manner of Porfirio Rubirosa wins him the title of husband no. 5 for fifty-three days (*The Associated Press*)

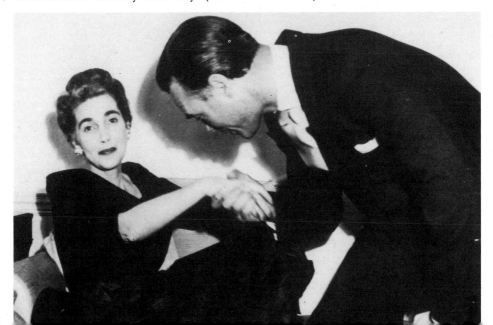

At Wimbledon with old friend and ex-tennis champion, Baron Gottfried von Cramm, prospective husband no. 6 (*UPI/Bettmann*)

Barbara and husband no. 7 (her last), Raymond Doan, are met at Los Angeles airport by Lance and his second wife, Cheryl Holdridge (*The Associated Press*)

of Barbara's, was very much in love with Alexis as a result of his pressing courtship. He was honest enough not to pretend that he was in love with her; it did not seem to matter to Louise. She was determined to marry him in spite of her family's strong objections. During the four months between his engagement and his marriage to Louise, Alexis carried on an amorous courtship with Barbara whom he sensed was attracted to him. This courtship was carried on mostly by letter at a time when Barbara was preparing for her presentation at the British court. Immediately upon his marriage to Louise, he established a joint bank account with her and proceeded to lavish upon himself all the trappings of one born to immense wealth. He bought himself a complete new wardrobe, the quantity of which would have served a whole regiment of well-dressed dandies. This included the obligatory collection of Cartier studs and cuff-links. He then purchased a Rolls Royce and a couple of sports cars, and finally he acquired a stable of eight of the best polo ponies obtainable in England.

Curiously, in spite of having access to Louise's unlimited fortune, Alexis did not bother to pay his bills and was forever being hounded by creditors and threatened with court action. This was typical of all the Mdivani brothers and sisters. They all left enormous debts throughout the cities of the world, with luxury hotels and shops such as furriers and jewellers swearing never to let them through their front doors again. The Mdivanis just moved on and used other hotels, other shops. It is amazing how many hard-headed business people will extend credit to people who call themselves 'Prince' or 'Princess'.

When Louise and Alexis married in May 1931, she was nineteen and he twenty-three. Barbara was allowing Alexis to woo her even before his marriage to her childhood friend. He continued to court Barbara during his honeymoon with Louise. Why should he limit himself to one millionairess if he could have two? He loved neither of them; he was in love with Barbara's close friend, the ravishing Silvia de Rivas who was not rich and whose family would not let her marry him. So, as he harvested, with Louise's full approval, the financial benefits of being one of the world's best-kept men, he wrote love letters to Barbara when they were apart. He had been married to Louise for less than two months, when, during the height of the season in Biarritz, he and Barbara were seen together, tête-à-tête, in all the fashionable spots. There was a lull in Barbara's romantic life and the idea that Alexis was married to someone else made him more attractive and desirable. She encouraged his attentions. There was no subterfuge in their meetings. Alexis, being the amoral person he was, saw no wrong in juggling other women in his life while his sweet and patient bride stayed waiting in their hotel suite. Barbara, on the other hand, was indulging in vanity, in having a good time at the round of parties, polo matches, picnics and night-clubs. She was attracted to Alexis and the streak in her character which enjoyed creating havoc and scandal was clearly already present.

Barbara's father disapproved of her cavorting openly with Alexis whom he considered as a total debauchee and libertine. Why could she not be interested in some of the very respectable and titled European suitors who were at her feet – if she must have a European. The answer to that is that trait in Barbara's character which caused her a great deal of frustration during her life-time. Barbara did not appreciate anything that came easily, she longed for the unattainable. She needed the challenge, she enjoyed a good chase. Once she had conquered her desired object, she then lost interest in it. To a certain extent we probably all have this trait – the grass always looks greener beyond our immediate boundaries. But in Barbara this peculiarity was pushed to an extreme. It was a perversion. It obscured her better judgement, her intelligence, her experience. Again and again it led her into disastrous situations from which she was only able to extricate herself because of her money.

So here, at the age of eighteen, Barbara was publicly stating, 'I want this man whom I know to be in love with Silvia, who is making his bride miserable at the same time as spending her money at an alarming rate, and I don't care how many people are upset or hurt by it.' How well that suited Alexis! It was the realization of Roussie's machinations. She had discovered all she could about Barbara's favourite things and provided Alexis with the appropriate books of poetry, pieces of jade (for Barbara had started collecting in her teens), and so on to use with his devastating charm in his pursuit of Barbara. Barbara's friends and family did all they could to dissuade her from her friendship with the whole Mdivani clan who were always found in the same fashionable spots as Barbara – something that was no coincidence. Father and step-mother, the guardians of the under-age girl, took her away on interesting trips to try to take her mind off Alexis. It had the opposite effect on Barbara: strengthening her resolve to get away from parental interference in any way she could.

Barbara and Alexis no longer bothered to maintain even a veneer of social decorum, while everyone in their set noted Louise's incredible forbearance. Before she had celebrated her first wedding anniversary, Louise realized that she had no marriage to speak of. She finally sued for divorce after eighteen months of married life, giving Alexis a reputed $1 million cash settlement. Nina's Dutch husband negotiated the very favourable terms on Alexis' behalf. The friendship between Barbara and Louise, once so strong, strained and broke.

Characteristically, once Alexis was free, Barbara's interest in him cooled. But since he had shed Louise for a bigger prize, he was not going to be thwarted by a lukewarm shoulder. Barbara set off on a trip to South-East Asia with a few friends to get away from her father. Nor did she want to seem too eager to grab what Louise had cast off. Alexis, with the money he had obtained from Louise, pursued her, determined to extract from Barbara an acceptance to his proposal of marriage. This swashbuckling impudence was more than Barbara could resist and she agreed to Alexis' proposal in the restaurant of her hotel in Bangkok. She only needed to wait six months to reach her majority and be free to marry without parental consent. But she could not wait that long. Wanting things *immediately* was part of Barbara's fundamental temperament. She suspected that her father would completely and utterly disapprove of the match. Not only had he lost his temper with Barbara on the subject on many occasions, but he had stated quite categorically to enquiring journalists that his daughter would only marry this 'money-mad Georgian blackmailer' over his dead body. Knowing what was waiting for her at the other end of the telephone, Barbara called her father from Bangkok and asked for his consent to her marriage to Alexis. She added that if he did not give it, she would be married immediately by some local civil servant who would easily overlook minor details of a legal nature. Faced by this threat, Franklyn Hutton felt forced to give his consent to avoid a scandal. He suggested that they marry in style back in Europe, secretly hoping that in the meantime his hare-brained daughter would change her mind. Barbara, on the other hand, was looking forward to a wedding to outshine all weddings, especially that of Louise Van Alen. Then, when she came into her inheritance, she was looking forward to being an even more generous benefactress to her husband than Louise had been, if that were possible. In fact, Barbara was not prepared to wait until her birthday to start

149

spending on Alexis. When she arrived in Paris, where Alexis was a resident, to start the wedding arrangements, Barbara demanded, and obtained, half a million dollars as spending money in addition to her usual allowance.

Luckily for Barbara, her father, despite his drinking and womanizing, had a first-rate financial brain, and was well aware that his daughter needed protecting from the Alexises of this world. Later, Graham Mattison was to fulfil the same role. Had it not been for such level-headed people, Barbara would have become penniless at the drop of a wedding contract, many times over. Because Alexis was a French resident and because the wedding was to take place in Paris, in the normal course of events the French law of common property would have automatically applied to the couple. Under this law everything that a wife brought into the marriage became the property of the husband to dispose of exactly as he pleased. Barbara was prepared to walk down the aisle without benefit of legal safeguards of her inheritance. Franklyn Hutton, still his daughter's legal guardian, insisted on a prenuptial agreement. There was a period of hard bargaining between Hutton and Alexis' lawyers who naturally argued for the French common property law. Because of the legal wrangle there was a risk that the wedding, scheduled for 20 June 1933, might have to be postponed. Alexis insisted on abiding by the French laws. He could not see why he should not go for the total prize. His own lawyers counselled him against it and the outcome was a settlement of $1 million as a pre-wedding gift, plus an annual emolument of $50,000. Alexis was not at all offended at being branded a fortune-hunter, after all, wasn't he one of the best? He was not happy with the marriage settlement, but reassured himself that, once married, there were many ways to skin a cat.

Alexis understood Barbara very well. She could not do enough for him and started to behave in a slave-like manner. She insisted that they go through a religious ceremony in the Russian Orthodox Church, although neither of them belonged to it. She wanted the pageantry and the mysterious Eastern rites as part of the wedding. It suited Barbara's taste to have an elaborately adorned setting which hinted at an unconventional tradition. It had to be anything but run-of-the-mill. It reflected her independence of mind even at that age. In order to give Barbara what she wanted, Alexis had to go through the formalities of being received into the Russian Orthodox Church. Much to his discomfiture he was obliged to meet the priests and hear a few lectures about the conduct of his life – which Barbara found highly amusing.

France, upon becoming a Republic, separated church and state, so that, legally, only a civil ceremony was necessary. If a religious one was desired, it had to be celebrated separately and after the civil one. The wrangle over the prenuptial agreement was settled in time for the civil ceremony to go ahead as planned, on 20 June 1933, in the fashionable Mairie of the 16th Arrondissement. Barbara's witnesses were her father and her Aunt Jessie; Alexis' were his sister Roussie's husband José Maria Sert, and a member of the Georgian Embassy's staff. Such a large crowd assembled to try to get a glimpse of the couple, that a large number of gendarmes was needed. Barbara made a handsome contribution to both the police station of the 16th Arrondissement and to the Municipalité. The world press was in attendance to photograph Barbara in a light grey ensemble designed especially for the occasion by Coco Chanel. Alexis also looked very smart in his morning suit, but people remarked that he looked very sleepy and somewhat jaded. Did he find the scene at the Mairie a little too familiar? A great deal of international publicity had been given to the vast amounts spent by Barbara on her trousseau bought from the most expensive boutiques and couturiers in Paris, in amounts that seemed unreasonable even to the rich. Barbara, unaware of the meaning of poverty, became the target of very unfavourable press comment at a time when the world was still struggling with the Depression. It was reminiscent of the press attacks at the time of her coming-out party. The American press was the most vitriolic. Marrying a foreigner was an affront to the insular Americans. But, even worse, they blamed her for spending her money abroad when there was a dire need for economic recovery back home. They felt that, having inherited an American fortune, she should spend it to benefit her countrymen in hard times.

The non-essential religious ceremony took place two days after the civil event, in the Eglise Russe at 12 rue Daru in the 8th Arrondissement. Of the handful of Parisian Russian Orthodox churches, this one was in the best district, between Parc Monceau and the Arc de Triomphe. Alexis insisted on including on the invitation the church's description as 'the official church of exiled Russian nobility since the Revolution'. He became more and more royal as he got closer to Barbara's money. Although there was doubt that the bridegroom would be able to attend his wedding – he had been served with a writ for a $5,000 debt that very morning. Barbara paid off the debt just in time.

Eight hundred guests, chosen from the social élite, were invited to attend the celebration. Not surprisingly, a large crowd gathered to look at the bride in her wedding dress. A reported eight thousand people charged through the police cordon to get a closer view. Those who managed to see the bride were not disappointed. Barbara was dressed from head to foot in ivory satin and lace, a creation by the couturier Jean Patou, with a diamond tiara on her head. Inside the church the setting was worthy of a film with Greta Garbo. The fairy-tale symbolism must have delighted Barbara. Here she was, living a fable which included rituals heavy with romantic meaning, although she understood not one word of the Russian dialogue. The five priests were themselves bedecked with heavy, ornate liturgical garments. A choir intoned the Gregorian chants in thanksgiving. Bejewelled crowns were held over the heads of the bride and groom who concluded the hour-long ceremony by drinking a toast to each other from an ornamental cup. The whole scene was surrounded by religious icons, candle-light, incense, thousands of flowers, not to mention the hundreds of elegant guests.

Immediately after the religious ceremony there followed a wedding lunch at the Ritz, where Barbara was living. The Ritz's factotum, Max Charrier, told me that the hotel had to reorganize its storage space in order to accommodate the wedding presents that came pouring in from all corners of the world. Max said that many of the gifts were never paid for, and quite a few of them had been charged to Barbara's running petty cash account at the Ritz. One thing is certain, there were very few gifts that Barbara could use. On her return from her honeymoon, she gave away virtually all of them. Max and his family were still using some of the household items which he had been given twenty-five years before. One present that did delight Barbara was from her father. It was a sixty-foot power-driven luxury motor boat to be used in Venice where Barbara had bought a palace on the Grand Canal. She paid $90,000 for the property and had put it in the name of Prince Alexis Mdivani.

It is not certain how many pieces of luggage accompanied the bridal pair on their honeymoon in Italy. From my own experience of working for Barbara I know that it was always exaggerated in any newspaper article which mentioned her travelling. It is an easy way of emphasizing the excesses of a rich person. The truth was that Barbara always travelled with members of her personal staff, and with a few friends as well. The press, however, regarded the luggage of the whole party as Barbara's – and then usually multiplied the number of items to impress the readers. Barbara herself found it amusing that pieces of luggage should be distorted to make a point. And, naturally, she never knew how many pieces she travelled with. She did not pack them, nor did she arrange for their transport. She did, however, insist on Vuitton travel cases and, at the time of her marriage in 1933, each case bore a closed crown in gold indicating 'Prince' or 'Princess'.

The honeymoon started in a train from Paris, making for Venice. The marriage, however, was not sexually active. Indeed, Barbara later told people that it was never consummated. Whether this is true, or whether she was wishfully thinking back to a very unsatisfactory physical experience with Alexis, I cannot tell. I do know that there was no love between them. Barbara often said, and used the argument in court, that she wanted to get away from her father and that Alexis had a way of giving her comfort and understanding. He was flattering and sweet, and for that she was grateful enough to marry him. Barbara complained, at the time of her divorce from Alexis, that he was so busy playing polo and so exhausted from it that he was no use as a husband. The truth is, more likely, that he did not find her sexually attractive. This is illustrated by his now historic comment on their wedding night. Barbara had put on her most beautiful satin and lace nightie only to be told by Alexis that she was too fat, thereby implying that she was repulsive. That one hurtful remark, made at the most vulnerable moment, changed her life. She immediately went on a crash diet and stayed on a diet for most of her life; a source of considerable irritation to at least one of her subsequent husbands. Later, she even resorted to surgery to reduce the size of her breasts.

In Venice, despite the devastation to her morale caused by Alexis' cruel gibe, Barbara made the most of her new role. She found definite social advantages in being married and having a title, instead of being just Miss Barbara Hutton. The newly-married couple were included in the festivities of the season and there were many activities to interest Barbara. She particularly enjoyed setting her husband up in a way to put Louise to shame. Whatever Alexis had been given by his first heiress-wife, Barbara improved on it. Two new strings of polo ponies had to come from the best Argentinian stables. His dress studs and cuff-links were more valuable than his previous ones. And they had not one, but two new custom-built Rolls Royces: 'His' and 'Hers'. In Venice that summer, Barbara formed several long-lasting friendships among the Italian aristocracy, including Marina Volpi Luling-Buschetti. For the first time, she felt she was appreciated as an adult. She absorbed the culture that Venice and its surroundings offered. She learned the vagaries of European society. Her dress sense improved and, as she lost weight, so did her appearance and she became appreciated as a generous and gracious hostess.

Barbara's immediate world was still dominated by her in-laws. Alexis was not the only member of the family who managed a financially-advantageous union. Serge first married Pola Negri, the star of many silent films. When her career began to wane, Serge divorced her to marry the more wealthy opera singer Mary MacCormick. The latter demanded a divorce after a short and bumpy marriage during which Serge went through her considerable fortune. Before dying on the polo field, kicked on the head by his pony, Serge had married Louise Van Alen who had failed to learn her lesson with Alexis. Brother David married the wealthy star Mae Murray and left her penniless and with a ruined career. Elder sister, Roussie, carved herself a very desirable place in society, but it led, nevertheless, to drug addiction. The younger sister, Nina, in spite of being the least good-looking of the family, still managed to make two marriages in quick succession which brought her status and money, if not happiness.

At the time of Barbara's marriage to Alexis, the whole Mdivani troupe lived off Barbara's generosity, using their undoubted charms and their gifts for being highly entertaining.

Barbara had been a Mdivani for barely five months when Serge and David were charged with theft, embezzlement and larceny in which Alexis was implicated. Barbara paid the bail and whisked her husband off on a tour of the Far East before a summons could be issued for him. Ultimately, with the help of the best legal advice, the course of justice was rendered as leniently as circumstances would allow. Serge and David were sentenced to pay a fine which was once again settled by their benefactress and sister-in-law.

Meanwhile, in the Far East, Barbara indulged herself in buying jade, porcelain, screens and lacquered furniture for her collection, and jewellery for Alexis. The couple went on to Japan where she was given royal treatment. They were entertained by the Emperor and his family who wanted to make sure that their visit should be as pleasant as possible. All obstacles and red-tape were overcome and they were given a motorcycle escort wherever they went. From that visit onwards, Japan became a permanent and regular fixture on Barbara's itinerary. Japan has been described as 'A country in love with art', and that was the way it seemed to Barbara. She remained friends with the Emperor's daughter. The friendship had to go into abeyance during the war but it resumed, unscathed, after hostilities ceased. Barbara often said, in the face of criticism for her love of Japan, that people's souls did not change with their country's military or political inclinations. She tended to think of people as individuals and not as one of a group or a nationality. The Japanese way of life, the simple lines of the houses and furniture, had great appeal for Barbara. It was then that she decided that some day she would have a house in the Japanese style. It was in Barbara's nature to go overboard about something. Japan became a bee in her bonnet and she could not see enough of the country, visiting not only the tourist attractions but also the more remote and contemplative areas. It was not Alexis' scene and he grew restless, bored, argumentative. The marriage started to experience its first strains.

From Japan, Barbara and Alexis went to China. If Barbara embraced Japan for its art, she identified with China for its history and civilization. It overwhelmed her in every aspect, and had done for as long as she could remember. As I am Chinese, I was fascinated that she should be so attuned to everything and remarked on it. Barbara merely commented that it was probably because she had been Chinese in another life. During her trip to Shanghai and Peking with Alexis, Barbara started her serious study of calligraphy and spoken Mandarin. She travelled with a teacher who also taught her Chinese history and philosophy. Barbara wanted with her someone who could translate and explain to her the writing on historic monuments, the inscriptions on tombs, the annotation on the base of porcelain objects, the peculiarities of ornamental seals. The trip inspired many of Barbara's poems, which were later published as a collection entitled *Peking Pictures*. The poems could be said to reflect a youthful enthusiasm for the exotic. A fragment from the book, written by Barbara at the age of twenty-one, reads:

> I bring you my poor dreams
> Caught in a green jade bowl
> Carved untold years ago
> Out of a Chinese soul.

The fact that Barbara was writing poetry on this trip might be an indication that all was not well in the marriage. Certainly, Alexis did not share his wife's enthusiasm for cultural matters. He missed his polo games. Like a spoiled child, he resented Barbara's complete absorption in something in which he had no interest.

It was during this trip that Barbara announced that she intended to adopt a Chinese child, and applied to the authorities in Shanghai to adopt and take away a little girl during her stay in the city. Unfortunately she had made her intentions public. As a result she was promptly deluged by hopeful parents, newspaper reporters, policemen and the curious. The American consulate had to intervene and make an announcement in the newspapers to deny the story. The Grand Hotel was cordoned off for five days, making it very inconvenient for the other guests. Barbara had also omitted to consult her husband about her intentions. Alexis was furious, being totally against the idea of children, let alone an adopted one. Occasionally Barbara would sentimentalize to me about the Chinese daughter she might have had, adding: 'You are my Chinese daughter.'

The next leg of the journey took Barbara and Alexis to India where they met people they had known in Europe. This time they were to be pampered guests of the maharajahs in their sumptuous palaces: Kapurthala, Cooch-Behar, Jaipur, Baroda. Alexis was able to enjoy games of polo and big game hunting. He had more in common with the Europeanized maharajahs who enjoyed a good old carousal, ending sometimes in a good natured brawl. Alexis' behaviour was alienating Barbara from him, for at that time she disapproved of any drinking at all. She wanted to see the real India – the ordinary people – but her friends did not know any ordinary people.

Alexis had by now dropped his mask of assiduous Romeo and emerged as an immature, superficial egotist for whom Barbara was fast losing respect. She continued to put up a good front for the benefit of the press and in order not to prove her father right in such a short time. Privately, Barbara turned more and more to writing poetry, all of which revealed a strong thread of disappointment and hopelessness, remarkable in someone only at the threshold of life. In spite of the public face and assurances that everything was wonderful, rumours were already spreading both in the press and among Barbara's friends that it was only a matter of time before the end of the marriage. Instead of an affectionate husband, she had

156

been saddled with a selfish pleasure-seeker who needed his debts paid to stay out of jail.

The next step in that short-lived marriage was to become a familiar pattern in Barbara's behaviour. Having been disappointed in her husband, she looked for a way out. She became cold and distant towards him, implying 'I wish you would just disappear,' while at the same time continuing to keep him in the luxury which he now expected. In fact, she even started to step up her generosity (perhaps out of guilt), so making him hang on the more. Paradoxically, therefore, when she wished to be rid of someone she only managed to make him want to stay. If only she had been strong enough to stop the flow of finance, she would have been rid of him that much sooner. Basically, Barbara was quite unable to face a confrontation; she also disliked scandal and the attendant bad publicity, so she preferred to be cowardly and generous.

Having decided that Alexis was the wrong man, Barbara was ready to fall in love and start again. This, she often said to me, is where it is a definite advantage to be rich. As a woman, if you have money, there is no need to be stuck with someone you hate. So, because Barbara's nature was insecure, impulsive and romantic, none of her friends was surprised to learn that she had found her new knight in shining armour on a train journey through Germany on her way to Venice. She admitted readily that with Count Kurt von Haugwitz-Reventlow, it was love at first sight. In her own words, 'He was the most handsome man that I had ever seen.' Indeed, this tall, fair and aristocratic man, seventeen years her senior, was the total antithesis of her first husband. Where Alexis had thick features, Kurt's profile was noble and refined. Where Alexis was fawning and blubbery, Kurt was masterful, dominating and proud. She could feel, at their first meeting, that he had enormous strength of character and she felt utterly drawn to him. She was the one who spoke first and she was further gratified when she found that he had not recognized her. What she discovered about him only confirmed her first impresssion, that he was *the* man for her. He was extremely well connected, with a title which was real, 'Not like some titles I could mention', Barbara said to newsmen. The title was further supported by a castle in Denmark and a village bearing the family name. Everything she learned about the man attested to the solid respectability of impeccable reputation, without a hint of scandal or loose-living. Barbara did not need much to convince her that she wished to make Kurt her second

157

husband. What is more, she felt for the first time the sensations of physical desire. This love was not only romantic, it was also passionate.

The switching of husbands was always an awkward transition, because Barbara consciously avoided any confrontation. She preferred to carry on with the new man, allowing the old one to draw his own conclusions. Eventually, though, if only for legal reasons, there would have to be a show-down. For Alexis, it happened in London in the spring of 1935. While Kurt was in the next room, Barbara told Alexis that the marriage was over. Alexis was all too aware of the situation, having read in the papers about Barbara's new love. Having announced her decision to Alexis, Barbara took the next boat to New York and then travelled to Reno to establish residence in order to qualify for a 'quickie' divorce. 'The quicker the better,' she told the newsmen in New York.

Everywhere, she was mobbed by journalists, photographers and curious crowds. The police had to be present in force everywhere Barbara went, to contain the now hostile crowd. Barbara's activities – her trips, her parties, her purchases had been widely publicized. Everything she did was blown up to illustrate the dichotomy between the wasteful spending in Barbara's life and the innocent victims of the Depression. The newspapers made it seem as if Barbara was responsible for the economic misfortune of anyone who was less fortunate. She was condemned for the personnel policy of the management of the Woolworth stores in the US and elsewhere. The public jeered, jostled and spat at her whenever they saw her. Further, there was resentment and anger at her friendship with foreigners, and even worse: titled foreigners. It was during that year, 1935, that Barbara realized the extent of hatred felt by Americans towards her and made up her mind to avoid any unnecessary or prolonged visit to her native country. The only reason for her visit would be to see Aunt Jessie and Cousin Jimmy, but even they could visit her abroad.

The divorce obtained in Reno on 13 May 1935 was conducted in as quiet a manner as could be possible for anything concerning Barbara. It was heard in closed session with Alexis represented by a lawyer. The divorce was granted upon proof that residence had been established and Barbara's testimony that Alexis had married her only for her money and that she had married to get away from her father. Alexis had been handsomely provided for. Barbara set up for him a second very generous trust fund which would provide for all his spending needs. He still had two strings of polo ponies, the house in Venice and the motor boat, a Rolls Royce and all the presents, in terms of jewellery, clothes and furniture, that Barbara had given him. A large parting gift in Barbara's terms meant, 'Thank you for being my escort and companion, thank you for the use of your name, thank you for introducing me to your crowd and *do* say nice things about me on your further travels in life.'

Her marriage might have made Barbara a 'Princess' for the first time, but she was now aware that she could do better in social terms. Still, her basic instinct was to stay on good terms with the Mdivanis. She achieved that by continuing to be generous to them, at the same time staying out of their way as much as possible. She was still doing that thirty years later.

On the very same day as the divorce hearing, Count Kurt Reventlow arrived unnoticed in Reno and joined Barbara at Lake Tahoe, not far away, where she had quietly completed her required residence status. Less than twenty-four hours later, they were married in a simple and almost anonymous ceremony. They spent a couple of days in San Francisco but everywhere they went they met hoards of aggressive protesters, and the threat of violence. They left for New York where they were greeted by the same type of demonstrations. They were relieved when they stepped aboard a steamship bound for Europe. They could finally settle down, relax and get acquainted without having to hide. The courtship leading up to the semi-secret wedding had been conducted furtively, not so much to avoid legal complications but mostly to outsmart the Mdivani clan.

Aboard the ship crossing to Europe, Barbara was eager to learn and discuss everything about the man she had just married. She had fallen for the packaging, now she wanted to know the contents. Her friends who had met Kurt did not much like him. They found him hard, autocratic and mean. They had tried diplomatically to suggest to Barbara that she should get to know him better before taking the plunge, which only strengthened her resolve to swap her adolescent Alexis for an honest-to-goodness hero as quickly as possible. What she knew about Kurt impressed her very much and once her mind was made up it was no use trying to change it. Even her father could not object to Kurt's background, which he had investigated. Kurt was by all accounts a real nobleman and gentleman. His education and training were consistent with his lineage. His family had been feudal lords and landowners in Denmark for eight centuries. His

159

ancestors had had connections with the Danish royal family during that period. Barbara was thrilled when Kurt, as feudal landlord and subject to royal protocol, had to obtain permission to marry her from King Christian X. It was only a formality but it appealed to Barbara's romantic nature. She visualized the fairy-tale castle that would be her home. Kurt had a reputation of being one of the best amateur skiers in Europe. He was an all-round athlete and had led a clean, irreproachable life.

Aboard the *Bremen*, on their honeymoon, Barbara discovered for the first time certain other facts about Kurt's background. He had not been born Danish, as she had believed, but Prussian. His father had been a German and his mother of Austro-Danish descent. Kurt had been an officer in the German army in the First World War, and had earned the Iron Cross for bravery. His education and upbringing had been totally Prussian. He and his brother inherited the manor house of Hardenberg Castle after the First World War when they became Danish citizens, and turned their land to dairy farming. They led modest, hard-working and quiet lives with no luxuries except for vacations on the European ski slopes. On their honeymoon, Barbara also discovered that Kurt was anything but a Prince Charming. He showed himself to have an uncontrollable temper and a view of marriage which was not at all what Barbara had expected. He believed in a wife being obedient and yielding. He was censorious of luxuries and easy living. He believed that Barbara could put her money to good use back on the farm in Denmark.

Barbara found her new husband to be completely transformed immediately after their marriage. He become intolerant and rigid and seemed to be angry all the time. He appeared to enjoy being cruel to servants and children. There was a sadistic streak in him which alarmed her. Kurt, on his side, came to a rude awakening. He told newsmen that he was disturbed by Barbara's eating habits – or more to the point, her non-eating habits. He wanted to enjoy his meals and was unable to do so at the same table with Barbara who would just drink black coffee. The subject of meals became a constant irritant which affected Kurt's mood. Kurt also detested the publicity which accompanied Barbara wherever she went. The realization that it would now be a permanent feature of his life was having a depressing effect on him.

On arrival in Europe, Barbara summoned her cousin Jimmy Donahue to liven up the scene, and to dilute the heavy atmosphere between Kurt and herself. Jimmy and Kurt took an instant dislike to each other. It only encouraged Jimmy to do everything he could to annoy Kurt. This amused Barbara during that summer as they went from Germany, Egypt, Palestine and back to Paris. There, one evening, Kurt persuaded Barbara to leave the others and go to a show with him. The show turned out to be a sex show and on their return to the Ritz, Kurt raped her. Barbara was to use this as evidence in the divorce court when she branded him as a wife beater, extremely cruel and a sexual deviate.

During the course of the summer Barbara learned that Alexis had killed himself at the wheel of the Rolls Royce she had given him. He had been driving much too fast down a narrow road in Spain, when he hit something on the road which made the car hurtle off the road and into a ravine, killing him instantly. His passenger was his latest girl-friend, Baroness Maud von Thyssen, the wife of the German steel tycoon, Baron Heinrich von Thyssen. She recovered from her injuries. Barbara was a beneficiary of Alexis' will, together with his brothers and sisters. His estate was to be shared out amicably. Barbara, however, had no intention of wrangling over Alexis' estate. She gave her share, which included the palace in Venice, back to the Mdivani family.

Alexis' death was a great shock to Barbara. In a strange way she had missed his carefree, boyish company. He was certainly a lot more fun than Kurt. She went into mourning for a while which irritated Kurt intensely. It was also at this time that Barbara found she was pregnant. She decided it was the right moment to visit Kurt's ancestral seat in Denmark. She was given a warm welcome by Kurt's older brother who kept the farm going. The neighbours and villagers held a feast in honour of Barbara's marriage into the family. The visit did not, however, live up to Barbara's imagination. The castle was not her idea of a castle. It was only partially occupied and there was no heating in the rooms. Everything was bleak and artless. She felt uncomfortable in this modest and frugal atmosphere. The visit did not last long and anyone who thought that Barbara would make her home in the castle was soon disabused. The villagers were disappointed; they had hoped to benefit from the immense fortune they had heard belonged to the new Countess von Reventlow. It was not to be. Barbara never lived in Denmark, but neither was she there long enough to retain any bad memories of it.

Barbara and Kurt decided to make their home in London, believing it to be the safest place to bring up a child. Barbara had several good friends in London, including the Kennerleys, the Droghedas (then called Moore). The social life in London was reputed to be more elegant than anywhere else, what with Royal Ascot, Wimbledon and invitations to Buckingham Palace. Another advantage of London, Barbara would point out, was that it was not far from Paris.

Barbara and Kurt first moved into a twenty-seven-bedroom Victorian mansion on the borders of Hampstead Heath. It stood in seven acres of secluded land. It was meant to be a temporary residence until they found something permanent. At the same time Barbara bought Ashwood House, near Woking in Surrey, to be done up for week-ends. Barbara soon realized that she did not enjoy week-ends in the country and never stayed at Ashwood House. It was not until 1938 that Barbara at last found exactly what she wanted, a private residence situated in Regent's Park which she named Winfield House and turned into a magnificent mansion. When Barbara left London she gave Winfield House to the American government to be used for the Ambassador's residence. It is still the residence of the US Ambassador to Britain.

Denmark and the United States are two countries which do not allow dual nationality. Barbara had to decide on being a citizen of one or the other. In making the decision, she had to consider several aspects of the problem. Firstly, on an emotional level Barbara was keen to turn her back on the country that had rejected her. She would never forget the hatred she had seen in the eyes of the people who formed mobs to jeer and spit at her in the streets of New York. Barbara herself was more at home in the company of Europeans than of Americans. She spoke with no trace of an American accent and she rarely used American idioms except in jest. She certainly had no personal attachment to the United States. She said that every time she saw references to herself as 'Babs' or 'the Huttentot', she wanted to puke. Not that she had any patriotic feelings for Denmark. What did matter to her, though, was the opportunity for her son to inherit a Danish title if he so wished when the time came. Quite apart from these sentimental and emotional considerations, there was the financial one which concerned a whole battery of financial and legal experts, including her father. By renouncing her American citizenship, Barbara would be able to save herself over half a million dollars annually in income tax. Furthermore, in the event of her death, her son would benefit as a Danish citizen by not having to pay more than half his inheritance to the US Treasury. As was natural for Barbara, she went overboard for the idea of becoming a Danish subject. She was especially pleased to be able to give back what she had got from the American public. She could, and did, say that she had been hounded out of her own country. Years later, when Kurt Reventlow himself had become an American citizen by being a long-term resident, Barbara was pleased to travel on her Danish passport. Denmark, she discovered, is a non-controversial country that elicits no hatred from anybody, and there are few passports in the world that are as welcome in so many countries. Had Barbara regretted her assumption of Danish citizenship, it would not have been difficult to arrange a reversal. Successive American governments tried to woo her back, but Barbara never considered it for one moment.

The financial and legal side of Barbara's act of renunciation was masterminded by Graham Mattison. From then on, he was to negotiate all her financial affairs and later on he acquired power of attorney which gave him a free hand in handling her fortune. As Mattison was conducting the business he came to London, for he realized that Barbara's marriage to Kurt was not likely to last much longer. Their arguments were now conducted quite openly. Kurt could not bear to be contradicted. Barbara enjoyed baiting him in front of people when he would lose his temper and stalk off in absolute rage. He tried in vain to discipline Barbara to his way of life – cheerless, stern and prim. He openly showed his disapproval of most of her friends, especially of the Mdivanis whom Barbara still saw occasionally. Kurt was rude and arrogant to Barbara's servants, taking it upon himself to dismiss them on a whim. Barbara could not tolerate this and made a point of humiliating Kurt publicly. She would say that she who pays chooses. Since it was her money, she had the right to choose her house, her servants, her friends and he had no rights and nothing to say about any of them.

Once again, Barbara used the same ploy when she wanted to get rid of a husband. She showed an intense interest in the tennis player Baron Gottfried von Cramm who was in London and playing in the Wimbledon finals against the American, Don Budge. She invited von Cramm, making him the guest of honour at her dinner parties. She openly set out to charm him; she only had eyes for him. This was the way she told people that Kurt was no longer in her favour. It was also a way of forgetting that she was married to someone she could no longer bear to be in the same room with. Kurt was a very jealous man and he was unable to disguise his intense vexation at his wife's behaviour. However, he was not prepared to leave the marriage. There was a son who meant a great deal to him, and there was the prospect of being in charge of Barbara's fortune. He was convinced that he could manage the spending of her money in a much more sensible manner. He had waited forty years to get married and honestly believed that marriages last a lifetime. To Kurt, hatred between the spouses was no reason for separation.

Mattison knew about the prenuptial settlement imposed on Alexis Mdivani by Franklyn Hutton. Under French law Alexis would have been the recipient of Barbara's entire fortune by the very act of their marriage. Mattison suspected that Kurt would not be averse to the same thing happening when Barbara became a Danish subject, since a similar law existed there. Mattison required Kurt to sign a contract waiving all rights to Barbara's assets. Kurt felt in a position to drive a bargain as he knew how keen Mattison and Barbara were on the renunciation of her American citizenship. Mattison calculated that it would be well worth buying off Kurt for the savings on English and American taxes. Mattison offered Kurt $1 million, take it or leave it. Kurt signed. Mattison estimated that the sum would be amortized in two years and it would further save Barbara from feeling obliged to settle a large amount when the divorce took place. All in all, Mattison had concluded an excellent deal. 'Darling, in your hands,' Barbara said to him, 'I will have no more financial problems.'

Upon repudiating her American birthrights, Barbara incurred the ultimate wrath of the xenophobic Americans. It was the last insult and released a renewed torrent of abuse against her in the American press. She was now an out and out traitor. 'Babs Renounces Citizenship But Not Profits' was a typical headline. It was difficult, if not impossible, for the average American to understand how anyone would want to be anything but American if given the choice. In their history, most people of the world have clawed their way to the land of opportunity; people were prepared to risk their lives to be part of the golden melting pot. My own experience of living in the United States for eight years was that people took personal offence if you told them that you did not wish to become an American citizen. In later years when Barbara spoke about that episode, she said that people in the public eye have no right to live their own lives. Barbara compared her ostracism by

Americans with that suffered by Ingrid Bergman when she had a child out of wedlock. 'The difference is that I don't need the public to make a living,' she said. 'They don't own me.'

The effect of the new wave of adverse publicity resulted in more strikes by Woolworth employees whose discontent was increased by the reminders of the disparity between their income and Barbara's. Woolworth shops were shutting down in the crisis and even people in the Woolworth management felt that Barbara had a duty to spend her money in the country where her grandfather had made it. Barbara never felt any more responsibility to Woolworth employees than to any poorly-paid worker in the world, although she did sympathize with the less fortunate. Those of us who were aware of her generous good deeds know how much she identified with such people. She felt a tremendous guilt for being rich. She did not, however, identify with the sales girls of the Woolworth stores. With Graham Mattison directing her investments, Barbara was gradually relinquishing her interests in the Woolworth company anyway. Mattison was wisely investing her money in the more lucrative field of oil shares.

Although Barbara knew within weeks of her marriage to Kurt that she could have no affinity with such a person, she basically needed a strong husband by her side and she also decided to compromise for the sake of the baby who was born in London in 1936. Her life continued in its usual way whether Kurt was there or not. He enjoyed most of the social events which he considered part of an aristocrat's pleasant duties. Barbara was a popular hostess in London and provided Kurt with an entrée to Mayfair society, to such an extent that he would not have considered going back to farm with his brother in Denmark.

On a trip to India in the spring of 1938, Barbara decided to force an open rupture with Kurt by having an affair with Prince Muassam, the young Nizam of Hyderabad. Muassam introduced Barbara to the beauties of the Koran, large tracts of which she memorized and could still recite thirty years later. With him she discovered the works of Tagore which were to be part of her life subsequently. I often heard her discussing in depth certain passages with her Indian friends. It was a reflection of her involvement and knowledge of the East. It is doubtful that Barbara was ever in love with Muassam, but he was in love with her. She taunted Kurt by saying that at least Muassam was not interested in her money for he had ten times more than she had. While Kurt was taken on a tiger hunt, Barbara visited the Taj Mahal with Muassam. She commemorated the trip with the following poem:

> O look! If look it be
> To look, and not to dream
> Of this loveliness beyond
> All loveliness has been!
>
> Can it be of pearl
> This wonder that I see?
> The palace of a mermaid
> Arisen from the sea?
>
> Can it be the moon
> Now fallen from the skies
> This miracle in white
> Here before my eyes?
>
> What god created it?
> What god, upon a time,
> Created the perfection
> And glory of its line.
>
> And those who may behold
> This beauty, such as I –
> What need have we to know
> A heaven when we die.

On returning to London, Barbara once more engaged in her social activities, but now she felt a definite need to remove Kurt from her house. He had been terribly unpleasant during their trip to India and it got to the point where a civil word between the two, even for appearances' sake, was impossible. Barbara started to attend functions without Kurt and it seemed to everybody that she was once again available to choose a new partner. At a ball attended by royalty from several countries, Barbara met Prince Frederick of Prussia, a direct descendant of Queen Victoria and Kaiser Wilhelm II. Barbara was very flattered by this young man's obvious attraction for her. She lost no time in inviting him to Winfield House the following day. The next move was to ask him to stay, since he obviously enjoyed playing tennis and using the swimming pool. When he accepted this invitation, Barbara proceeded to install him in Kurt's room; it was, after all, her house. Barbara succeeded in her intention of making it so mortifying for Kurt that he would leave. Nevertheless it took about a month of being in the ignominious position of finding another man in his bed to force Kurt to move to a hotel. For a man of such pride and short temper, he must have gone through hell before moving out.

Once Kurt was out of her house, Barbara felt able to instruct a lawyer to act on her behalf to obtain a divorce. The lawyer involved was William Mitchell. Barbara told him that she was prepared to pay a substantial sum to have a quick and clean divorce with as little publicity as possible. Kurt was not prepared to consider any settlement. He oscillated between despair and rage. Jimmy Donahue believed that Kurt was stalling for a bigger settlement. Kurt told Mitchell that two could play Barbara's game, especially since he was the injured party. In the midst of the emotional arguments back and forth, most of which were carried by the press, finances were discussed. 'I just want to lead a happy life,' said Barbara, 'and it is impossible with Kurt.' Kurt replied, 'I love my wife very much indeed, and despite everything I still love her and always will.' Mitchell offered Kurt $1 million over and above the $1 million agreed when Barbara took Danish citizenship, in return for a quiet divorce and unconditional custody of Lance. Kurt replied that he would not even consider $5 million.

It was a stalemate which could obviously not be resolved amicably. In the dialogue carried on by the two protagonists through Mr Mitchell, Kurt had sworn to shoot Prince Frederick like a dog if he saw him with his wife again. Barbara took advantage of this statement to have Kurt arrested on the grounds that, with his violent temper and the possession of a gun, he was putting lives in danger. She sent Lance with Sister, Tiki and two bodyguards to a comfortable out-of-the-way hotel in north Yorkshire, until things blew over. There was no telling what Kurt would do in desperation. The trial that followed was the beginning of litigation between Kurt and Barbara that lasted for over a decade, all of which provided material for the tabloid press, most of it to Barbara's detriment.

The adverse publicity over the divorce affected Barbara so much that her love of England turned into a need to get away from the country forever. The last thing that Barbara did before leaving London was to sign in an English court a deed of separation with

Kurt, stipulating that she would have custody of Lance until he reached school age, when Kurt could have him for half of the school holidays. Kurt was awarded no additional financial settlement. He could have had another $1 million. Henceforth there would be continuous litigation between Barbara and Kurt over the interpretation of each parent's rights over Lance. Accusations on both sides continued, each parent argued that Lance was being corrupted. Each was prepared to sue the other over minor things such as an article in the papers giving inaccurate quotation, rumours of slander, and so on. They were field days for the lawyers. In the meantime, Barbara was enjoying the life of a single person, accepting homage from many aspirants.

The most notable suitor was Bobby Sweeney, the American champion golfer of Irish descent and charm. Here was an intelligent, educated and handsome escort who was cheerful and amusing, a good dancer and just the type of company that Barbara craved. She took full advantage and embarked on a full-blown romance with him. They travelled together from England to France, then to Egypt and Greece. The papers carried the news of their impending marriage. Perhaps if Barbara had been free, she might have made Bobby husband number three.

12

In Sickness and in Health

In the year that Europe was plunged into the Second World War, Barbara met Cary Grant on a ship going from New York to Southampton. They found themselves included in the same group at the Captain's table. They had mutual friends and they were both, in a way, Anglo-Americans. Barbara said that she did not fall for Cary when she first met him. She did find him remarkably pleasant and unassuming for a famous film star, but she did not give him another thought after that journey ended. She was still involved with Bobby even though they spent periods apart. Americans were pleased that Barbara had apparently given up her craze for foreigners with titles. What is more she was pictured helping the war effort by knitting socks for the European soldiers. Americans had come out of the Depression and now had other preoccupations. Barbara's image took an upward turn. She was pleased to be back in the States and went on to California to visit friends and to show four-year-old Lance her favourite places in San Francisco. It was in the summer of 1940 that Cary Grant's and Barbara's paths crossed again. This time the relationship developed into something more serious. And, in 1941, they started their courtship by going to Mexico for a holiday with three friends.

It was not surprising that Barbara helped to precipitate the relationship. It was a good two years since she had had a husband as such. Her insecurity and romantic nature would not allow this state of affairs to be prolonged any more. She liked the idea that Cary was a self-made man who had attained the summit of his profession, and that as such he could not be branded a kept man. He was, in fact, more famous than she was; but that gave her reassurance. On 26 July 1942, Cary Grant, having helped in the war

169

effort, became an American citizen. Sixteen days earlier he and Barbara had married in a short ceremony at Lake Arrowhead at the home of Frank Vincent, his manager. Cary had not taken off a day from work. The marriage was played down due to adverse publicity. He was very sensitive about being called a fortune-hunter or a social climber. The studio agreed that there should be as little publicity as possible. They could not afford to have his image tarnished. Cary and Barbara had nothing in common in terms of background and education. It was true that they were both motherless from an early age, but they reacted to it differently.

The couple lived on Amalfi Drive in Pacific Palisades in a house rented from Douglas Fairbanks Jr. Elegant living is not enough to make a marriage. Cary was away from home a great deal, for his work and in the war effort. He was infuriated by the publicity of his marriage, not least by their nickname 'Cash & Cary'. In the rare interviews he accorded to the press, Cary did not like to talk about himself. He hated the additional attention brought on by his marriage.

Barbara made a conscious effort to make friends among Cary's colleagues. She threw herself into a healthy life, playing a lot of tennis. She was able to give Lance a secure home and wanted to give him the chance of putting down some roots, which he managed to do. It was, however, plain to everyone that the newly marrieds shared very little besides the fact that they were celebrities. Grant was as stingy as they come and Barbara was the opposite. They were bound to clash on this. It was not long before Barbara reverted to her old ways, surrounding herself with sycophants, leading an aimless life that irritated Cary. The marriage lasted, on and off, for three years, but when it ended, the two remained friends.

Towards the end of her marriage to Cary, Barbara was as usual looking in other directions to replace the current man in her life. In Hollywood, there was no shortage of good-looking escorts, though they might have lacked culture or intellect. Barbara had a fling with Philip Reed, for a short time. She then became smitten with a dashing adventurer, a friend of Errol Flynn's, by the name of Freddie McEvoy. Freddie was a professional gambler, a smuggler, a con-man, a larger-than-life character full of daring and charm. Barbara could not resist this handsome hunk in spite of his reputation. He had been married twice to very rich women and made a superhuman effort to make Barbara his third. The reason why Barbara did not fall for it was probably because he lacked the proper background, his breeding distinctly left something to be desired. Nevertheless, Barbara indulged him with the usual expensive gifts plus $100,000 during their six-month affair, conducted mostly in New York. When Barbara returned to Paris, she started seeing Count Alain d'Eudeville, a wealthy French nobleman. They were inseparable for several months. The press followed them from Paris to the Côte d'Azur. Barbara was back in her familiar Europe after a prolonged period in America. Barbara's cultural dichotomy made her seesaw between the two. From the likeable American rogue she threw herself into the arms of a member of the rigid French upper class. But whatever their social rank, they had to be good looking.

Although Barbara assured the press that she had no intention of getting married again, that she was enjoying the freedom of doing what she pleased, she was subconsciously looking for husband number four. She was well aware that every time a marriage of hers failed, she made a fool of herself. She was really ashamed of it, and yet she could not help it. When she met Prince Igor Troubetzkoy, who was a friend of Freddie McEvoy's, she looked at him in a most favourable light. Here was an exceptional man. He was the same age as Barbara, of Russian aristocracy. His family had fled from Russia before the Revolution and Igor had been born and educated in France. By culture, he was one hundred per cent French. By nature he was noble, simple, unpretentious and down-to-earth. He was penniless but had no aspiration to wealth. His all-consuming interest was cycling; he had been a champion cyclist, lean, muscular, with a profile like John Barrymore's. This utterly charming, unassuming and uncomplicated man stepped into Barbara's world. It was a world he could not fathom and, I believe, he never did. He was so oblivious to material goods, so guileless that he was unable to imagine anyone with ulterior motives, much less have any himself. To Igor, a wife was a wife – as simple as that. He certainly landed up with the wrong wife. At thirty-five years old, Igor longed for the very qualities of life that would have bored Barbara to death.

From the first evening they spent together at Barbara's invitation, she realized that Igor was a completely different type of man from any other she had met. He was pure, innocent and money had no effect on him – either the lack of it or large amounts of it. He was a free spirit, unaffected by worldly considerations. Because of this, Barbara nicknamed him 'Pixie'. Here was one person who could enjoy a huge meal while she had black coffee and cigarettes, and not be affected, not even notice. He enjoyed anyone's company, did not try to run Barbara's life or curb her excessive spending. If he disapproved of something, he kept it to himself and then forgot about it. He did not let things upset him, he was a happy person and enjoyed life on any terms. He and his brother had been brought up very modestly in Nice. The boys had no money of their own. Since Igor was cycling mad, he never had time for a full-time job. He bummed along with no great ambition and no regrets. He was very modest about his title, indeed was really embarrassed by it. Barbara scooped him up from this simple life and transported him into hers, deciding that being Princess Troubetzkoy was better than being ex-Mrs Cary Grant.

There was no mad passion for Igor. Barbara found him extremely sweet and a refreshing change from the vain, demanding and calculating type of men she knew. Igor did not even want a car! He went everywhere on his bike. He was not interested in polo; he enjoyed painting in the countryside. All Barbara's friends adored Igor. He was handsome, free and had a genuine title. Igor, on the other hand, had naïvely fallen in love with a 'beautiful woman with a sensitive soul', in spite of her money which he believed was an obstacle between them. At first he just could not believe the sums spent on clothes, hotel bills, donations to unworthy causes. But Igor looked optimistically on the bright side of life. Since it was not his money, it was none of his business. Barbara found Igor an ideal companion and friend, if not terribly exciting. They went together to St Moritz where Igor enjoyed the skiing and Barbara did the social rounds. Barbara thought it would be a good idea to have a small wedding in St Moritz but the news leaked out and the usual hoards of journalists materialized from all parts of the globe. Instead of marrying the couple went into hiding.

The marriage eventually took place in Chur, a small village outside Zurich, on 1 March 1947, attended only by Anya and Savely Sorine, friends from New York who had joined Barbara's skiing party in St Moritz. Almost from the beginning, the marriage was ill-starred. Barbara had developed the habit of taking drugs to control her appetite. These gave her insomnia for which she took sleeping pills. The matter was further complicated by her increasing dependence on alcohol. Her life was taking on a nightmarish atmosphere. Igor was relegated to the role of a helpless observer. He was pushed further and further into the background by the growing number of people attending Barbara's semi-darkened bedroom around the clock. She did not eat, could not sleep, the pills had suppressed her sex drive and she was becoming the victim of her addictions. Igor's presence in her life was superfluous.

In the three years following her marriage to Igor, Barbara was to see more of the inside of Swiss clinics than the mountain scenery. She underwent four major operations in three years. In addition, and perhaps as a result of, her drink/drug/diet condition, she was beset by a series of abdominal complaints which included intestinal occlusion and an ovarian tumour. Her abdomen, she said, was now a patchwork. In spite of the vast amount of reportage in the press, the operations were shrouded in obscure terms. Hélène, who was at Barbara's bedside throughout that period, told me that no one seemed to know what was going on. There was no evidence or medical proof of the specific necessity for these operations. It was the opinion of many of Barbara's friends, including Cary Grant, that doctors became knife-happy when they saw a rich person. In one of the operations in Switzerland, Barbara was relieved of her remaining ovary without permission. (The first had been taken away during the complications arising immediately after Lance's birth.) Some of Barbara's close friends held the preposterous belief that Igor had persuaded the surgeons to remove any possibility of further children in the hope of being her main beneficiary. I personally never believed that to be true, not least because Hélène told me that Igor was kept constantly well out of the way. No one asked his opinion about anything and he said nothing.

Because Igor was inconspicuous and did not interfere, Barbara treated him as inessential. As a result of the removal of her ovary, Barbara experienced overnight the effects of the menopause. She felt her youth slipping away and she discovered the approach of forty and the appearance of wrinkles a most distressing experience. The fear and frenzy she felt pushed her to heavy drinking. She also became hooked on barbiturates of which she needed ever-increasing doses.

During her convalescence, Barbara would enjoy telephoning her friends. At that time, she would often call Baron Gottfried von Cramm of whom she was still extremely fond. She admired him for his tennis, for his aristocratic lineage, and she enjoyed his good manners and taste. It was a great pity that he was a homosexual. In fact Barbara had a girlish crush on him, a kind of hero-worship, mainly because she could not have him. From her bed in the clinic

173

near Bern, she would have long conversations with Gottfried at his castle in Hanover. She persuaded him to visit her in Switzerland and he stayed several days. She showered him with attention and expensive gifts and was obviously paying more attention to him than to Igor who was told that she could not see anyone, although he knew perfectly well that Gottfried was there holding her hand.

In this, his first experience of marriage, Igor had expected a normal husband–wife relationship. He woke up to something totally different. First of all, he was given his own bedroom when he thought he would be sharing a bed with his wife. He was pushed further away from the person he loved and summoned occasionally when he was required. He complained that Barbara's dog saw more of her than he did. Barbara's health problems completely wrecked any chance of a real marriage. Still, Igor became resigned to the fact that he had no role as a husband. He was an onlooker, a non-participant. Back in Paris, he could at least visit his old haunts instead of living in a hotel room or waiting in the ante-room of a clinic. He thought of taking up motor racing but Barbara talked him out of it. Igor hated the Ritz and wanted a home somewhere in the country for himself and Barbara to get away from all the phoney superficiality around their lives. For Igor, real luxury was to be in his own home, surrounded by beautiful things, by silence, by the quality of the people you have around, by the quality of their thoughts, and feelings. Barbara could not be persuaded to spend one day in the countryside, let alone live there for any length of time. She remembered her country house in England which she had never used. But she went along with his idea, agreeing with him that it might be a possibility. She allowed Igor to search seriously for a home outside of Paris; it occupied his time. After some time, he found a charming house in Gif-sur-Yvette. It was not far from Paris and the area's beauty attracted many of Paris' wealthy residents, including the Duke and Duchess of Windsor. Barbara let Igor purchase it and encouraged him to do it up himself which is what he wanted to do. He put in a great deal of time and effort in the hope that this might be the place to start afresh a two-year marriage that had never really taken off.

For Barbara the marriage had already gone stale. She was unable to treat Igor with any respect. When he was waiting around, she did not wish to see him and when he was at Gif working on the house she resented his interest in something outside her life. She had reached the point where she wanted Igor out. The opportunity arose when she met Prince Henri de la Tour d'Auvergne-Lauraguais, and publicly conducted a love affair with him across two continents. In exactly the same way that Kurt Reventlow had been provoked by Prince Frederick of Prussia, Igor came to the end of his patience, packed his bags and left the Ritz. He took the train to the Côte d'Azur to stay with his mother. This was August and he had been locked out of Barbara's bedroom since the spring. He saw himself as the injured party. As a Frenchman he would have been acquitted of murdering his wife's lover. He felt that, as the aggrieved person, he would be able to demand the terms of a just settlement. He employed a lawyer named Melvin Belli and asked him to demand a reconciliation and that Barbara should resume conjugal relations under threat of legal action. He told the press as much and it was plastered all over the evening papers: 'PRINCE DEMANDS BABS COME HOME AND ACT LIKE A WIFE.' The threat to sue Barbara immediately brought Graham Mattison to France. He soon impressed on Mr Belli that Igor was in no position to threaten or to demand anything. Belli was not even sure of obtaining his fee, since Igor had no money. Unlike his predecessors, Igor had not amassed anything that could be turned into cash. He had to come to terms with the fact that he had lost his wife without compensation. It took another year before the divorce was pronounced, during which time Igor continued to hope for a reconciliation. As usual with Barbara there were no half measures. The settlement on Igor was modest. Barbara did not forgive him for attempting to sue her. He was accorded a trust which would yield a modest income for his modest needs and he was given the house which he had done up in the hope of sharing it with Barbara. He also gained peace of mind to pursue a simple life.

The next episode in Barbara's life was dominated by drink and drugs. Her social life was passed in a haze of semi-awareness. Her friends felt that Barbara had a death wish which pushed her relentlessly on this road to self-destruction. Time and again she was persuaded to try some treatment or other. No organic ailment could be detected and every treatment always ended without any improvement in her condition. Barbara did not seem to believe in anything any more. At times, she would ring Igor for a comforting chat. Whenever she felt particularly depressed, she would call him and he would come to visit her and soothe her with his gentle manner. He was a happy man with the life he made for himself. He

175

wanted no more. Barbara would ask him to marry her again, but Igor would just smile sweetly.

Barbara's next escapade in marriage was the most disastrous, costly and degrading of them all. It was the marriage in which she made herself the complete laughing stock of the world's gossip columnists. One could say that she was not herself. From meeting to courtship to marriage to divorce, the whole affair was conducted in a cloud of alcohol which never lifted for an instant. Porfirio Rubirosa worked a perfect put-up job and he came out of it the winner. Rubi's reputation as a great lover was notorious but his talents were not confined to the bedroom. He had such charming manners that he was appreciated not only by the ladies. People said that when Rubi came in, it was sunshine. Men like Rubi were not sterling characters but they were colourful and gave the international scene great animation. He did not so much fleece rich women; his victims were a type born to be fleeced. Barbara was the best example of that type. Although neither handsome nor tall women fell for his excellent manners, his graciousness and suavity. They fell for the veneer that hid his unscrupulous mentality. He was intelligent and played polo at international level. He was undoubtedly a versatile and talented man. He came from a diplomatic family in the Dominican Republic, went to the best schools and belonged to the international upper-crust. He spoke several languages fluently and had studied law before making a career in the army. He came to the notice of his country's dictator, Rafael Trujillo Molino, and became a personal friend of the Trujillo family. The dictator's daughter, Flor de Oro (Flower of gold), fell in love with this irresistible young officer. They were married and Trujillo set the bridegroom on the start of a diplomatic career in Europe. Rubi's life in Europe included playing polo, gambling and wooing the ladies. Flor stood it for five years and then asked for a divorce. Far from incurring the wrath of Trujillo for being a faithless husband and for using his diplomatic position as a springboard for his various social activities, Trujillo promoted Rubi within the diplomatic hierarchy until he eventually reached the rank of ambassador. It really is an exceptional man who can combine business and pleasure with such success.

Rubi then fell in love with the French film star Danielle Darrieux who was to gain enormous popularity starring opposite Charles Boyer in *Mayerling*. Danielle divorced her husband, a film director, to marry Rubi in Paris during the German occupation. This

176

marriage lasted no longer than his first but he and Danielle had an amicable divorce and remained good friends. In 1947, Rubi married Doris Duke. This American tobacco heiress, a friend of Barbara's who had come out at the same time as her, had four times Barbara's fortune yet she rarely appeared in the headlines. Doris had a head for figures and managed her own fortune. She had an income of $4 million a year, tax free, led a good life and did not throw her money away. Barbara always envied Doris' business acumen. The Rubi-Duke marriage lasted just over a year and even though Doris was anything but generous, Rubi came out of it with a heap of goodies including a mansion in Paris, some new polo ponies, a sports car, an airplane and half a million dollars in cash. Credit must be given to his diplomatic skills. Doris told Barbara that Rubi was fun, charming and wonderful. Her grounds for divorce was 'extreme mental cruelty' – she could not bear his infidelities.

Although Barbara had met Rubi before at Doris' home in Hawaii, it was at a small dinner party in Deauville that the romance took off. At the time Rubi was having an affair with Zsa Zsa Gabor, the Hungarian actress, who was rather an expensive item. Rubi was going through a bad financial patch and had been sacked by Trujillo for having been named as co-respondent in two highly unsavoury divorce cases. He saw in Barbara the possibility of replenishing his coffers. He used his well-known seduction routine which no woman in her right mind could possibly resist. Barbara was fascinated to find out why Doris had been attracted to him. The fact that he was courting Zsa Zsa Gabor was a further challenge. When Barbara showed signs of falling for the notorious Romeo, everyone tried to avert the disaster. Aunt Jessie, Cousin Jimmy, Graham Mattison, Cary Grant, all her friends begged her not to marry in haste.

At that time, Barbara had been through the painful episode of being rejected by Prince Henri de la Tour d'Auvergne-Lauraguais. She was alone and did not enjoy being in that state. Drink made her more depressed and vulnerable. Here was this impeccably-mannered man who used his magnetism on her by serenading her outside her window, this man with all the most desirable women in the world at his feet. It did not take Barbara long to convince herself that she was in love with Rubi. Perhaps a sensible woman would have stopped short of marriage, but Barbara did not like to have her lover branded a gigolo. Barbara never thought of the cost, so she made up her mind and set the date. The wedding was to take place on 30 December 1953, at the residence of the Dominican Consul, Rubi's friend. Barbara agreed to it because by marrying in what was considered official Dominican territory, as was the legal status of the Consul's residence, she could dodge the New York State laws requiring certain formalities such as a blood test. What Barbara was unaware of was that by marrying on Dominican territory she would have acquired Dominican citizenship which would have given her husband legal rights over her fortune. For the third time, Barbara had to be saved from losing everything she owned in one foolish starry-eyed moment. Graham Mattison had foreseen the stratagem and had requested Rubi to sign a prenuptial contract. Rubi was prepared for it and demanded $5 million against his signature. After some hard negotiations, Rubi accepted half that amount. With his marriage to Barbara, Rubi was reinstated by Trujillo as Minister Plenipotentiary to France.

At the wedding reception at the Pierre, Barbara, aged forty-one and wearing a Balenciaga dress of black taffeta, faced the newsmen. She sat next to Lance who looked dejected and embarrassed. She was barely able to slur her words and had she tried to stand up would have fallen on her face. To the outsider, she looked tired but happy. She said to one reporter, 'I'm so tired I could die.' Rubi behaved in his customary suave manner, kissing his bride's hand to show how moved and speechless he was on this occasion. Later the first guests had hardly arrived when Barbara collapsed and had to be carried off to bed. Barbara had been drunk throughout her wedding day. Hélène told me that they were terrified something worse would happen in front of the journalists.

It took less time than usual for Barbara to realize that she had made another dreadful mistake. Instead of a loving husband who read poetry and whispered sweet nothings in her ear, she found Rubi carrying on his normal life of flying his own plane, playing polo, visiting Zsa Zsa and others. Things were not helped by the fact that Barbara had fallen on the day after the wedding and broken her leg. She was to spend her honeymoon in plaster up to her hip. The truth was that Rubi had contracted this marriage for business reasons – something not unknown in Latin countries. The marriage lasted fifty-three days and was turned into a farce by Zsa Zsa Gabor's continuous dialogue with the newsmen. She milked the situation for all it was worth and her performance in this episode helped her towards an acting career. In this case Zsa Zsa proved to be the one who had the last laugh; Barbara was the loser. Zsa Zsa delighted in the publicity. She told the press that Rubi had proposed to her and when she refused, he gave her a black eye and married Barbara Hutton instead. Rubi denied it. Whatever the truth, Barbara spent her wedding night drunk and on her own. Rubi went on the town and spent the night at a bachelor friend's apartment with a dancing girl. According to Hélène and Tiki who were at Barbara's side throughout the marriage, it was never consummated, if only because they hardly saw each other. Rubi dropped his pretences immediately after the wedding and returned to his bachelor life. He was not inclined to perform his husbandly duty and the plastered leg was as good an excuse as any. The couple went to Palm Beach where Rubi continued to have a good time with any woman he fancied. He spent Barbara's money on himself as fast as he could. By the time Barbara realized that she had again made a fool of herself, she had already given Rubi $2½ million, a twin-engined North American B-25 airplane, a property in his own country worth half a million dollars and approximately $1 million in other gifts. Even though the marriage lasted less than two months, Barbara had to wait two years for her divorce. Because the marriage was under Dominican law she could not get it without Dominican consent. By the law of that country, she had to wait for Rubi to sue her for divorce. She finally obtained it on 30 July 1955.

During 1954, Barbara played the field, drank a lot and tried to forget her mistake with Rubi. Her most publicized escort at the time was the tall, handsome English actor, Michael Rennie, of *Third Man* fame. Their outings often made the newspapers, making it appear a long and serious romance. In fact, it did not last more than a few weeks. Sexually they were incompatible. Barbara had a low libido as a result of the drugs, and she turned to her old friend Baron Gottfried von Cramm, the person she had idolized since 1937. At least he never made sexual demands on her.

By now von Cramm had an import/export business in Hamburg as well as a school for training young tennis players. His time was also very taken up by various family responsibilities. Barbara was more inclined to stay at home and she often phoned Gottfried, begging him to take time off to visit her. He finally accepted an invitation to Tangier in the summer of 1955. The attraction that Barbara felt was mostly spurred on by the fact that he was unattainable. He had been married for a short time, an experience which permanently turned him against women. It suited Barbara to believe that his imprisonment for homosexuality while Hitler was in power was really because of his outspoken comments against the Nazis. This may have been true, but Barbara was deluding herself if she believed that von Cramm was not a homosexual. He had himself admitted as much. Von Cramm was no fortune-hunter. Grandpa Woolworth would not have been able to brand him as either a foreign gigolo or a work-shy aristocrat. Von Cramm was refined, polite and cultured. He treasured his friendship with Barbara whose culture and refinement he was able to appreciate. Here was one friend who was worthy of Barbara's intellect. But, in her need for all or nothing, she was not satisfied with a marvellous friendship with Gottfried, she had to make it into something which it could never be.

It is true that at Sidi Hosni it was possible to imagine oneself living a fairy-tale. Von Cramm had no ulterior motives when he agreed to join Barbara in Tangier. He probably did not count on her persuasive pressure. The outcome of this visit was that Barbara announced to everyone that she and Gottfried were to be married, that she had been in love with him for eighteen years and that had she married him then, her life would have been one long period of bliss. Barbara announced to her friends that Gottfried had become her lover. Subsequently she had to admit that it was for the first and last time. And in that one moment, Barbara found both a personal triumph and a public vindication of Gottfried's reputation. In Barbara's mind, this was going to be the perfect marriage. Her hero-worship after all those years was about to have a happy ending, proving that true love did conquer all.

Barbara wanted to marry Gottfried immediately, and with no publicity. Barbara's friends were all delighted, they all heartily approved of Gottfried, an honourable and upright man without pretention or pettiness. No one who had ever met him could have found any objection to the match. The marriage took place on 8 November 1955, at the Mairie of Versailles, arranged in secrecy by the curator of Versailles, Gerald Van der Kemp. This was one favour returned to Barbara for making the largest individual contribution to the Versailles restoration fund. Gerald was Barbara's witness and one of Gottfried's brothers was his. There followed a reception at the Ritz for close friends. The press was naturally in attendance. Both bride and groom spoke of their eighteen-year friendship and how their marriage had been greatly overdue, but better late than never. Barbara wore black again, not because she expected marriage to be like a funeral, but because she thought it made her look thinner. As usual, the marital bliss was to be short lived, and difficulties started to appear almost immediately. Barbara had expected Mattison to arrange for the US government's ban on homosexuals to be lifted so that she and Gottfried could visit the US together. But his efforts were in vain. The request was unequivocally turned down by the authorities. They could not afford to make this exception, knowing the amount of publicity it would receive. So, unable to make her usual Christmas visit to Aunt Jessie and Cousin Jimmy, Barbara rented a villa in Cuernavaca, Mexico, thus setting in motion the realization of her long-term dream of building a Japanese-type house.

Although no specific plans had been discussed before the marriage, Gottfried had not intended to abandon his successful business in Hamburg. He had just expected to spend his holidays with Barbara and for her to spend some of her time in Hamburg. Barbara, on the other hand, needed a husband to fit in with her life and certainly not to have any interests of his own such as a job. In a sense it was just as well that Gottfried left the scene periodically to attend to his business and his tennis school. He was not happy in any prolonged period of relaxation, especially when Barbara was drinking heavily. It also became apparent that Gottfried much preferred the company of young men. He became less circumspect about being seen with them, and he would invite them to stay the night in his bedroom. It was humiliating for Barbara and she turned more and more to drink for comfort. Not surprisingly, they drifted apart and Barbara resumed her visits to New York, San Francisco and Hawaii – without Gottfried. She even went to Venice without him. All pretence was dropped in the second year of their marriage.

At the time someone described Barbara as 'a tumbleweed blown on an aimless pathway by the mistral of her lonely life'. In November 1957, she attached herself to a handsome gigolo who had some family pretensions although he himself had led an unsuccessful, shady life which left him with no money, but a taste for the good life. His name, Philip van Rensselear, suggests the type of person he was. He would probably have succeeded in his mission as a gigolo if he only had the talent for discretion. Unfortunately, his arrogance let him down. He talked to all and sundry about Barbara's most private habits; he told newsmen that they were going to be married. Not surprisingly, he did not last very long and Barbara paid him off magnanimously a couple of months later. He then proceeded to write a couple of trashy books about his experiences during the few weeks he was Barbara's escort, so full of inaccuracies that they could be classified as fiction.

If experiences such as the one with van Rensselear, proved that Barbara was a victim and a fool, she was not always as unlucky. About the same time she met Jimmy Douglas, a handsome, intelligent and sensitive person, who gave Barbara the happiest three years she was to experience in her life. Unfortunately, she experienced the same problem with Jimmy as with Gottfried, and eventually she had to leave him because she could not compete with Jimmy's men friends. But, at first, Jimmy helped her regain her youth and her will to live. She recaptured the beauty of living, her love of the Orient and travel by initiating him into the world that had enchanted her in her own youth. At that time, Barbara was still legally married to Gottfried. Otherwise, she would have wanted to marry Jimmy. It was at that time that I joined Barbara's household. We all thought the world of Jimmy Douglas. He was one of the finest men we could encounter and the only person who was able to stop Barbara from drinking.

They had met in Venice in 1957, at a time when Barbara was beginning to realize the folly of her marriage to von Cramm. Jimmy was then one of the most handsome men in American café society. His father was the Secretary of the Air Force in the US government and Jimmy had money from his mother's family which afforded him a comfortable life among his wealthy contemporaries. He was unusually cultured, played the piano beautifully and had a charming personality. He was enjoying the season in Europe, as part of the Princess Margaret set. His looks, intelligence and charm opened any door he wished to enter. Although a good many years younger than Barbara, Jimmy felt a great deal of sympathy towards this pathetic figure. He shared Barbara's love of beautiful things and he rose to the challenge of saving this lost soul. He determined to try and stop her from drinking and Barbara found in this beautiful young man a reason to live. The doctors marvelled at her ability to recover; her resilience in the face of bad health throughout her life was quite incredible.

It did not take long for Barbara to install Jimmy Douglas in her apartment in Paris. She even agreed to house Jimmy's snakes which he kept as pets. She listened with admiration as he played Chopin on her grand piano. He also shared Barbara's taste for the Orient. He had his room lined with Thai silk and Barbara gave him the best stereo equipment on which to play his classical records. But he did not like to be caged, so Barbara also bought him a flat on the Left Bank where he could entertain his own friends and get away when he wanted. At the beginning of the relationship, as always, Barbara gave him *carte blanche*. She took great pleasure in planning the furnishings of his flat. He could have anything he wanted and she would foot the bill. Barbara was so happy with Jimmy that she stopped drinking altogether for over a year.

On their return from Japan in 1959, the first heady passion had passed. Barbara became angry every time Jimmy played the piano because it meant that he was not paying attention to her. Whereas previously she would ask him to play on, now she was in a bad mood if he so much as entered the music room. She was also aware that Jimmy was spending more and more time in his own flat with another young man. It became obvious that some of the things that Barbara was giving to Jimmy were benefiting his friends who had no part in Barbara's life. The humiliation had an all too familiar pattern: first her generosity is accepted with gratitude, then it is abused. The immediate effect on Barbara was that she started to drink again.

Things really began to crumble between Barbara and Jimmy when he stopped hiding the fact that he preferred other company. He was the only person who could keep her from drinking, and therefore who could save her life. He enjoyed this power over her, the challenge, and he was genuinely attached to Barbara. She blackmailed him by drinking; it was a way to keep him near. But relationships grow stale at the best of times and we could see that Jimmy could no longer stand the strain of it. Barbara was too demanding. He coped with the situation by staying away more and more. Barbara tried hard to include Jimmy's friends at her parties. She extended a friendly hand but there was jealousy and suspicion on both sides.

In her younger days, in order to get out of a relationship, Barbara would simply have started a new romance and installed the new man in Jimmy's room. But now she was pushing fifty it was not so easy. What she eventually did was to wait for Jimmy to go on a trip to Venice. While he was away, she asked Hélène to pack all his belongings and she had them delivered to his flat. With it, she left a dignified, poetic but final letter. It would be years before they could meet again as friends. Jimmy was also relieved. He felt rather a fraud, living off a woman knowing his interests lay elsewhere, for he was basically a sincere and honest person. There was also the fact that Jimmy's parents were scandalized by his relationship with Barbara. They had refused to meet her when she travelled through the US with Jimmy. That had been a great blow to her pride. The break was inevitable, although regrettable to those of us who felt he alone could stop the drinking. Barbara was never to love as deeply again. She started to look for a substitute. Alas, nothing she saw was comparable and she continued her life as best she knew how.

When Jimmy departed, Barbara started drinking again and she was obviously ripe for another liaison. She took on the next available man, and that was Lloyd (Frank) Franklin. He stayed with Barbara for three years. It was not love on her part, although she was very fond of him. She needed someone to fill the place Jimmy Douglas had left vacant. Lloyd was charming and considerate but she was always aware of the difference in age and his very modest family background. She never considered marriage to him, although I am sure he would have wanted it.

Barbara was not really happy not being married. There was a residue of American respectability in her that needed to be fulfilled. But it became more and more difficult to find anyone suitable. She no longer had all the eligible bachelors from wealthy and privileged backgrounds begging for her hand in marriage. She was now in her fifties, with a doubtful reputation and a drink/drug problem. In the summer of 1963, Barbara attended an exhibition in Marrakesh of the work of an amateur painter, Raymond Doan, born of a French mother and a Vietnamese father. He was of the same generation as Barbara. She considered him suitable, but he was happily married with two sons, and he worked as an engineer for a French company in Marrakesh. Subconsciously, Barbara had been looking for a more appropriate partner than Lloyd Franklin. Such details as a job or a wife did not seem to be obstacles to Barbara. The all-important consideration was that he would fit the bill – with a few embellishments such as a proper wardrobe and a title. From the very beginning, Barbara disliked Doan's paintings but since this was what brought them together, she bought all his works. She invited Doan to visit her at Sidi Hosni and installed him as an honoured guest while Lloyd looked on. Within a month, Barbara had arranged a payment to Doan's firm to release him from his contract. Graham Mattison managed to persuade Doan that his future would be greatly enhanced without his wife and children.

We found Raymond Doan to be a dour, cheerless person with no humour or conversation, in spite of having been educated in France. At the beginning of the whirlwind romance, I don't believe that Doan knew what was happening. I was instructed by Barbara to take him to the tailor's in Gibraltar and order him some clothes as he had nothing decent to wear. He chose the material for three suits, all of the most questionable quality and taste. Later, when we all returned to Paris, Barbara asked me to choose his clothes. I'd already had that experience with Jimmy Douglas and Lloyd Franklin and knew what he would need. In Paris, Barbara already showed signs of irritation with Doan. These were to increase as time went on. She enjoyed humiliating him in front of people, and she would sometimes scream insults at him, something she had never done to anyone before. Doan just took it all with a bewildered and resigned expression. He never argued with her. He had already burned his boats in Morocco; he had to wait until he and Barbara were married before he could make any kind of objection. It was a mystery to us why Barbara wished to marry him since it was obvious that she held him in contempt. Did she need someone to hit out at for all the frustrations she felt? Was she so insecure without a husband? Barbara was full of contradictions. They tore her apart and prevented her from facing the realities of life. She knew only self-destruction.

My chief project in that autumn of 1962 was to try and contact the ex-Emperor of Indochina, Bao Dai, with a view to negotiating the purchase of a title for Doan. Emperor Bao Dai, an avowed anti-Communist, had been a key national figure in Vietnam. But in the events of the Second World War and after the takeover of the North by the Viet Minh, the French backed him as the head of an independent state within the French Union, refusing to recognize the nationalist aspirations of the people. By then, these aspirations had gathered such momentum that any French-backed person would be unacceptable to the people and Bao Dai spent his remaining days on a comfortable pension provided by the French government. He lived on the Côte d'Azur, a regular client at the roulette tables. When I tracked him down in Cannes, I found that he had no power to grant any title and he was not prepared to invent a phoney one even for a price. Eventually, Barbara found an impoverished titled Laotian family who was prepared to adopt Doan, thus giving him the title of Vinh Na Champassak. It only cost her $250,000.

When they married in Cuernavaca on 7 April 1964, Barbara

185

became a Princess for the third time. The bride and groom had gone all hippie and Oriental, wearing trinkets on their hands and bare feet, each one with some magical significance. They had a handful of guests and there was a seven-tier wedding cake which was not meant to represent the bride's seven husbands although the coincidence was rather unfortunate. The seven tiers were actually meant to represent the seven levels of Buddhist consciousness, the highest being Nirvana the state of total emancipation and beatification.

Once married, Doan found himself an identity. He flaunted his title and demanded obeisance. He personally took responsibility for Barbara and distanced all her friends and staff so he was in sole charge of the decisions. All phone calls had first to be referred to him. He grew his hair and dressed himself up like a guru. As usual, Graham Mattison came in with a prenuptial contract and a deal was struck at $3 million payable in advance. Even though Barbara had no respect for Doan, she had bought herself, via him, a semblance of self-respect. The comforting illusion for her was being able to answer to the title of Princess de Champassak, with her Prince at her side. She needed that prop to travel through life. They hobbled along in their imperfect marriage; they parted and were reconciled several times. Doan learned to exercise patience and submission. Barbara continued on her physical and mental decline.

There was no real end to Barbara's seventh marriage although she and Doan were legally separated. Barbara was her usual magnanimous self on bidding farewell to her last husband. She gave him a house in Tangier and jewels worth millions. Mattison made an agreement with Doan and allowed him to retain his annual allowance on condition he did not ask for a divorce. Mattison had retained some respect for Doan and preferred him to be Barbara's last husband. In the event, Barbara was no longer looking for another husband. It indicated that she had lost all interest in life.

And as her own life drew inexorably towards its close, Barbara had to come to terms with the deaths of many of those once close to her. Freddie McEvoy had drowned in a yachting accident in 1951. In 1964 Rubi killed himself in a car crash in the Bois de Boulogne a few hundred yards from her apartment. In 1966 her favourite cousin Jimmy died of an overdose. In 1968 Lloyd Franklin killed himself and his pregnant wife in the Maserati that Barbara had given him. In 1969 Kurt Reventlow died after major heart surgery. In 1971 Aunt Jessie died, but peacefully in her sleep, at the age of eighty-five. Then, in 1972, came the shock of Lance's death, distant though their relationship had been for many years. The following year both her Aunt Marjorie and cousin Wooly Donahue died. Finally in 1976, von Cramm was killed in Cairo, but by then Barbara's health was such that she may have been largely unaware of his death.

13

Cary Grant

Of all her husbands, Barbara retained a friendly relationship with only two: Cary Grant and Prince Igor Troubetzkoy. The latter remained a loyal and loving friend. He treated Barbara like a little sister and she often turned to him for comfort in times of sorrow. She would have been happy to marry him again, if only to be a Princess once more, but Igor was far too wise for that.

Cary Grant was a long-distance friend. Although their paths no longer crossed because they really belonged to different worlds, they kept up a correspondence and whenever Barbara spoke of Cary, it was with affection. He had been one husband who had not socially humiliated her. She would say half-jokingly, 'Of all the actors to marry, I chose the best there was.'

At the time of her marriage to Cary, he was at the height of success in his acting career. He was loved and respected throughout the world and what was more, his income was equal to Barbara's, although he had to work for it. He had retained his self-respect by pursuing his profession and thus avoided the label of gigolo or kept man. Not only did he continue in his career after his marriage to Barbara, but he kept his friends and activities. It was inevitable that the marriage should be doomed. Barbara, in the long run, was unable to fit into his life-style and Cary refused to pander to her entourage made up mostly of hangers-on. Nevertheless, it was through Cary that Barbara made many friends in Hollywood, such as Sonia Henie, Ingrid Bergman, Joseph Cotten and Douglas Fairbanks Jr, who enriched her life for many years afterwards.

In April 1961, while Barbara was on her annual trip to the Far

East and I was in Paris dealing with the affairs of her three homes, I received a cable from Japan:

CARY GRANT INCOGNITO ARRIVING IN PARIS WITH CHAUFFEUR TUESDAY 29TH STAYING TWO WEEKS STOP PLEASE ARRANGE ALL COMFORTS IN GUEST ROOM STOP KEEP THE PRESS FROM FINDING OUT STOP SEND BEST LOVE TO ALL BARBARA.

I had four days to prepare for his arrival. I did tell one of my close friends about this exciting prospect. She was ever so envious. Most women would have given their right arm to be allowed a glimpse of Cary Grant in the flesh. Unfortunately I could not oblige, since he was coming to Paris in secret. Even Herminie, who had seen crowned heads, went all girlish when she knew of the visit. Nothing ever impressed Herminie, but she began to pester me: 'What do you think Cary Grant will want to eat?', 'Could you persuade him to have a few dinner parties?', 'Will you ask him to write down his favourite menus?', 'Will you ask him to autograph a picture for me?'

Maria, our fiery and volatile chambermaid, had just worked hard during the visit of Lord Drogheda who came to stay (also in Barbara's absence) during one of his business trips to Paris. Although, at the time, Lord Drogheda had complained that he would have preferred a manservant. Thinking that I was doing Maria a kindness I asked Araceli, the other chambermaid, to get the room ready for Cary Grant. Immediately, I had a livid Maria threatening to leave unless she (being the senior maid) was assigned to Cary Grant's room. It almost came to blows between Maria and Araceli. I decided the only fair thing in the circumstances was to allow them to take turns. Instead of gratitude from either of them, I managed to make two enemies. I had never heard of chambermaids being upset at not having to do work.

Not long after the cable arrived, I started to get phone calls from the press regarding Cary Grant's visit to Paris. I firmly denied everything. Still the rumours persisted and appeared in the papers. I was worried that either Barbara or Cary would think I had talked to the press. French reporters were in the habit of paying for information and Barbara's Swiss chauffeur, Fernand, made a sizeable extra income feeding the gossip columns with information. Could one of the staff have told Fernand even though they had been asked not to? I doubted it because they all disliked him for his habit of talking to the press, nor did they like the superior airs he gave himself.

Cary Grant was coming to Paris to discuss a new film with the producer Stanley Donen. Cary was by then not only a star, but a joint-producer of his films. The idea that Cary Grant was staying in Barbara Hutton's apartment appealed to the press, who were busily resurrecting the old Cash and Cary days. I believe that the rumour might have been leaked by Stanley Donen's office, or even by Cary himself. His attitude to publicity was similar to that of many stars: he disliked the disruption and annoyance of media attention, but became paranoid if they ignored him.

Cary was arriving from London with his Rolls Royce (registration number CG 1 – incognito?) and Tony, his English chauffeur. I had been in touch with Tony by telephone to plan the arrival. Since our building had started to gather reporters who had obviously been tipped off about the date of the arrival, we arranged for Cary to arrive at the tradesmen's entrance in an ordinary taxi at 2 am. Tony would follow two hours later with the luggage in the Rolls. The reporters had not bothered to wait up. But they were there early the next morning and it was then difficult to hide the fact that he had arrived and was living in the third floor flat: there was a Rolls Royce CG 1 outside the door. I had to say that Mr Grant was giving no interviews whatsoever, that his visit was private, so don't bother to wait. Still, they waited . . .

However nervous I might have been at meeting Cary Grant, the minute I set eyes on him it was like meeting an old friend. His face was so familiar, his manner so warm and friendly. He looked older than I expected but his ways were exactly the same as in his films. The suit he wore was that familiar type – well-cut single-breasted and worn with the casualness of someone with a perfect physique. His face was tanned and his hair was beginning to show some grey – very distinguished. He was most humble, apologizing for the inconvenience, expressing gratitude for the hospitality and saying, with such sincerity, how much he had looked forward to meeting me. For the two weeks we were to be in each other's constant company I was to marvel at his ability to say just the right thing at the right time – and always in such a pleasant manner. It occurred to me that in his movie roles, he was behaving naturally and that he did not need to 'act' as such. Perhaps, I thought, it was his English origins, the perfect gentleman, the light wit, the banter. But by the

190

end of the two weeks, I came to feel that in fact he had no personality of his own, his persona was made up of his film roles. His wit came from his old scripts, his social manner came from the roles he had assumed. And what a marvellous result! I was to learn later, when meeting other stars, that many of them were also non-persons, and they assumed the characters in the scripts they learned. Recently I read in a magazine article remarks made by Ronald Reagan and it named the films from which each quote came.

Another attribute Cary had, which again is typical of so many actors, was his narcissism. The flat's long central hall leading to the bedrooms was hung on both sides with Japanese silk prints. Between these panels were glass-fronted display cabinets which housed Barbara's valuable collection of snuff boxes and mounted jade pieces. These shelves were illuminated at night giving the whole an exquisite effect. Between the show cases and silk prints there were narrow vertical strips of mirror. Whenever Cary walked down this hall, which art connoisseurs used to ask permission to see, he would only look at his own reflection. I don't believe he once cast a glance at all the marvellous treasures, nor did he admire the total décor which must have been the most beautiful in Paris. He would stop to take a closer look at his hair, or he would look worriedly at his face, to see if it was a bit puffed up under the eyes. His biggest preoccupation was his appearance.

This was to be the despair of Herminie. Here she was, poised to prepare the best meal she could for her idol, and all he wanted at every meal was one poached egg. These were, of course, served in exquisitely delicate porcelain, but that could not compensate Herminie for the meals she had planned. Cary was very concerned about his weight – it was not by accident that he always looked perfect, it was by dint of hard work and sacrifice. His year-round tan was no coincidence either, he worked hard to maintain it. He told me that at one time he was drinking too much and he cured that by hypnosis. He said that drink would have ruined his looks and that's why he stopped. He also used hypnosis to help him give up smoking. He was, in fact, a great advocate of this method, and I can't think of a better advertisement.

He did not even give Herminie the pleasure of producing one of her well-known calorie-laden dinners. He spent his time like a recluse, only seeing a few friends and refusing to offer them a meal because he did not enjoy watching people eating food he would not

191

allow himself to eat. For Herminie it was a deprivation and frustration. She fumed and ranted to me; she felt that I had let her down, for surely I could have persuaded him to give a dinner party. Had she spoken English, I am sure she would have knocked on his bedroom door and argued with him.

One of our guest's more tiresome quirks was his inability to make a decision as to how he would spend his time. Even more frustrating, he would make a decision and then change his mind, so arrangements would have to be cancelled. He spent a great deal of time on the phone, talking to various people all over the world. My tasks of being his telephone operator and travel agent were made almost impossible. One evening I would be making reservations for him to fly to Hong Kong, Los Angeles, Rome and New York the following day. In the morning he would decide to stay in Paris. Fortunately, the travel agencies knew me, otherwise they would have thought I was a hoaxer using Cary Grant's name.

Cary's habit of indecision was demonstrated when Herminie asked on the very first day if she could have an autographed picture. 'Of course,' he said ever so sincerely, 'nothing could give me greater pleasure.' He sounded as if he really meant it and he flashed that famous broad smile of his, with a direct gaze of his shining eyes. He had stacks of pictures of himself and every day he would remind me that he would be signing one for Herminie – but not today. He put it off and put it off until he left. And he left without doing it, all the while proclaiming that he was about to do it. He then solemnly promised he would send one as soon as he was back in the States. It never arrived. The charm always oozed out of him and every time we would fall under the spell and the charm. He was always so grateful for everything and his promises always sounded so sincere. He left, thanking me profusely for all my help. He truly made me feel that there was no one else on earth quite as marvellous as I was. In fact, he thought so much of me that he said he would send me a present the minute he returned home. Like Herminie's autographed picture, it never arrived. I did not even receive a thank-you note typed by a secretary at the studio.

Cary Grant's sexuality has been a topic for considerable speculation. He was said to be bi-sexual and he lived for some years with Randolph Scott. It would appear that his bi-sexuality took the form of alternate preferences. One period of his life it would be men, then he would be heterosexual for several years. I often wondered if he was capable of real genuine feelings, so obsessed was he with his own public image. At that time in Paris, he had just gone through his divorce from Betsy Drake, and he was experiencing a period of fascination for very young women because, I thought, he was very preoccupied with growing old. The long phone calls were mostly to young women in all the various cities he was planning to visit. He would make each of them believe that they were the only love in his life. I think it is true that a man can love more than one woman, but I cannot believe that he could possibly be in love with all those young ladies at the same time. I believe it was an ego-massaging exercise to reassure himself that he could still pull them. He had just been released from a period of work and he wanted to promise all of them 'I am coming to see you tomorrow'. Hence the travel reservations. He was believing his own fantasies.

After a few days I found it wearing to have to deal with both the actual world and his fantasy world. I found his constant need to indulge in it irritating. Occasionally Cary and I would peer out the window to see if the reporters were still there. Cary would count how many there were as a measure of his continued popularity. He always seemed delighted if the number increased, although I felt sorry for them having to wait for nothing. One day, Cary saw amongst the reporters an attractive young brunette. Cary said to me, 'Let her come up, I'll give her an interview.' I was quite put out; I felt it was unfair to all the others who had waited much longer. I wondered if she had been sent especially to bait him. He gave her half an hour of his time and the girl was triumphant. Perhaps it helped her career; I hope so. The fact was that Cary did not do this for her. He needed to have this young woman look adoringly at him. He was visibly delighted at having impressed her.

After the initial niceties, making conversation with Cary Grant was not a very stimulating activity. He was not interested in much outside himself and his films. He told me that *North By Northwest* was his best film. He was too much of a gentleman to give in to gossip about the Hollywood scene which would have fascinated me, and he did not have opinions about many things. There was really a rather two-dimensional person behind the fantastic charismatic image. He had a happy disposition, if somewhat shallow. He did get upset when he found out that when a film in which he starred with Tony Curtis was shown, it was Curtis who had top billing. He looked genuinely hurt when he said, 'That's the new generation; they want younger stars.' He said that when people saw him in public he would hear them say, 'That's Gary Cooper,

193

doesn't he look old!' Cary did not enjoy growing old, however gracefully he did it.

Occasionally, he would talk about his ex-wives, and always in the most self-deprecating way. 'All my ex-wives are very happy, especially since they are ex,' he would joke. Yet, he never once mentioned Barbara by name. When I referred to her, he would not continue the subject. He did not seem to appreciate any of the furniture or paintings in the place. He was neither interested nor curious. He said he did appreciate the hospitality at the apartment because it meant privacy and saving on a hotel bill.

He was, however, interested in one kind of art. Since he was unable to leave the apartment, he asked me to go to an address in the Latin Quarter where he had been before. It was the atelier of a painter who specialized in *trompe l'oeil* paintings. This particular type of painting would falsify the environment and give it an illusion of depth. For example, a canvas depicting a scene to cover a wall which would make the room look as if it were double in length. Another of the artist's favourite subjects was paintings of eggs – an egg on a table, the egg looking truly three-dimensional. I was allowed to take some back on approval. Cary showed obvious fascination for this kind of painting. He was bowled over at how real the painted egg looked; he kept saying, 'Isn't it amazing, truly amazing!' I went back and forth several times while Cary chose some of the paintings and changed his mind. He first exchanged one for another. Then he wanted the first one again. In the end, he had me return the lot. The painter seemed rather relieved. She told me she had dealt with Mr Grant for years and it was difficult to get payment from him.

During his stay in Paris, some of Cary's friends came to the apartment to see him. Notable among them were Sophia Loren and Ingrid Bergman. Rumour had it that he had had love affairs with both of them. These two actresses proved to me that not all members of their profession are vain and empty-headed. They both exuded natural charm and simplicity. They were both unaffected and both adored pottering about at home, cooking meals for their husbands. Ingrid at the time was living like an ordinary housewife, just outside Paris with her Swedish husband. When you rang her up, she answered the phone herself. Neither woman had allowed fame to spoil her view of herself.

Barbara Hutton always spoke with affection about Cary even though they had not made a go of their marriage. Her stories about that period of her life were full of humour. One of her favourites demonstrated just how seriously Cary took his role in the public eye. Barbara herself did not give a fig about her reputation, as her behaviour testifies all too clearly. One day, Cary was reading an article in a magazine when he looked up at Barbara and said, 'Do you realize that we are the most important couple in the world after the Duke and Duchess of Windsor?' When Barbara told this story she would be doubled up in hysterical laughter. She thought it was the funniest remark ever, and she would add, 'And you should have seen his face, he *really* was serious!!' But his stinginess still rankled with her, even in the years that I worked for her. Whenever Barbara spoke about a stingy person, she would refer to him as 'a Cary Grant'.

During their marriage Barbara was as generous to Cary as she was to all her husbands. She not only paid for all the household expenses, but she bought new clothes for him, gave him cars, jewels and works of art. When they divorced, the studio was quick to make it clear that Cary was not getting any settlement. There was no need for it, he had been living off Barbara for three years, had increased his capital, was a millionaire in his own right and still earning. As Barbara was not an ideal person to be married to, so Cary was not an ideal marriage mate either. In his usual self-deprecating way he said that he had hurt all the women he loved. About his divorce from Barbara, he said, 'Barbara was looking for affection and I didn't know then how to give it.'

195

14

The End of the Affair

My personal relationship with Barbara was bound to deteriorate after three years. It had started at the very summit. It was like a love affair where I could do no wrong. She praised me to everybody – in my presence and in my absence. Whenever she was in New York, visiting her cousin Jimmy at his Long Island mansion, she would invite my father to dinner and say the most flattering things about me. She felt lucky to have found me. The most important aspect for her was the joy of having an Oriental presence about her. She delighted in that. On the practical side of the situation, she had for the first time an efficient social secretary whereas previously she had no one in that position. Sister Latimer had dealt with the travel arrangements but was not up to doing accounts or correspondence. Barbara also felt that she had become bossy and interfering. With me, Barbara had a young person who was just the opposite: under-confident and dead eager to please. I got along well with the French staff and shopkeepers, as French was my first language, and I had been recommended by Graham Mattison who was the main protagonist in all her important financial transactions. She appreciated the fact that I did not try to run her life. 'All my life,' she would complain, 'people have wanted to run my life for me. They think they know better how to spend my money.' I could see how easy it was to feel protective towards this seemingly helpless creature whom everybody tried to cheat.

It did not take me long to note that Barbara would dictate to me that I had to grow my hair and keep it straight. She wanted to use me like a doll. I had to make sure that I wore whatever clothes she gave me, to parade in front of her wearing what she chose for me to wear. If it did not fit me perfectly, she would have her own Lanvin seamstress do any necessary alterations. Sometimes she would give me clothes I disliked intensely; sometimes they would be beautiful but very uncomfortable to work in – no matter, I had to wear them. I remember one particular couturier dress of black and white taffeta. It had a tight and narrow skirt and an enormous bow on one shoulder. Barbara seriously expected me to work in it. Little did she know how I longed to wear a pair of trousers and a sweater! I would be cued by Hélène as to how pleased Barbara was with me, with my appearance, with my performance. It was extremely rare for Barbara to show disapproval to anyone's face. If she was displeased with someone, she would avoid them.

With Herminie's cooking it was very easy to put on weight. Barbara had an obsession for slimness. I was told, via Hélène, that I should trim down and I was sent to a local masseur who beat me up black and blue, ostensibly to disengage the water from my body's cells. It was so painful that I accelerated the slimming by hardly eating anything.

When I first started working at rue Octave Feuillet, I was engaged to a banker, Philippe Senat, who was very prudish and somewhat provincial. Barbara very generously included him at her dinner parties. It was a disaster from the beginning. Philippe disapproved of her life-style and of my involvement in it. The very first time he came to dinner, he intimated to her that she led an immoral life and that she would do well to think about the poor in this world instead of wasting her money on trivialities. No wonder she took an instant dislike to him! She told me that I would be making a mistake if I were to marry him. She enlisted all her friends to put pressure on me to break off my engagement. She arranged for me to be paired off with other escorts among her friends. When Colin Fraser visited Paris and when he and I were in Cuernavaca at the same time, Barbara made a point of arranging for us to visit the restaurants and night-clubs together at her expense. 'Sooner or later,' she would say with a wink, 'You will forget Philippe.' She encouraged me in a flirtation with the heart specialist, Dr Henri Deschamps, who had looked after Tiki in her last illness. Barbara was delighted the time I was paired off with Marlon Brando when he was visiting Paris. She thought it would impress me. Equally, she encouraged me in a romance with the ex-guardsman, Jeremy Eldridge, Lloyd Franklin's friend. Philippe was quite right when he said that I would be tainted by this immoral way of life. I did break off our engagement but it was not because of Barbara or her way of life. I had used my job, which involved travelling, as an excuse for postponing the wedding date. I realized that the reason I was making excuses was that I did not want to get married. There was nothing Barbara disliked more than for the people around her to get married and settle down. She enjoyed seeing and causing discord. She had a need for mischief. She enjoyed stories of adultery and infidelities. She actively encouraged it among her friends.

During the summer of 1961, while Jeremy Eldridge was supervising the building of stables and a bungalow for Lloyd, I spent every available minute with Jerry, having a good excuse in that he needed an interpreter in his work for Lloyd, Jerry being a typical Englishman who spoke only English.

One week-end the Tangier polo team was invited to play in Marbella and Lloyd asked Jerry to be part of the team. I very much wanted to go along and asked Barbara if she would mind my taking the week-end off; Ira Belline had promised to cover for my duties. 'Of course, you go, darling. And have a *lovely* week-end,' Barbara replied giving me a warm kiss. I was as thrilled and excited as a schoolgirl. I was by now very involved in horses myself and enjoyed looking after them on the ferry crossing to Algeciras. We stayed at the Marbella Club; the group included besides Jerry and me, Lloyd, Dr Little, a Moroccan officer from Tangier and the groom, Peter. It was a wonderful week-end and I was in love.

On my return to Tangier, I went to see Barbara in the morning as usual and was told by Ira that Barbara did not wish to see me. Ira explained that Barbara had been upset that I preferred to go off to Spain rather than stay with her. 'But,' Ira added, 'come tomorrow morning as usual.' I did that and again I was told that Barbara did not wish to see me. I left again. On the third day, when Barbara was still angry and refused to see me, I said to Ira, 'Look, call me at the Rembrandt [the hotel where I always stayed, there being only four bedrooms at Sidi Hosni] when Barbara needs me.' 'Oh! No!', Ira exclaimed, 'You must wait here every day otherwise she'll never forgive you.' It was the eighth day before Barbara asked that I go up to her room. I knew that the honeymoon was over; Barbara had discovered that I was not perfect. I was in her eyes yet another person who only used her. From then onwards I felt that at times I irritated her. I knew that I myself had changed. I had become more aggressive and short with people. I had gained confidence and exercised my authority. I was no longer the sweet little Chinese doll. What is more, I was very disenchanted with the job. It was not a bad job as such, but I had discovered that I needed a different way of life. I needed to express myself without looking over my shoulder all the time. Here I felt crushed, ground down. I had to get out and I looked for a way. I don't suppose that Jerry suspected that when I accepted his offer of marriage, I used it as a key to let me out of my cell. Whereas with Philippe I had used the job to get out of marriage, now I was using marriage to get out of the job.

On my return to Paris at the end of that season, I wrote to Graham Mattison telling him that I was going to leave Barbara's employment and I told Barbara the same. I felt that getting married was about the most solid justification for leaving a job. No one could blame me for it. I was wrong. Barbara could not accept it as a valid reason. She argued with me that she was an authority on marriage (hadn't she tried it six times and failed?) and it doesn't work. 'Marriage,' to quote Barbara, 'is for the birds.' She wasn't married at the time. It was difficult to argue with her. All I could do was listen to her and then repeat what I had already said. But I could not bring myself to tell her that I was fed up to there with her lot. She had, after all, been more than kind and generous, there is no denying that. She finally agreed to let me go when she could find a replacement. She said that she knew where to find someone suitable. I waited and waited and realized after three months that she had done nothing, and had never intended to do anything. In the meantime, she was starting to exclude me from her normal evening functions and I learned from the other staff that Barbara was very angry. She was telling everybody that I was an ungrateful brat. She also told people that I was butch and that she suspected I was a lesbian.

My daily routine continued normally and our meetings face-to-face were cordial and mildly affectionate. Barbara offered to set up an office in London for me to continue to do the paperwork from my homebase. It was a generous offer; I could have named my terms. However, I knew well enough that when she pays you, she owns you body and soul. Sooner or later, she would demand that I join her somewhere else in the world. I was not prepared to do that. I had to cut myself off; there could be no half measure. One evening after I had assured her again that I really meant to leave, Barbara had been drinking and I was at my usual post sitting at the foot of her bed trying not to nod off. 'Do you know, darling, that no one has ever left me before? You are the first person that I can't buy and I hate you for it,' she added with a smile. In fact, she had not tried to buy me. Had she offered me $1 million, perhaps I would have stayed.

Clearly no progress was being made about finding a replacement for me, so I decided to go ahead with my plans to get married and leave. Jerry had been married before so had to get a divorce first. On my side, being a Catholic, I had difficulties with getting permission to marry a divorced man. In the end it proved impossible, so I married outside the Church.

The marriage took place in London at Marylebone Registry Office. It was the most private of weddings with just Jerry's parents as witnesses. It was Saturday, 15 October 1962, and I was back at work on Monday in Paris. I said to Barbara that I would leave in exactly three months, whether she had found someone else or not.

A few weeks later a very pleasant English accountant came to audit my books. He worked in my office for several days. At first he was rather brusque, but slowly he relaxed and we got on very well. He spoke perfect French and had chosen to live in Paris. When he finished his work he told me that Graham Mattison had asked him to check my books because Barbara had called him in New York to tell him that I was embezzling funds. He added that he found everything in order and would be pleased to put it in writing if I wished. I replied with hurt pride, 'No, thank you. I don't need written proof that I am honest.' If they only knew how easily I *could* have been dishonest in my position. I had become a baddie because Barbara could not have her way. It did not, however, prevent her from giving me $30,000 when I left, although she had already given me $20,000 three months previously when I was married.

Postscript

The Death of Barbara Hutton

Immortality

Nothing ever dies, neither joy nor pain,
A flower is not born but to blossom again;
No rapture once known, no anguish, no need
Lies barren and was wasted for want of a seed.

No darkness remains in the ultimate light
Where shadows are suns at the closing of night;
And blessed is all that seemed ugly and sore,
Most beautiful this which was hurtful before.

Nor nothing may die, neither passion nor shame,
But in death is immortal, a spirit, a flame
Of life without ending, of love without cease,
Of love everlasting! O glorious peace!

Barbara Hutton, *The Wayfarer*

Barbara died on 11 May 1979, at the age of sixty-six. She was no more than a skeleton. She had been dying for several years, of malnutrition, inactivity and overall decay. Her organs and muscles were spent from being either misused or unused. It was the end of the gossip columnists' dream. In the last three years of her life, Barbara had lost all her teeth, was unable to walk and was only semi-conscious of the financial problems surrounding her. Her employees had not been paid since 1976 and hotels were suing her for thousands of dollars' rent. Her life ran out at the same time as her money.

She was buried in the Woolworth Mausoleum in the Woodlawn Cemetery in the Bronx, New York, where she joined her son Lance. Only ten people attended the funeral and the press, for once, was unaware of the occasion. When I learned of Barbara's death from the newspapers, I was saddened because part of my life had died, but I was not surprised. Although only sixty-six, she had lived at least two lifetimes and, in the end, she must have been, I felt, pleased to be released.

At Christmas 1982 during a holiday in Mexico, I went to visit Sumiya. It had been sold to a Mexican restaurant chain. Only one small part of the superb estate was used. The food was barely mediocre. The rest of the property had been allowed to deteriorate. The beautiful swimming pool was dry, with a few unhealthy-looking pots of plants occupying some of the space. There were some poorly-fed peacocks strutting about. I wondered if they were the same ones I had known, and if they remembered. I wished I had not gone back.

Bibliography

Bryan, J. III & Murphy, Charles J. V., *The Windsor Story*, St Albans, Herts: Granada Publishing Ltd, 1979

Griffing, Robert P. Jr, *The Barbara Hutton Collection of Chinese Porcelain*, Honolulu: Honolulu Academy of Arts, 1956

Heymann, C. David, *Poor Little Rich Girl*, London: Hutchinson & Co (Publishers) Ltd, 1985

Randall, Monica, *The Mansions of Long Island's Gold Coast*, New York: Hastings House, 1970

Smith, T. V., 'A Successful Experiment in Cultural Transplanting: Barbara Hutton's House in Cuernavaca, Mexico' *House Beautiful*, January 1962

Winkler, John K., *Five and Ten: The Fabulous Life of F W Woolworth*, New York: Robert M. McBride & Co., 1940

Index

209